Advanced SDL Game Engineering: Expert Techniques for Professional Developers

Kameron Hussain and Frahaan Hussain

Published by Sonar Publishing, 2024.

ADVANCED SDL GAME ENGINEERING: EXPERT TECHNIQUES FOR PROFESSIONAL DEVELOPERS

First edition. January 17, 2024.

ISBN: 979-8224062935

Written by Kameron Hussain and Frahaan Hussain.

Table of Contents

Chapter 1: Mastering Complex Game Systems

1.1 Designing Robust Game Architectures

1.2 Advanced Systems for Game Logic

1.3 Managing Large-Scale Game Worlds

1.4 Integrating Complex Gameplay Mechanics

1.5 Performance and Memory Optimization Techniques

Chapter 2: High-Performance Rendering with SDL

2.1 Optimizing Rendering Pipelines

2.2 Advanced Techniques in 2D and 3D Graphics

2.3 GPU Acceleration and Its Utilization

2.4 Implementing High-Resolution Support

2.5 Balancing Visual Quality and Performance

Chapter 3: Multi-Threaded and Asynchronous Programming

3.1 Understanding Threads in Game Development

3.2 Asynchronous Operations in SDL

3.3 Thread Synchronization and Safety

3.4 Scalable Multithreading Techniques

3.5 Maximizing Performance with Parallel Processing

Chapter 4: Network Engineering for Online Games

4.1 Advanced Networking Concepts in SDL

4.2 Building Scalable Multiplayer Servers

4.3 Network Security Best Practices

4.4 Efficient Data Transmission Techniques

4.5 Creating Seamless Online Experiences

Chapter 5: Advanced AI and Simulation

5.1 Complex AI Algorithms for Games

5.2 Simulating Realistic Behaviors and Environments

5.3 AI in Large-Scale World Dynamics

5.4 Integrating Machine Learning in Games

5.5 Challenges in Balancing and AI Design

Chapter 6: Physics and Real-Time Interactions

6.1. Realistic Physics for Game Dynamics

6.2. Implementing Advanced Collision Detection

Basic Collision Detection

Advanced Collision Detection Techniques

Performance Considerations

6.3. Fluid and Soft Body Dynamics

Fluid Dynamics

Soft Body Dynamics

Performance Considerations

6.4. Real-Time Environmental Effects

Weather Simulation

Day-Night Cycle

Dynamic Wind and Vegetation

Performance Considerations

6.5. Integrating Physics with Game Logic

Physics Engines

Physics and Gameplay Interaction

Performance Considerations

7.1. Spatial Audio and 3D Soundscapes

The Importance of Spatial Audio

Sound Positioning

Sound Attenuation

Doppler Effect

Implementing Spatial Audio

Listener and Sound Source

Environmental Effects

Real-Time Calculations

Performance Considerations

7.2. Advanced Audio Processing Techniques

Real-Time Effects

Dynamic Mixing

Spatialized Audio

Interactive Music Systems

Performance Optimization

7.3. Dynamic Sound Systems in Games

Dynamic Sound Generation

Environmental Audio

Interactive Soundscapes

Player-Centric Audio

Performance Considerations

7.4. Integrating Adaptive Music

The Role of Adaptive Music

Dynamic Layering

Interactive Crossfading

Musical Emotion Mapping

Player-Centric Music

Performance Considerations

7.5. Audio Optimization for Various Platforms

Platform-Specific Audio Considerations

Audio Compression and Formats

Audio Streaming

Memory Management

Cross-Platform Audio Middleware

Platform-Specific Audio Effects

Testing and Quality Assurance

Chapter 8: Developing for Emerging Technologies

8.1. Virtual Reality (VR) Integration with SDL

Understanding Virtual Reality (VR)

SDL and VR Integration

Conclusion

8.2. Augmented Reality (AR) in Game Development

Understanding Augmented Reality (AR)

SDL and AR Integration

Conclusion

8.3. Exploring Haptic Feedback and Sensory Inputs

Understanding Haptic Feedback

SDL and Haptic Feedback

Sensory Inputs

Conclusion

8.4. Adaptive Gaming with AI and IoT

AI in Gaming

IoT Integration

Challenges and Considerations

Examples of Adaptive Gaming

Conclusion

8.5. Preparing for Future Gaming Technologies

Embracing Emerging Trends

Cross-Platform Development

Future-Proofing Game Assets

Adaptive Game Engines

Collaboration with Research Institutions

Ethical Considerations

Continuous Learning

Conclusion

Chapter 9: Profiling and Performance Tuning

9.1. Advanced Profiling Techniques

Profiling Tools and Frameworks

CPU Profiling

GPU Profiling

Memory Profiling

Multi-Threading Profiling

Automated Testing and Continuous Integration

Conclusion

9.2. Identifying and Solving Performance Bottlenecks

Common Performance Bottlenecks

Profiling and Analysis

Optimization Strategies

Continuous Testing and Optimization

9.3. Memory Management and Leak Detection

Memory Management Techniques

Detecting Memory Leaks

Preventing Memory Leaks

9.4. Cross-Platform Performance Considerations

1. Hardware Variability

2. Input Methods

3. Operating System Differences

4. Screen Resolutions and Aspect Ratios

5. Performance Optimization

6. Battery Life and Resource Management

7. Cross-Platform Testing

8. Updates and Patches

9.5. Tuning Games for Optimal Performance

1. Profiling and Benchmarking

2. Code Optimization

3. Asset Optimization

4. Threading and Parallelism

5. Memory Management

6. Render Batching and Draw Calls

7. Runtime Optimization

8. Cross-Platform Considerations

9. Player Feedback

10. Testing and Optimization Iteration

Chapter 10: Scalable Game Server Architecture

10.1. Designing High-Availability Game Servers

1. Redundancy and Failover

2. Scalability Strategies

3. Data Persistence and Backup

4. Monitoring and Alerting

5. Geographic Distribution

6. Security and DDoS Mitigation

7. Disaster Recovery Planning

10.2. Load Balancing and Resource Allocation

1. Load Balancing Strategies

2. Elastic Scaling and Auto-Scaling

3. Resource Allocation and Game Instances

4. Monitoring and Performance Metrics

10.3. Server Scaling Strategies

1. Horizontal Scaling

2. Vertical Scaling

3. Hybrid Approaches

10.4. Handling Massive Concurrent Player Bases

1. Load Balancing

2. Caching and Data Optimization

3. Asynchronous Processing

4. Database Scaling

5. Real-Time Monitoring and Scaling

10.5. Cloud-Based Solutions and Integrations

1. Benefits of Cloud-Based Solutions

2. Cloud-Based Game Servers

3. Cloud-Based Databases

4. Cloud-Based Game Analytics

5. Cloud-Based Asset Storage

6. Continuous Integration and Deployment (CI/CD)

7. Multi-Platform Support

8. Data Backups and Disaster Recovery

Chapter 11: Advanced Shader and Visual Effects

Section 11.1: Writing Custom Shader Programs

Understanding Shaders

Shader Languages

Anatomy of a Shader

Creating Visual Effects

Section 11.2: Real-Time Lighting and Shadow Techniques

Lighting Models

Types of Light Sources

Shadow Mapping

Global Illumination

Light Probes

Deferred Rendering

Post-Processing Effects

Section 11.3: Special Effects with Particle Systems

What Are Particle Systems?

Basic Components of a Particle System

Particle System Workflow

Particle Effects Examples

Optimization and Performance

Section 11.4: Advanced Rendering Techniques for Realism

Physically Based Rendering (PBR)

Global Illumination (GI)

High Dynamic Range (HDR) Rendering

Screen-Space Reflections (SSR)

Post-Processing Effects

Performance Considerations

Section 11.5: Shader Optimization and GPU Resources

Shader Optimization

GPU Resource Management

Chapter 12: Cross-Platform Development Challenges

Section 12.1: Managing Platform-Specific Features

Section 12.2: Strategy for Universal Input Handling

Section 12.3: Ensuring Consistent Performance Across Platforms

Section 12.4: Automated Testing for Multi-Platform Support

Section 12.5: Navigating Different Distribution Models

Chapter 13: Advanced User Interface and HUD Design

Section 13.1: Designing Intuitive and Dynamic UIs

Section 13.2: Customizable and Scalable HUD Systems

Section 13.3: Implementing Touch and Gesture Controls

Section 13.4: Accessibility and Universal Design Principles

Section 13.5: UI Animation and Interaction Techniques

Chapter 14: In-depth Analytics and Player Tracking

Section 14.1: Implementing Game Analytics Tools

Section 14.2: Analyzing Player Behavior and Preferences

Section 14.3: Utilizing Data for Game Improvements

Section 14.4: Ethical Considerations in Player Data Usage

Section 14.5: Real-Time Analytics and Reporting

Chapter 15: Advanced Level and World Design

Section 15.1: Techniques for Dynamic Level Generation

Section 15.2: Creating Interactive and Responsive Environments

Section 15.3: Narrative-Driven World Building

Section 15.4: Integrating Levels with Game Mechanics

Section 15.5: Balancing Aesthetic Appeal and Functionality

Chapter 16: Monetization and Business Models

Section 16.1: Innovative Monetization Strategies

Section 16.2: Balancing Profit and Player Experience

Section 16.3: Exploring Subscription and Freemium Models

Subscription-Based Monetization

Freemium Monetization

Section 16.4: Managing In-Game Economies

Core Components of In-Game Economies

Strategies for Effective In-Game Economy Management

Section 16.5: Ethical Considerations in Game Monetization

Player-Centric Ethical Practices

Community and Social Responsibility

Ethical Advertising and Marketing

Social Responsibility

Chapter 17: Advanced Debugging and Error Handling

Section 17.1: Complex Bug Tracking and Resolution

1. Logging and Instrumentation

2. Crash Dump Analysis

3. Profiling Tools

4. Reproducible Test Cases

5. Static Analysis

6. Code Reviews and Pair Programming

7. Version Control and Issue Tracking

8. Automated Testing

9. Root Cause Analysis

10. Documentation

11. Post-Mortems

Section 17.2: Automated Testing and Continuous Integration

1. Types of Automated Tests

2. Test Automation Frameworks

3. Continuous Integration (CI) Pipelines

4. CI Platforms

5. Benefits of CI

6. CI Best Practices

Section 17.3: Handling Runtime Errors and Crashes

1. Runtime Errors vs. Crashes

2. Error Reporting and Logging

3. Exception Handling

4. Memory Management

5. Crash Dumps and Minidumps

6. Automatic Crash Reporting

7. Continuous Testing

8. User-Friendly Error Handling

9. Debugging Tools

10. Monitoring in Production

Section 17.4: Debugging Multiplayer and Network Issues

1. Understanding Networked Systems

2. Network Emulation and Simulation

3. Logging and Diagnostics

4. Packet Inspection and Wireshark

5. Reproducible Test Cases

6. Peer-to-Peer Debugging

7. Latency Compensation

8. Synchronization and Authoritative Server

9. Load Testing

10. Cross-Platform Compatibility

11. Security Audits

Section 17.5: Establishing Effective QA Processes

1. Test Planning and Strategy

2. Test Case Design

3. Automated Testing

4. Regression Testing

5. Bug Tracking and Reporting

6. Usability Testing

7. Performance Testing

8. Localization and Accessibility Testing

9. Continuous Integration and Delivery (CI/CD)

10. User Acceptance Testing (UAT)

11. Documentation

12. Feedback Loops

Chapter 18: Legal and Ethical Considerations

Section 18.1: Intellectual Property Rights in Game Development

Section 18.2: Navigating Licensing and Compliance

Section 18.3: Addressing Privacy and Data Protection

Section 18.4: Ethical Dilemmas in Game Content

Section 18.5: Promoting Fair Play and Community Standards

Chapter 19: Post-Launch Management and Evolution

Section 19.1: Strategies for Post-Launch Game Support

Continuous Updates and Content

Monetization Strategies

Community Engagement

Data-Driven Decision Making

Cross-Platform and Cross-Progression

Marketing and Promotion

Player Feedback and Iteration

Section 19.2: Managing Community Feedback and Expectations

Active Communication

Prioritizing Feedback

Feedback Analysis

Handling Negative Feedback

Setting Realistic Expectations

Section 19.3: Iterative Development and Updates

The Power of Iteration

Planning Updates

Content Updates

Community Involvement

Post-Launch Monetization

Community Celebrations

Conclusion

Section 19.4: Keeping Your Game Relevant in a Changing Market

Market Research and Trends

Continuous Innovation

Community Engagement

Data-Driven Decision Making

Consistent Quality Assurance

Monetization Considerations

Evolving Marketing Strategies

Conclusion

Section 19.5: Planning for Longevity and Legacy

Sustainability in Game Development

Post-Launch Support and Updates

Legacy Support

Building a Community and Brand

Ethical Considerations

Leaving a Lasting Impact

Chapter 20: Future Directions in Game Development

Section 20.1: Emerging Trends and Technologies

1. Metaverse and Virtual Worlds

2. Cloud Gaming

3. Augmented Reality (AR) Gaming

4. Blockchain and NFTs in Gaming

5. AI and Procedural Content Generation

6. Cross-Platform Play and Compatibility

7. Sustainability and Environmental Initiatives

8. Neurogaming and Brain-Computer Interfaces (BCIs)

9. Accessibility and Inclusivity

10. AI-Generated Content and Stories

11. Ethical Game Development

12. Remote and Distributed Development

13. Retro and Nostalgia Gaming

14. Sandbox and User-Created Content

15. Game Streaming and Content Creation

Section 20.2: SDL's Role in Future Game Development

1. Cross-Platform Development

2. Performance and Optimization

3. Multi-Threaded and Asynchronous Programming

4. Integration with Emerging Technologies

5. Community and Ecosystem

6. Open Source and Accessibility

7. Simplicity and Versatility

8. Legacy Support

9. Middleware Integration

10. Licensing and Business Models

Section 20.3: Preparing for Next-Generation Platforms

1. Hardware Advancements

2. Resolution and Display Technologies

3. Ray Tracing and Realistic Graphics

4. Input and Interaction

5. Cross-Platform Compatibility

6. Networking and Multiplayer

7. Performance and Optimization

8. Scalability

9. Accessibility and Inclusivity

10. Ethical Considerations

Section 20.4: The Evolving Landscape of Game Design

1. Immersive Experiences

2. Narrative Complexity

3. Live Services and Continuous Content

4. User-Generated Content

5. Esports and Competitive Gaming

6. Accessibility and Inclusivity

7. Ethical Game Design

8. Sustainability and Environmental Responsibility

9. Cultural Sensitivity and Global Markets

10. Emerging Platforms and Technologies

Section 20.5: Visionary Thinking for Future Game Creators

1. Metaverse and Virtual Worlds

2. AI-Generated Worlds and Stories

3. Haptic Feedback and Immersion

4. Neurogaming and Brain-Computer Interfaces

5. Blockchain and Ownership

6. Sustainable Game Development

7. Mixed Reality Experiences

8. Ethical AI and Inclusivity

9. Education and Skill Development

10. Global Collaboration

Chapter 1: Mastering Complex Game Systems

1.1 Designing Robust Game Architectures

In the world of game development, creating a robust game architecture is fundamental to building successful and sustainable games. A well-designed game architecture forms the backbone of your project, ensuring that it can evolve, scale, and adapt to changing requirements. In this section, we will delve into the key principles and strategies for designing robust game architectures.

1.1.1 The Importance of Game Architecture

Game architecture is the blueprint of your game, defining how different components and systems interact with each other. It provides a structured framework for organizing your code and assets, making it easier to manage and maintain as your project grows. Without a solid architecture, you risk facing code spaghetti, making it challenging to implement new features or fix bugs.

1.1.2 Modular Design

A modular design approach involves breaking down your game into smaller, manageable modules or components. Each module should have a specific responsibility and interface, allowing for easy integration and testing. This design philosophy promotes reusability, as well as collaboration among team members.

```
# Example of a modular design in Python

class Player:

def __init__(self, name):

self.name = name
```

```
self.health = 100

class Enemy:

def __init__(self, name):

self.name = name

self.health = 50
```

In the example above, we have two distinct modules, Player and Enemy, each responsible for managing different aspects of the game.

1.1.3 Separation of Concerns

Separation of concerns is a principle that encourages keeping different aspects of your game separate. For instance, you should separate the rendering, physics, and game logic components. This separation makes it easier to modify or replace individual parts without affecting the entire system.

1.1.4 Data-Driven Design

Data-driven design involves storing game data, such as level layouts, enemy behaviors, and item properties, in external files rather than hardcoding them into the code. This approach enhances flexibility and allows for rapid iteration and testing without modifying the codebase.

```
<!—Example of data-driven level design in XML—>

<level>

<name>Level 1</name>

<background>forest.jpg</background>

<enemies>
```

```
<enemy type="goblin" position="100,200" />

<enemy type="skeleton" position="300,150" />

</enemies>

</level>
```

By using external files, you can tweak game parameters without needing to recompile the game.

1.1.5 Scalability and Extensibility

A robust game architecture should be scalable and extensible, capable of accommodating new features and content seamlessly. This requires careful planning and adherence to design patterns that promote flexibility.

1.1.6 Design Patterns for Game Architecture

Various design patterns, such as the Entity-Component-System (ECS) pattern, can be valuable in structuring your game architecture. These patterns provide clear guidelines on how to organize and manage game entities, components, and systems.

```
# Example of an ECS architecture in Python

class Entity:

def __init__(self):

self.components = {}

class Component:

def __init__(self, name):

self.name = name
```

```
class System:
def __init__(self):
self.entities = []
def update(self):
# Update logic for entities with relevant components
```

Design patterns like ECS help you achieve a clean and maintainable architecture that can adapt to the complexity of your game.

In summary, designing a robust game architecture is a critical step in game development. It involves modular design, separation of concerns, data-driven design, scalability, and the use of design patterns. A well-thought-out architecture sets the foundation for creating engaging and sustainable games. In the following sections of this chapter, we will explore advanced systems for game logic, managing large-scale game worlds, integrating complex gameplay mechanics, and performance and memory optimization techniques.

1.2 Advanced Systems for Game Logic

In the realm of game development, creating captivating gameplay experiences is at the core of every successful game. To achieve this, game logic plays a pivotal role in determining how the game behaves, responds to player actions, and provides challenges. In this section, we will explore advanced systems and techniques for implementing game logic that engages players and enhances their gaming experience.

1.2.1 Finite State Machines (FSM)

Finite State Machines are a powerful concept for managing game logic. They allow you to represent an entity's behavior as a set of states and transitions between them. Each state defines how the entity behaves under specific conditions. FSMs are particularly useful for modeling character behaviors, enemy AI, and interactive objects.

Here's a simple Python example of an FSM for a character's movement:

```
class Character:

def __init__(self):

self.state = "idle"

def update(self):

if self.state == "idle":

# Handle idle behavior

elif self.state == "walking":
```

```
# Handle walking behavior

elif self.state == "attacking":

# Handle attacking behavior
```

1.2.2 Behavior Trees

Behavior Trees provide a hierarchical way to structure game logic. They are well-suited for complex AI behaviors where decision-making is involved. Nodes in a behavior tree represent actions, conditions, or composite tasks. Behavior trees offer flexibility in defining AI behaviors and make it easier to create dynamic and responsive NPCs.

```
# Example of a simple behavior tree in Python

class BehaviorTree:

def __init__(self):

self.root = SelectorNode(

SequenceNode(

IsEnemyInRange(),

AttackEnemy()

),

Wander()

)

def update(self):

self.root.execute()
```

In this example, the behavior tree decides whether an NPC should attack an enemy or wander around based on conditions.

1.2.3 Rule-Based Systems

Rule-based systems are a classic approach to game logic. They use a set of rules or conditions to determine the game's behavior. These rules can range from simple if-then statements to more complex rule sets. Rule-based systems are effective for defining game rules, triggering events, and managing in-game systems.

```
# Example of a rule-based system in Python

if player_health <= 0:

game_over = True

elif enemy_count == 0:

level_completed = True

elif player_position.distance_to(treasure_position) < 10:

collect_treasure()
```

Rule-based systems are intuitive and can be used for a wide range of game logic scenarios.

1.2.4 Scripting Languages

Many game engines and frameworks support scripting languages that allow you to define game logic outside of the main codebase. This separation of logic from code offers flexibility and eases iteration. Common scripting languages used in game development include Lua, Python, and JavaScript.

```
—Example of Lua scripting in a game engine
```

```
function onPlayerCollision(player, obstacle)

if obstacle.type == "enemy" then

player:takeDamage(obstacle.damage)

elseif obstacle.type == "powerup" then

player:applyPowerup(obstacle.effect)

end

end
```

Scripting languages enable designers and game developers to tweak and experiment with game logic without altering the core engine code.

1.2.5 Event-Driven Programming

Event-driven programming is prevalent in game development. It involves responding to events or signals triggered by player actions, system events, or game conditions. Event-driven architectures are essential for handling user input, managing game state transitions, and creating interactive gameplay.

```
# Example of event-driven input handling in Python

def on_key_press(key):

if key == "SPACE":

player.jump()

def on_mouse_click(x, y):

if button.contains(x, y):
```

```
button.click()
```

In event-driven systems, callbacks or event handlers execute specific actions when triggered by events.

In conclusion, advanced systems for game logic are instrumental in creating engaging and immersive gameplay experiences. Finite State Machines, Behavior Trees, Rule-Based Systems, Scripting Languages, and Event-Driven Programming are essential tools in a game developer's toolkit. These systems empower game developers to craft intricate gameplay mechanics, realistic AI behaviors, and interactive game worlds that captivate players and keep them coming back for more. In the subsequent sections of this chapter, we will delve into managing large-scale game worlds, integrating complex gameplay mechanics, and optimizing performance and memory to further enhance your game's quality and player experience.

1.3 Managing Large-Scale Game Worlds

As games continue to evolve, the demand for expansive and immersive game worlds has grown exponentially. Managing large-scale game worlds presents unique challenges, from efficiently storing and streaming assets to creating dynamic and interactive environments. In this section, we will explore strategies and techniques for effectively managing large game worlds that captivate players and deliver seamless experiences.

1.3.1 Level of Detail (LOD) Techniques

Level of Detail (LOD) techniques are essential for optimizing large-scale game worlds. LOD involves adjusting the level of detail in objects or terrain based on their distance from the player's viewpoint. This technique reduces computational load and memory usage while maintaining visual quality.

```
# Example of LOD for terrain rendering in a game engine

if camera_distance > threshold_distance:

render_low_detail_terrain()

else:

render_high_detail_terrain()
```

By dynamically adjusting the level of detail, you can render only what the player can see in high detail, conserving resources for other aspects of the game.

1.3.2 Spatial Partitioning

Spatial partitioning is crucial for efficiently managing game world data. It involves dividing the game world into smaller regions or cells, making it easier to cull objects that are not within the player's view or are too far away. Common spatial partitioning techniques include quad-trees, octrees, and grid-based systems.

```
# Example of a grid-based spatial partitioning system

grid = create_grid(world_bounds, cell_size)

objects = get_objects_within_grid_cell(player_position, grid)
```

Spatial partitioning minimizes the number of objects that need to be processed and rendered at any given time, improving performance.

1.3.3 Streaming and Loading

Streaming and loading assets dynamically as the player explores the game world is essential for large-scale environments. This prevents long initial loading times and reduces memory usage. Techniques such as asynchronous asset loading and streaming zones help maintain a smooth gaming experience.

```
# Example of asynchronous asset loading in Unity

LoadAsync("large_building", on_building_loaded)

def on_building_loaded(building):

instantiate(building)
```

Asynchronous loading allows the game to continue running while assets are loaded in the background.

1.3.4 Procedural Content Generation

Procedural content generation is a powerful approach to creating large game worlds. It involves using algorithms to generate terrain, environments, and even quests dynamically. Procedural generation reduces the need for extensive manual content creation and enables endless replayability.

```
# Example of procedural terrain generation in a game engine

terrain = generate_terrain(seed)
```

Procedural content generation can be used to create diverse and expansive landscapes without a massive storage overhead.

1.3.5 Scene Management

Efficient scene management is vital for large-scale game worlds. This includes techniques for seamlessly transitioning between different areas, managing scene loading, and ensuring a smooth player experience. Scene graphs and state machines are commonly used to orchestrate scene changes and transitions.

```
# Example of a scene transition in a game engine using a state machine

if player_position.crosses_boundary(new_scene_boundary):

change_scene(new_scene)
```

Effective scene management ensures that players can explore the game world without interruptions.

1.3.6 Dynamic World Interactions

Large-scale game worlds should offer dynamic and interactive elements to engage players. This includes dynamic weather systems, day-night cycles, and interactive objects. Game developers often use scripting languages or behavior systems to create these dynamic interactions.

```
# Example of a day-night cycle script in a game engine
def update_day_night_cycle(time_of_day):
lighting.set_sun_position(time_of_day)
if time_of_day == "night":
spawn_nighttime_enemies()
```

Dynamic interactions contribute to a living and immersive game world.

In conclusion, managing large-scale game worlds is a critical aspect of modern game development. Level of Detail techniques, spatial partitioning, streaming and loading, procedural content generation, scene management, and dynamic world interactions are key strategies for creating expansive and engaging game environments. These techniques ensure that players can explore vast worlds seamlessly, without sacrificing performance or visual quality. In the following sections of this chapter, we will explore further complexities in game development, including integrating complex gameplay mechanics and optimizing performance and memory.

1.4 Integrating Complex Gameplay Mechanics

Game development thrives on innovation and creativity, and integrating complex gameplay mechanics is at the heart of creating unique and compelling experiences for players. This section delves into the process of seamlessly integrating complex gameplay mechanics into your game, ensuring that they enhance the player's immersion and enjoyment.

1.4.1 Core Gameplay Loops

Complex gameplay mechanics often revolve around core gameplay loops. These loops define the essential interactions and activities players engage in throughout the game. Identifying and refining your core gameplay loops is crucial for creating a cohesive and engaging player experience.

```
# Example of a core gameplay loop in a platformer game

while not game_over:

handle_input()

update_player_position()

handle_collisions()

render_game_scene()
```

In this example, the core gameplay loop handles player input, character movement, collision detection, and rendering.

1.4.2 Player Progression Systems

Player progression systems are fundamental for keeping players engaged over extended play sessions. These systems include character leveling, skill trees, unlockable content, and resource management. Balancing these progression mechanics to provide a sense of achievement and challenge is essential.

```
# Example of a skill tree system in a role-playing game

class PlayerCharacter:

def __init__(self):

self.level = 1

self.skill_points = 0

self.skills = {"attack": 0, "defense": 0}

def level_up(self):

self.level += 1

self.skill_points += 1

def spend_skill_point(self, skill_name):

if self.skill_points > 0:

self.skills[skill_name] += 1

self.skill_points -= 1
```

Player progression systems should provide meaningful choices and rewards.

1.4.3 Interactive Mechanics

Complex gameplay often involves interactive mechanics that challenge players' problem-solving abilities. Puzzles, physics-based interactions, and interactive environments add depth to gameplay. Careful design and testing are crucial to ensure that these mechanics are intuitive and enjoyable.

```
# Example of a physics-based puzzle in a game engine

def solve_puzzle(puzzle_objects):

if puzzle_objects_connected(puzzle_objects):

open_secret_door()
```

Interactive mechanics should align with the game's narrative and world.

1.4.4 Narrative Integration

Story-driven games benefit from seamless narrative integration with gameplay mechanics. Choices made by players should impact the story's progression, and vice versa. Dialogue systems, branching storylines, and player agency are key components of narrative integration.

```
# Example of a branching dialogue system in a narrative game

def start_dialogue(npc):

available_choices = npc.get_dialogue_choices()

player_choice = present_choices_to_player(available_choices)

npc.react_to_choice(player_choice)
```

Narrative integration ensures that players feel connected to the game's story.

1.4.5 Balancing and Playtesting

Balancing complex gameplay mechanics is an ongoing process. Playtesting is invaluable for identifying potential issues, tweaking difficulty levels, and ensuring that the gameplay remains enjoyable and challenging. Gathering player feedback and iterating on the mechanics is essential for achieving balance.

```
# Example of using playtest feedback to balance enemy encounters

def adjust_enemy_stats(enemy):

if playtesters find the enemy too difficult, decrease its health.

if playtesters find the enemy too easy, increase its damage.
```

Balancing ensures that the gameplay remains engaging and fair.

1.4.6 Integration with Other Systems

Complex gameplay mechanics should seamlessly integrate with other game systems, including AI, physics, audio, and UI. Ensuring that these systems work harmoniously enhances the overall player experience.

```
# Example of integrating complex AI behavior with gameplay

def enemy_behavior(enemy):

if player_in_range(enemy):

chase_player(enemy)

else:

roam_randomly(enemy)
```

Integrating AI behavior with gameplay mechanics creates dynamic and challenging encounters.

In conclusion, integrating complex gameplay mechanics requires careful planning, testing, and iteration. Core gameplay loops, player progression systems, interactive mechanics, narrative integration, balancing, and integration with other game systems are key considerations. The successful integration of complex mechanics can elevate your game, providing players with memorable and immersive experiences. In the subsequent sections of this chapter, we will explore techniques for optimizing performance and memory, ensuring that your game runs smoothly and efficiently.

1.5 Performance and Memory Optimization Techniques

Optimizing performance and memory usage is paramount in game development, as it directly impacts the player's experience. In this section, we will explore various techniques and strategies to ensure that your game runs smoothly, efficiently utilizes hardware resources, and provides an enjoyable gameplay experience.

1.5.1 Profiling and Benchmarking

Profiling your game is the first step in identifying performance bottlenecks. Profilers provide insights into which parts of your code consume the most CPU or memory resources. Benchmarking tools help measure the performance of specific functions or components.

```
# Example of using a profiler in Unity

StartProfiling("Update")

# Game update logic

StopProfiling("Update")
```

Profiling helps pinpoint areas that require optimization.

1.5.2 Code Optimization

Code optimization involves improving the efficiency of your code. This can include reducing unnecessary calculations, optimizing loops, and minimizing memory allocations.

```
# Example of loop optimization in C++

for (int i = 0; i < arraySize; ++i) {
```

```
// Code to optimize
}
```

Optimized code can significantly boost performance.

1.5.3 Memory Management

Efficient memory management is essential to prevent memory leaks and excessive memory consumption. Use tools like memory profilers to track memory usage and ensure that objects are properly released when no longer needed.

```
// Example of memory management in C#

// Create an object

GameObject enemy = new GameObject();

// Destroy the object when it's no longer needed

Destroy(enemy);
```

Proper memory management prevents performance degradation over time.

1.5.4 Asset Optimization

Optimizing assets, such as textures, models, and audio files, is crucial for reducing loading times and memory usage. This includes using appropriate compression formats, mipmaps, and LOD techniques.

```
# Example of texture compression settings in a game engine

texture = load_texture("terrain.png", compression=BC7, generate_mipmaps=True)
```

Optimized assets strike a balance between visual quality and resource consumption.

1.5.5 Multithreading

Utilizing multithreading can significantly improve performance, especially for tasks that can be parallelized, such as physics calculations or AI processing. Implement thread pools and synchronization mechanisms to make efficient use of CPU cores.

```
# Example of multithreading in Java using Executors

ExecutorService executor = Executors.newFixedThreadPool(numThreads);

executor.submit(() -> perform_parallel_task());
```

Multithreading can distribute the workload and reduce processing time.

1.5.6 GPU Acceleration

Leveraging GPU acceleration is essential for rendering complex graphics. Utilize modern graphics APIs and shaders to offload rendering tasks to the GPU, allowing for more advanced visual effects and improved frame rates.

```
// Example of a simple fragment shader for GPU acceleration

#version 330 core

in vec2 TexCoord;

out vec4 FragColor;

uniform sampler2D texture;

void main() {
```

```
FragColor = texture(texture, TexCoord);
}
```

GPU acceleration enhances graphics performance.

1.5.7 Asset Streaming

Asset streaming involves loading assets dynamically as the player progresses through the game. This reduces initial loading times and memory overhead by only loading what is currently needed.

```
# Example of asset streaming in Unreal Engine
load_streamed_level("level_1")
```

Asset streaming ensures that the game uses resources efficiently.

1.5.8 Cross-Platform Optimization

Optimizing for different platforms requires tailoring your game to the specific hardware capabilities of each platform. Adjust graphics settings, resolution, and resource usage to ensure a consistent and smooth experience across various devices.

```
// Example of platform-specific optimization in Unity
#if UNITY_ANDROID
QualitySettings.SetQualityLevel(1); // Lower graphics quality for Android
#elif UNITY_IOS
QualitySettings.SetQualityLevel(2); // Medium graphics quality for iOS
#endif
```

Cross-platform optimization ensures your game performs well on a variety of devices.

1.5.9 Continuous Testing

Continuous testing throughout development is crucial for identifying and addressing performance and memory issues as they arise. Automated testing tools and profiling during development cycles help maintain optimal performance.

```
# Example of automated performance testing in a game engine

RunPerformanceTests()
```

Continuous testing prevents performance regressions and memory leaks.

In conclusion, performance and memory optimization techniques are essential to ensure that your game runs smoothly and provides an enjoyable player experience. Profiling, code optimization, memory management, asset optimization, multithreading, GPU acceleration, asset streaming, cross-platform optimization, and continuous testing are key strategies to achieve optimal performance and resource usage in your game. By applying these techniques, you can deliver a high-quality gaming experience that keeps players engaged and satisfied.

Chapter 2: High-Performance Rendering with SDL

2.1 Optimizing Rendering Pipelines

Efficient rendering is a cornerstone of any visually appealing game. In this section, we will explore techniques for optimizing rendering pipelines using the Simple DirectMedia Layer (SDL), a popular library for 2D and 3D graphics.

2.1.1 Understanding Rendering Pipelines

Rendering pipelines are the sequence of steps that transform 3D objects and scenes into 2D images on the screen. SDL provides a simplified rendering pipeline for 2D graphics, but understanding the stages involved is essential for optimization.

```
// Example of a simplified rendering pipeline in SDL

SDL_Surface* surface = load_image("texture.png"); // Load texture

SDL_BlitSurface(surface, NULL, screen_surface, NULL); // Blit texture to screen

SDL_UpdateWindowSurface(window); // Update the window
```

The pipeline involves loading textures, blitting (drawing) them to the screen surface, and updating the window.

2.1.2 Texture Atlas

Texture atlases are a powerful optimization technique that reduces the number of texture swaps during rendering. Instead of loading multiple small textures, pack several sprites into a single larger texture atlas.

```
// Example of using a texture atlas in SDL
```

SDL_Surface* atlas = load_image("atlas.png"); *// Load the texture atlas*

SDL_Rect source_rect = {x, y, width, height}; *// Define the source rectangle*

SDL_Rect dest_rect = {screen_x, screen_y, width, height}; *// Define the destination rectangle*

SDL_BlitSurface(atlas, &source_rect, screen_surface, &dest_rect); *// Blit sprite from atlas*

Texture atlases reduce the overhead of loading and switching textures.

2.1.3 Batch Rendering

Batch rendering involves grouping similar objects together and rendering them in a single draw call. This minimizes the overhead of making individual rendering calls for each object.

// Example of batch rendering in SDL

SDL_SetRenderDrawColor(renderer, 255, 255, 255, 255); *// Set rendering color*

SDL_RenderDrawLine(renderer, x1, y1, x2, y2); *// Render multiple lines in one call*

SDL_RenderDrawLine(renderer, x3, y3, x4, y4);

SDL_RenderPresent(renderer); *// Present the rendered frame*

Batch rendering is efficient for rendering multiple objects with the same characteristics.

2.1.4 Occlusion Culling

Occlusion culling is a technique used to avoid rendering objects that are not visible to the camera. This optimization prevents unnecessary rendering of objects hidden behind others.

```
// Example of occlusion culling in SDL
if (is_object_visible(camera, object)) {
render_object(object);
}
```

Occlusion culling minimizes rendering overhead and improves performance.

2.1.5 Level of Detail (LOD) Models

LOD models involve using different versions of a 3D model with varying levels of detail based on the object's distance from the camera. SDL's 2D rendering doesn't directly apply to LOD models, but understanding the concept can be useful for 3D games.

```
// Example of LOD models in a 3D game engine
if (distance_to_camera(object) < threshold_distance) {
render_high_detail_model(object);
} else {
render_low_detail_model(object);
}
```

LOD models reduce the GPU load for distant objects.

2.1.6 Shader Optimization

Shaders play a vital role in modern rendering pipelines. Optimizing shaders by minimizing the number of instructions and calculations can lead to significant performance improvements.

```
// Example of shader optimization in OpenGL

void main() {

gl_FragColor = texture2D(texture, texCoord) * lightColor; // Optimized shader code

}
```

Shader optimization ensures that the GPU processes graphics efficiently.

2.1.7 GPU Acceleration

SDL provides support for GPU acceleration, which offloads rendering tasks to the graphics card. Utilize GPU acceleration for better performance and the ability to render more complex scenes.

```
// Example of enabling GPU acceleration in SDL

SDL_Renderer* renderer = SDL_CreateRenderer(window, -1, SDL_RENDERER_ACCELERATED);
```

GPU acceleration enhances rendering speed and quality.

2.1.8 Efficient Blending Modes

Blending modes determine how pixels are combined when rendering overlapping objects. Choosing the appropriate blending mode for different objects can reduce overdraw and improve rendering efficiency.

```
// Example of setting a blending mode in SDL
```

```
SDL_SetRenderDrawBlendMode(renderer,
SDL_BLENDMODE_BLEND); // Set blending mode
```

Efficient blending modes ensure that pixels are combined optimally.

In conclusion, optimizing rendering pipelines is essential for achieving high-performance graphics in your game. Understanding rendering stages, using texture atlases, batch rendering, occlusion culling, LOD models, shader optimization, GPU acceleration, and efficient blending modes are key strategies to achieve smooth and visually appealing graphics. By applying these techniques, you can create games that provide a delightful visual experience while maintaining optimal performance.

2.2 Advanced Techniques in 2D and 3D Graphics

Achieving impressive and visually stunning graphics is a key goal for many game developers. In this section, we will delve into advanced techniques for both 2D and 3D graphics using the Simple DirectMedia Layer (SDL) as our framework of choice.

2.2.1 2D Graphics Techniques

SDL is renowned for its capabilities in 2D graphics. Below are some advanced techniques to enhance your 2D graphics:

- **Particle Systems:** Implementing particle systems can add visual effects like fire, smoke, or explosions to your game. You can control particle behavior, size, and movement to create captivating visual effects.

```
// Example of a simple particle system in SDL

ParticleSystem particles;

particles.createEmitter(ParticleType::Fire, position, velocity);
```

- **Shader Effects:** Utilizing shaders in 2D rendering can create stunning visual effects. You can apply shaders for post-processing effects like bloom, motion blur, or color grading.

```
// Example of applying a shader effect in SDL

SDL_SetRenderDrawColor(renderer, 255, 255, 255, 255); // Set rendering color
```

SDL_RenderCopy(renderer, texture, NULL, &destRect); *// Render a texture*

SDL_RenderPresent(renderer); *// Present the rendered frame*

- **Framebuffers:** Using framebuffers allows you to render to a texture instead of the screen. This technique is useful for creating mirrors, reflections, or complex texture effects.

// Example of rendering to a framebuffer in SDL

SDL_Texture* targetTexture = SDL_CreateTexture(renderer, SDL_PIXELFORMAT_RGBA8888, SDL_TEXTUREACCESS_TARGET, width, height);

SDL_SetRenderTarget(renderer, targetTexture); *// Set the render target*

// Render to targetTexture

SDL_SetRenderTarget(renderer, NULL); *// Reset the render target*

2.2.2 3D Graphics Techniques

While SDL is primarily a 2D framework, it can be used in conjunction with OpenGL or other 3D libraries to achieve impressive 3D graphics. Here are some advanced techniques for 3D graphics:

- **Dynamic Lighting:** Implementing dynamic lighting can enhance the realism of 3D scenes. You can use techniques like Phong shading or normal mapping to achieve realistic lighting effects.

```
// Example of dynamic lighting in a 3D game using OpenGL

glEnable(GL_LIGHTING); // Enable lighting

glEnable(GL_LIGHT0); // Enable a light source

glShadeModel(GL_SMOOTH); // Use smooth shading
```

- **Shadow Mapping:** Shadow mapping is crucial for creating realistic shadows in 3D environments. It involves rendering the scene from the perspective of a light source to create shadow maps.

```
// Example of shadow mapping in a 3D game using OpenGL

// Render scene from light's perspective to create shadow map

// Apply shadow map when rendering the scene from the camera's perspective
```

- **Post-Processing Effects:** Post-processing effects such as depth of field, motion blur, or ambient occlusion can greatly enhance the visual quality of a 3D game.

```
// Example of applying post-processing effects in a 3D game using OpenGL

// Render the scene to a framebuffer

// Apply post-processing shaders to the framebuffer
```

- **Terrain Generation:** Creating procedural terrain is a powerful technique for open-world games. Algorithms like Perlin noise can generate realistic and varied landscapes.

  // Example of procedural terrain generation in a 3D game using OpenGL

  // Generate terrain heightmap using Perlin noise

  // Create terrain mesh based on the heightmap

2.2.3 Cross-Platform Considerations

When working with advanced graphics techniques, it's crucial to consider cross-platform compatibility. Different platforms may have varying levels of support for advanced graphics features. You should test and optimize your graphics code for each target platform to ensure a consistent and enjoyable gaming experience.

```
// Example of platform-specific graphics optimization in SDL

#if defined(__ANDROID__)

// Apply Android-specific optimizations

#elif defined(__APPLE__)

// Apply iOS/macOS-specific optimizations

#elif defined(_WIN32)

// Apply Windows-specific optimizations

#endif
```

In conclusion, mastering advanced techniques in both 2D and 3D graphics can significantly elevate the visual quality of your games. Whether you are creating visually stunning effects in 2D or immersive 3D environments, SDL provides a flexible platform to implement these techniques. Experimentation and creative use of graphics libraries and APIs will enable you to create memorable and visually captivating gaming experiences.

2.3 GPU Acceleration and Its Utilization

GPU acceleration is a critical aspect of modern game development, as it significantly contributes to rendering performance and visual quality. In this section, we will explore the importance of GPU acceleration and various techniques to effectively utilize the GPU for graphics rendering.

2.3.1 The Role of GPU in Graphics Rendering

The Graphics Processing Unit (GPU) plays a fundamental role in rendering graphics in games. Unlike the Central Processing Unit (CPU), which handles general-purpose tasks, the GPU is specialized for parallel processing and graphics rendering. GPUs are designed to perform numerous calculations simultaneously, making them ideal for rendering complex 2D and 3D scenes.

In a typical rendering pipeline, the CPU is responsible for game logic, physics, and preparing data for rendering. The GPU then takes this data and efficiently renders it to the screen. This division of labor allows for a seamless and efficient rendering process.

2.3.2 Hardware Acceleration with APIs

To effectively utilize the GPU, game developers often use graphics APIs (Application Programming Interfaces) like DirectX, OpenGL, Vulkan, or Metal. These APIs provide a bridge between the game code and the GPU, allowing developers to harness the full power of the graphics hardware.

```
// Example of initializing OpenGL in a game engine

glViewport(0, 0, screenWidth, screenHeight); // Set the viewport

glClearColor(0.0f, 0.0f, 0.0f, 1.0f); // Set the clear color
```

```
glEnable(GL_DEPTH_TEST); // Enable depth testing
```

Graphics APIs provide functions and tools for configuring rendering settings, creating shaders, and sending data to the GPU for rendering.

2.3.3 Parallelism and Pipelining

One of the key strengths of GPUs is their ability to execute tasks in parallel. GPUs are composed of thousands of small processing cores that can work simultaneously on different aspects of rendering. This parallelism allows for the efficient rendering of complex scenes with many objects.

To fully utilize GPU parallelism, game developers often employ techniques like multithreading. By separating rendering tasks into multiple threads, developers can take advantage of the GPU's parallel processing capabilities.

```
// Example of multithreading for rendering tasks

// Render thread

void RenderThread() {

while (isRunning) {

// Render the scene

}

}
```

Multithreading ensures that the GPU is kept busy with rendering tasks, leading to smoother frame rates.

2.3.4 GPU-Friendly Rendering Techniques

To make the most of GPU acceleration, developers should adopt rendering techniques that are GPU-friendly. These techniques include:

- **Batch Rendering:** Grouping similar objects together and rendering them in a single draw call reduces CPU overhead and minimizes the communication between the CPU and GPU.

- **Instancing:** Instancing allows rendering multiple instances of the same object with a single draw call, further reducing CPU-GPU communication.

- **GPU Shaders:** Writing optimized shaders that minimize unnecessary calculations and take advantage of GPU parallelism can significantly boost rendering performance.

```
// Example of an efficient shader in OpenGL

void main() {

gl_Position = projection * view * model * vec4(position, 1.0);

}
```

- **Texture Atlases:** Combining multiple textures into a single texture atlas reduces texture swaps, improving rendering performance.

- **Culling and LOD Techniques:** Implementing culling techniques like frustum culling and level-of-detail (LOD) can reduce the number of objects sent to the GPU for rendering.

- **Geometry and Occlusion Queries:** These techniques help determine which objects are visible to the camera and which can be skipped during rendering.

- **Asynchronous Loading:** Loading assets asynchronously in the background allows the CPU to prepare data for rendering without blocking the main game loop.

2.3.5 Cross-Platform Considerations

When utilizing GPU acceleration, it's essential to consider cross-platform compatibility. Different platforms may have varying GPU capabilities and support for specific graphics features. Game developers should test and optimize their GPU-related code for each target platform to ensure a consistent and enjoyable gaming experience across devices.

```
// Example of platform-specific GPU optimization in a game engine
#if defined(__ANDROID__)
// Apply Android-specific GPU optimizations
#elif defined(__APPLE__)
// Apply iOS/macOS-specific GPU optimizations
#elif defined(_WIN32)
// Apply Windows-specific GPU optimizations
#endif
```

In conclusion, GPU acceleration is a crucial aspect of modern game development, enabling developers to render complex and visually stunning graphics. Understanding the role of the GPU, utilizing graphics APIs, leveraging parallelism and pipelining, adopting GPU-friendly rendering techniques, and considering cross-platform compatibility are essential for harnessing the full potential of GPU acceleration. By implementing these strategies, game developers can deliver visually impressive and high-performance games that captivate players.

2.4 Implementing High-Resolution Support

High-resolution support is essential for modern games to provide players with visually stunning experiences on various devices. In this section, we will explore techniques for implementing high-resolution support in your game using the Simple DirectMedia Layer (SDL) and other relevant technologies.

2.4.1 Understanding High-Resolution Displays

High-resolution displays have become increasingly prevalent in gaming devices, from smartphones and tablets to desktop monitors and televisions. These displays offer higher pixel densities, resulting in sharper and more detailed visuals. To cater to this growing audience, it's crucial to implement high-resolution support in your game.

2.4.2 Resolution Independence

Resolution independence is the concept of designing your game to adapt to different screen resolutions seamlessly. It ensures that the game's visuals remain consistent and visually appealing, regardless of the user's device.

One way to achieve resolution independence is by using vector graphics for UI elements and sprites. Vector graphics scale smoothly to different resolutions without loss of quality. Additionally, using percentage-based layouts for UI elements allows them to adjust automatically to various screen sizes.

```
// Example of percentage-based UI layout in SDL

int screenWidth = GetScreenWidth(); // Get the current screen width
```

int screenHeight = GetScreenHeight(); // *Get the current screen height*

int buttonWidth = screenWidth * 0.2; // *Button width as a percentage of screen width*

int buttonHeight = screenHeight * 0.1; // *Button height as a percentage of screen height*

By using percentage-based calculations for UI elements, you can ensure they adapt to different resolutions.

2.4.3 Scalable Assets

Creating assets that can scale gracefully to high resolutions is essential. This involves designing textures, sprites, and UI elements with sufficient resolution and detail to accommodate larger screens.

// *Example of loading high-resolution textures in SDL*

SDL_Texture* highResTexture = LoadTexture("high_res_texture.png");

Loading high-resolution assets ensures that they look crisp and clear on high-DPI displays.

2.4.4 Multiple Asset Variants

To support different resolutions effectively, consider providing multiple variants of assets optimized for specific screen resolutions. This allows your game to load the most appropriate assets based on the user's device, reducing memory usage and improving performance.

// *Example of loading assets based on screen resolution in SDL*

if (screenWidth >= 1920 && screenHeight >= 1080) {

```
LoadHighResAssets();

} else {

LoadStandardAssets();

}
```

Loading assets dynamically based on resolution optimizes resource utilization.

2.4.5 Dynamic Scaling

Dynamic scaling involves adjusting the rendering resolution of your game based on the user's device. This can help maintain a consistent frame rate and ensure smooth gameplay, especially on devices with limited processing power.

```
// Example of dynamic scaling in SDL

int targetWidth = 1920; // Target resolution width

int targetHeight = 1080; // Target resolution height

SDL_SetWindowSize(window, targetWidth, targetHeight); // Set window size
```

Dynamic scaling can be particularly useful for mobile and lower-end devices.

2.4.6 User Interface (UI) Scaling

Scaling the game's user interface (UI) elements, including buttons, text, and menus, is essential for readability and usability on high-resolution displays. You can achieve this by adjusting the size and positioning of UI elements relative to the screen resolution.

```
// Example of UI scaling in SDL
```

int buttonWidth = screenWidth * 0.2; *// Button width as a percentage of screen width*

int buttonHeight = screenHeight * 0.1; *// Button height as a percentage of screen height*

button.SetSize(buttonWidth, buttonHeight); *// Set the button's size*

Proper UI scaling ensures that UI elements remain accessible and visually pleasing.

2.4.7 Testing and Optimization

Testing your game on various devices with different screen resolutions is crucial to ensure that high-resolution support works as intended. Identifying and addressing any issues related to scaling, asset loading, or UI layout is essential for providing a seamless gaming experience.

Additionally, optimizing your game's rendering pipeline, asset loading, and memory management can help maintain high performance on high-resolution displays.

In conclusion, implementing high-resolution support is vital for modern game development. By understanding resolution independence, using scalable assets, providing multiple asset variants, employing dynamic scaling, adapting the UI, and conducting thorough testing and optimization, you can ensure that your game looks and performs its best on a wide range of devices, catering to the diverse preferences of players.

2.5 Balancing Visual Quality and Performance

Balancing visual quality and performance is a critical aspect of game development. To create an enjoyable gaming experience, developers must find the right equilibrium between stunning visuals and smooth gameplay. In this section, we'll explore strategies and techniques to achieve this balance using the Simple DirectMedia Layer (SDL) and other relevant technologies.

2.5.1 Visual Quality Considerations

Visual quality encompasses various aspects, including graphics fidelity, special effects, texture details, lighting, and post-processing effects. While high-quality visuals can immerse players in the game world, they often come at the cost of performance. Here are some considerations to balance visual quality:

- **Texture Resolution:** Use appropriate texture resolutions for different objects and environments. High-resolution textures are essential for close-up objects, while distant objects may use lower-resolution textures.

- **Polygon Count:** Reduce the polygon count for distant or less critical objects. Level-of-detail (LOD) models are useful for this purpose, ensuring that complex 3D models are only used when necessary.

- **Dynamic Lighting:** Implement dynamic lighting for key scenes and objects, but limit the number of dynamic lights to maintain performance.

- **Post-Processing Effects:** Carefully choose and optimize post-processing effects like bloom, motion blur, and depth of field. Disable or reduce these effects on lower-end devices.

2.5.2 Performance Optimization Techniques

Optimizing performance without sacrificing visual quality is a continuous process throughout game development. Here are some performance optimization techniques:

- **Culling Techniques:** Implement frustum culling, occlusion culling, and backface culling to avoid rendering objects that are not visible to the camera.

- **Batch Rendering:** Group similar objects together and render them in a single draw call to minimize CPU-GPU communication.

- **GPU Shaders:** Optimize shaders to reduce unnecessary calculations and leverage the GPU's parallel processing capabilities.

- **Asynchronous Loading:** Load assets asynchronously in the background to prevent frame rate drops during loading.

- **Level Streaming:** Divide large game worlds into manageable chunks and stream them in and out as needed to reduce memory usage.

- **Memory Management:** Implement efficient memory management and detect memory leaks to prevent performance degradation.

```
// Example of memory management in C++
void* ptr = malloc(1024); // Allocate memory
// ...
free(ptr); // Free memory when it's no longer needed
```

- **Multi-Threading:** Use multi-threading to distribute CPU-intensive tasks across multiple threads, ensuring that the CPU and GPU are fully utilized.

```
// Example of multi-threading in C++
std::thread workerThread(DoWork); // Create a worker thread
workerThread.join(); // Wait for the worker thread to finish
```

2.5.3 Player Preferences and Device Performance

Consider the target audience and the devices your game will run on. Different players have varying preferences for visual quality and performance. Provide graphics settings in your game to allow players to adjust visual quality based on their device's capabilities and personal preferences.

```
// Example of graphics settings menu in a game
if (playerSettings.quality == HIGH) {
EnableHighQualityVisuals();
} else if (playerSettings.quality == LOW) {
DisableAdvancedVisuals();
}
```

By giving players control over graphics settings, you can cater to a broader audience.

2.5.4 Profiling and Testing

Regularly profile and test your game on a range of devices to identify performance bottlenecks and visual quality issues. Profiling tools can help pinpoint areas that require optimization, such as CPU-bound tasks or inefficient GPU usage.

```
// Example of profiling in a game engine

Profiler.Start("Rendering"); // Start profiling a specific task

// ...

Profiler.Stop("Rendering"); // Stop profiling the task
```

Testing on different hardware configurations, including both high-end and low-end devices, is essential to ensure your game performs well across the board.

2.5.5 Real-Time Adjustments

Consider implementing real-time adjustments during gameplay. For example, if the frame rate drops below a certain threshold, you can automatically reduce visual effects or adjust rendering settings to maintain smooth gameplay.

```
// Example of real-time adjustments in a game

if (currentFrameRate < targetFrameRate) {

ReduceVisualEffects();

}
```

Real-time adjustments help ensure a consistent gaming experience, even when unexpected performance issues arise.

In conclusion, balancing visual quality and performance is a complex but essential task in game development. By carefully considering visual quality aspects, optimizing performance through techniques like culling, batching, and multi-threading, providing player preferences for graphics settings, profiling and testing, and implementing real-time adjustments, you can create games that offer both stunning visuals and smooth gameplay, catering to a wide range of players and devices.

Chapter 3: Multi-Threaded and Asynchronous Programming

3.1 Understanding Threads in Game Development

Multi-threading and asynchronous programming are crucial techniques in modern game development, allowing games to efficiently utilize multi-core processors and deliver smooth gameplay experiences. In this section, we will delve into the fundamentals of threads and their role in game development using the Simple DirectMedia Layer (SDL) and relevant technologies.

3.1.1 Threads and Parallelism

In computing, a thread is the smallest unit of execution within a process. Threads enable parallelism, which means that multiple threads can execute tasks simultaneously, taking advantage of multi-core processors commonly found in modern devices. Parallelism is essential for distributing the workload across CPU cores, optimizing performance, and ensuring responsiveness in games.

3.1.2 Thread Creation and Management

In game development, threads are used to handle various tasks concurrently, such as rendering, physics simulation, AI calculations, and asset loading. SDL provides facilities for creating and managing threads efficiently.

```
// Example of creating a thread in SDL

#include <SDL_thread.h>

SDL_Thread* myThread = SDL_CreateThread(MyThreadFunction, "ThreadName", data);
```

In the above example, MyThreadFunction represents the function that the new thread will execute. data is a pointer to any data that needs to be passed to the thread.

3.1.3 Thread Synchronization

When multiple threads access shared resources or data simultaneously, thread synchronization is crucial to prevent data corruption and ensure consistency. SDL provides synchronization primitives like mutexes and semaphores for this purpose.

```
// Example of using a mutex in SDL for thread synchronization

#include <SDL_mutex.h>

SDL_mutex* myMutex = SDL_CreateMutex();

// Thread 1

SDL_LockMutex(myMutex);

// Access and modify shared data

SDL_UnlockMutex(myMutex);

// Thread 2

SDL_LockMutex(myMutex);

// Access and modify the same shared data

SDL_UnlockMutex(myMutex);
```

Mutexes ensure that only one thread can access the protected data at a time, preventing conflicts.

3.1.4 Task Parallelism

Task parallelism involves dividing a larger task into smaller, independent subtasks that can be executed concurrently by different threads. This approach can improve the overall efficiency of game code by parallelizing tasks that don't depend on each other.

```
// Example of task parallelism in game development

void Task1() {

// Perform task 1

}

void Task2() {

// Perform task 2

}

// Create two threads to execute Task1 and Task2 concurrently

SDL_Thread* thread1 = SDL_CreateThread(Task1, "Task1Thread", data1);

SDL_Thread* thread2 = SDL_CreateThread(Task2, "Task2Thread", data2);
```

By dividing tasks into smaller units, you can fully utilize CPU resources and improve performance.

3.1.5 Load Balancing

Load balancing is the process of distributing tasks evenly across available CPU cores to optimize resource utilization. Game engines often use load balancing techniques to ensure that all cores are actively working on relevant tasks.

```
// Example of load balancing in a game engine
```

```
// Determine the number of CPU cores available

int numCores = SDL_GetCPUCount();

// Create threads and assign tasks to balance the workload across cores

for (int i = 0; i < numCores; ++i) {

SDL_Thread* thread = SDL_CreateThread(WorkerThreadFunction, "WorkerThread", data);

}
```

Load balancing can prevent CPU cores from being underutilized, leading to better overall performance.

3.1.6 Thread Safety and Challenges

While multi-threading offers significant benefits, it also introduces challenges, including race conditions, deadlocks, and synchronization overhead. Game developers must carefully manage and synchronize threads to avoid these issues and ensure the correctness of their code.

In conclusion, understanding threads and their role in game development is essential for leveraging multi-core processors and optimizing game performance. Threads enable parallelism, allowing tasks to be executed concurrently, and SDL provides valuable tools for creating and managing threads. Thread synchronization, task parallelism, load balancing, and addressing thread safety challenges are critical aspects of effective multi-threaded and asynchronous programming in game development.

3.2 Asynchronous Operations in SDL

Asynchronous operations play a significant role in game development, enabling tasks to run independently without blocking the main game loop. SDL (Simple DirectMedia Layer) provides support for asynchronous programming, which is valuable for handling tasks like asset loading, network communication, and input processing while maintaining a responsive game experience. In this section, we will explore how to implement asynchronous operations using SDL and related techniques.

3.2.1 Asynchronous Asset Loading

Loading large assets, such as textures, models, or audio files, can be time-consuming and might cause the game to freeze temporarily if done synchronously. Asynchronous asset loading allows these tasks to happen in the background, ensuring the game remains responsive.

```
// Example of asynchronous asset loading in SDL using threads

SDL_Thread* assetLoadingThread = SDL_CreateThread(AsyncAssetLoader, "AssetLoaderThread", data);
```

In this example, the AsyncAssetLoader function runs in a separate thread, loading assets while the main game loop continues to execute.

3.2.2 Callbacks and Event Handling

SDL provides mechanisms for handling events and callbacks asynchronously. For instance, you can use SDL's event system to process input and respond to user interactions without blocking the main thread.

```
// Example of handling events asynchronously in SDL
```

```
SDL_Event event;
while (SDL_PollEvent(&event)) {
// Handle the event
}
```

By processing events asynchronously, you can ensure that the game responds to user input promptly.

3.2.3 Asynchronous Networking

Networking operations, such as connecting to game servers or fetching data from external sources, often involve latency and can't be executed synchronously without causing delays. SDL supports asynchronous socket operations, allowing network tasks to run independently.

```
// Example of asynchronous networking in SDL using sockets
SDLNet_SocketSet socketSet = SDLNet_AllocSocketSet(1);
TCPsocket clientSocket = SDLNet_TCP_Open(&serverIP);
// Add the socket to the socket set for asynchronous handling
SDLNet_TCP_AddSocket(socketSet, clientSocket);
// Wait for network events asynchronously
int numReadySockets = SDLNet_CheckSockets(socketSet, timeout);
```

Asynchronous networking prevents the game from becoming unresponsive during network operations.

3.2.4 Asynchronous Timers and Delays

SDL provides functions for creating timers and delays that operate asynchronously. These timers can be used for various purposes, including animations, timed events, and game logic that doesn't block the main thread.

```
// Example of asynchronous timers in SDL

Uint32 delay = 1000; // Delay in milliseconds

SDL_TimerID timerID = SDL_AddTimer(delay, TimerCallback, data);

// Timer callback function

Uint32 TimerCallback(Uint32 interval, void* param) {

// Handle timer event

return interval; // Set the timer to repeat

}
```

Asynchronous timers allow you to schedule tasks without disrupting the game's flow.

3.2.5 Thread Pools and Worker Threads

Managing multiple threads for asynchronous tasks can be complex. SDL allows developers to create thread pools, a collection of worker threads that can be used to execute tasks concurrently.

```
// Example of creating a thread pool in SDL

SDL_threadpool* threadPool = SDL_CreateThreadPool(numThreads);

// Add tasks to the thread pool for asynchronous execution
```

```
SDL_QueueWorkItem(AsyncTask, data, "Task1");

SDL_QueueWorkItem(AsyncTask, data, "Task2");
```

Thread pools simplify the management of worker threads, making it easier to parallelize tasks.

3.2.6 Asynchronous Input Handling

Handling input asynchronously is crucial for responsive gameplay. SDL's input handling mechanisms, including keyboard, mouse, and game controller events, can be processed asynchronously to ensure timely player input recognition.

```
// Example of asynchronous input handling in SDL

SDL_Event event;

while (SDL_PollEvent(&event)) {

// Handle input events asynchronously

}
```

By processing input asynchronously, you can maintain a smooth and responsive player experience.

3.2.7 Asynchronous Error Handling

Error handling is another area where asynchronous operations can be beneficial. Asynchronous error handling techniques can help diagnose and respond to errors without disrupting the main game loop.

```
// Example of asynchronous error handling in SDL

SDL_Thread* errorHandlingThread = SDL_CreateThread(AsyncErrorHandling, "ErrorThread", data);
```

By running error-handling tasks asynchronously, you can keep the game running even when errors occur.

In conclusion, asynchronous operations are essential for modern game development, enabling tasks to execute independently without blocking the main game loop. SDL provides various mechanisms for implementing asynchronous asset loading, event handling, networking, timers, input processing, error handling, and more. By effectively incorporating asynchronous programming techniques into your game, you can ensure a responsive and engaging player experience while efficiently managing time-consuming tasks in the background.

3.3 Thread Synchronization and Safety

Thread synchronization and ensuring thread safety are critical aspects of multi-threaded programming in game development. When multiple threads access shared resources or data concurrently, synchronization is necessary to prevent race conditions, deadlocks, and data corruption. In this section, we will explore thread synchronization techniques and best practices using SDL and relevant technologies.

3.3.1 Mutexes (Mutual Exclusion)

Mutexes, short for mutual exclusion, are synchronization primitives used to protect shared resources or data from concurrent access. In SDL, you can create and use mutexes to ensure that only one thread can access the protected resource at a time.

```
// Example of using mutexes for thread synchronization in SDL

#include <SDL_mutex.h>

SDL_mutex* myMutex = SDL_CreateMutex();

// Thread 1

SDL_LockMutex(myMutex);

// Access and modify shared data

SDL_UnlockMutex(myMutex);

// Thread 2

SDL_LockMutex(myMutex);

// Access and modify the same shared data
```

SDL_UnlockMutex(myMutex);

Mutexes provide a straightforward way to enforce exclusive access to resources, preventing data races and maintaining data integrity.

3.3.2 Semaphores

Semaphores are synchronization mechanisms used to control access to a resource by multiple threads. Semaphores allow a specified number of threads to access a resource simultaneously while blocking others.

// Example of using semaphores for thread synchronization in SDL

#include **<SDL_semaphore.h>**

SDL_sem* mySemaphore = SDL_CreateSemaphore(2); *// Allow up to 2 threads simultaneously*

// Thread 1

SDL_SemWait(mySemaphore);

// Access and modify shared data

SDL_SemPost(mySemaphore);

// Thread 2

SDL_SemWait(mySemaphore);

// Access and modify shared data

SDL_SemPost(mySemaphore);

Semaphores are useful when you want to control access to a resource based on a specific limit, such as the number of available worker threads.

3.3.3 Condition Variables

Condition variables are synchronization primitives that allow threads to wait for a specific condition to be met before proceeding. They are commonly used for thread coordination and notification.

```
// Example of using condition variables for thread synchronization in SDL

#include <SDL_thread.h>

SDL_mutex* conditionMutex = SDL_CreateMutex();

SDL_cond* conditionVariable = SDL_CreateCond();

// Thread 1

SDL_LockMutex(conditionMutex);

// Perform some work

SDL_CondSignal(conditionVariable); // Signal that the condition is met

SDL_UnlockMutex(conditionMutex);

// Thread 2

SDL_LockMutex(conditionMutex);

SDL_CondWait(conditionVariable, conditionMutex); // Wait until the condition is signaled

// Continue with the next task

SDL_UnlockMutex(conditionMutex);
```

Condition variables allow threads to efficiently wait for and respond to specific events or changes in shared data.

3.3.4 Atomic Operations

Atomic operations ensure that specific memory operations are executed without interruption by other threads. SDL provides atomic functions for performing operations like incrementing or swapping values atomically.

```
// Example of atomic operations in SDL

#include <SDL_atomic.h>

SDL_atomic_t atomicCounter = SDL_ATOMIC_VAR_INIT(0);

// Thread 1

SDL_AtomicIncRef(&atomicCounter); // Increment the value atomically

// Thread 2

SDL_AtomicDecRef(&atomicCounter); // Decrement the value atomically
```

Atomic operations are essential for ensuring that critical operations on shared data are performed without data races.

3.3.5 Deadlock Avoidance

Deadlocks can occur when multiple threads are waiting for each other to release resources. Avoiding deadlocks requires careful design and following best practices, such as always acquiring mutexes in the same order and using timeout mechanisms for locking operations.

```
// Example of using timeout for mutex locking in SDL
```

```
SDL_mutex* mutex1 = SDL_CreateMutex();
SDL_mutex* mutex2 = SDL_CreateMutex();
if (SDL_LockMutex(mutex1) == 0) {
if (SDL_LockMutex(mutex2) == 0) {
// Access shared resources protected by mutex1 and mutex2
SDL_UnlockMutex(mutex2);
}
SDL_UnlockMutex(mutex1);
}
```

By using timeouts and following consistent locking order, you can prevent deadlocks.

3.3.6 Testing and Debugging

Testing and debugging multi-threaded code is essential to identify and resolve synchronization issues. SDL provides debugging tools and profiling support to track and diagnose thread-related problems.

```
// Example of debugging and profiling multi-threaded code in SDL
SDL_threadID threadID = SDL_GetThreadID(); // Get the thread ID for debugging
SDL_SetThreadName(threadID, "WorkerThread"); // Set a name for the thread
// Use debugging and profiling tools to monitor thread behavior and identify issues.
```

Regularly testing and profiling your multi-threaded code can help ensure its correctness and performance.

In conclusion, thread synchronization and thread safety are vital considerations when developing multi-threaded game applications. SDL offers synchronization primitives like mutexes, semaphores, and condition variables, as well as atomic operations, to facilitate safe multi-threading. Careful design, deadlock avoidance, testing, and debugging are essential practices for creating robust and efficient multi-threaded game code.

3.4 Scalable Multithreading Techniques

Scalable multithreading is a crucial aspect of game development, allowing games to take full advantage of modern multi-core processors. In this section, we will explore various techniques and best practices for achieving scalable multithreading in game development using SDL and related technologies.

3.4.1 Task Parallelism

Task parallelism involves dividing a larger task into smaller, independent subtasks that can be executed concurrently by different threads. This approach can significantly improve the overall efficiency of game code by parallelizing tasks that don't depend on each other.

For example, a game engine might use task parallelism to process physics simulations for different objects in the game world simultaneously. Each object's physics calculations can be performed in parallel, reducing the overall time required for physics simulation.

```
// Example of task parallelism in game development

void Task1() {

// Perform physics calculations for object 1

}

void Task2() {

// Perform physics calculations for object 2

}

// Create two threads to execute Task1 and Task2 concurrently
```

SDL_Thread* thread1 = SDL_CreateThread(Task1, "Task1Thread", data1);

SDL_Thread* thread2 = SDL_CreateThread(Task2, "Task2Thread", data2);

By dividing tasks into smaller units and executing them concurrently, you can fully utilize CPU resources and improve performance.

3.4.2 Load Balancing

Load balancing is the process of distributing tasks evenly across available CPU cores to optimize resource utilization. Game engines often use load balancing techniques to ensure that all cores are actively working on relevant tasks.

// Example of load balancing in a game engine

// Determine the number of CPU cores available

int numCores = SDL_GetCPUCount();

// Create threads and assign tasks to balance the workload across cores

for (int i = 0; i < numCores; ++i) {

SDL_Thread* thread = SDL_CreateThread(WorkerThreadFunction, "WorkerThread", data);

}

Load balancing prevents CPU cores from being underutilized, leading to better overall performance.

3.4.3 Data Parallelism

Data parallelism involves processing multiple data elements in parallel using multiple threads. In game development, this technique is often used for tasks like rendering, where each thread is responsible for rendering a portion of the game world.

For example, in a game with a large open world, data parallelism can be employed to divide the world into chunks, and each thread can be assigned to render a specific chunk.

```
// Example of data parallelism in game development

void RenderChunk(int chunkID) {

// Render objects in the specified chunk

}

// Create multiple threads to render different chunks in parallel

for (int i = 0; i < numChunks; ++i) {

SDL_Thread* thread = SDL_CreateThread(RenderChunk, "RenderThread", chunkID);

}
```

Data parallelism is particularly effective for tasks that can be parallelized at the data level.

3.4.4 Thread Pools

Managing multiple threads for asynchronous tasks can be complex. Thread pools provide a convenient way to create and manage a collection of worker threads that can be used to execute tasks concurrently.

```
// Example of creating a thread pool in SDL
```

```
SDL_threadpool* threadPool = SDL_CreateThreadPool(numThreads);

// Add tasks to the thread pool for asynchronous execution

SDL_QueueWorkItem(AsyncTask, data, "Task1");

SDL_QueueWorkItem(AsyncTask, data, "Task2");
```

Thread pools simplify the management of worker threads, making it easier to parallelize tasks and ensure scalable multithreading.

3.4.5 Data Partitioning

Data partitioning involves dividing large datasets into smaller partitions that can be processed independently by multiple threads. In game development, data partitioning can be used in scenarios like pathfinding, where the game world's navigation grid is divided into partitions, and each thread calculates paths within its assigned partition.

```
// Example of data partitioning in game development

void CalculatePathsForPartition(int partitionID) {

// Calculate paths within the specified partition

}

// Create multiple threads to calculate paths for different partitions

for (int i = 0; i < numPartitions; ++i) {

SDL_Thread* thread = SDL_CreateThread(CalculatePathsForPartition, "PathfindingThread", partitionID);

}
```

Data partitioning allows for efficient parallel processing of large datasets, contributing to scalable multithreading.

In conclusion, scalable multithreading is essential for fully utilizing the processing power of modern multi-core CPUs in game development. Techniques such as task parallelism, load balancing, data parallelism, thread pools, and data partitioning are valuable tools for achieving scalability and optimizing game performance. By carefully choosing the right multithreading approach for specific tasks, game developers can create responsive and efficient games that take full advantage of today's hardware capabilities.

3.5 Maximizing Performance with Parallel Processing

Maximizing performance is a critical goal in game development, and parallel processing plays a pivotal role in achieving it. Parallelism allows games to utilize multi-core processors effectively, distribute workloads, and deliver smooth and responsive gameplay experiences. In this section, we will explore techniques and strategies for maximizing performance through parallel processing using SDL and relevant technologies.

3.5.1 Utilizing Multi-Core Processors

Modern CPUs often feature multiple cores, which can handle multiple threads simultaneously. To maximize performance, it's essential to design games that can utilize these cores effectively. This involves parallelizing tasks to run concurrently on different cores.

```
// Example of task parallelism in game development

void Task1() {

// Perform task 1

}

void Task2() {

// Perform task 2

}

// Create two threads to execute Task1 and Task2 concurrently

SDL_Thread* thread1 = SDL_CreateThread(Task1, "Task1Thread", data1);
```

```
SDL_Thread* thread2 = SDL_CreateThread(Task2, "Task2Thread", data2);
```

By distributing tasks across multiple threads, you can leverage the full potential of multi-core processors.

3.5.2 Parallel Rendering

Rendering is a resource-intensive task in game development, and parallel rendering techniques can significantly boost performance. One common approach is to divide the rendering workload among multiple threads, each responsible for rendering a portion of the game world.

```
// Example of parallel rendering in game development

void RenderChunk(int chunkID) {

// Render objects in the specified chunk

}

// Create multiple threads to render different chunks in parallel

for (int i = 0; i < numChunks; ++i) {

SDL_Thread* thread = SDL_CreateThread(RenderChunk, "RenderThread", chunkID);

}
```

Parallel rendering ensures that all available CPU cores contribute to rendering tasks, leading to improved frame rates.

3.5.3 Parallel Physics Simulation

Physics simulations are another computationally intensive aspect of game development. Parallelizing physics calculations, such as collision detection and rigid body dynamics, can lead to substantial performance improvements.

```
// Example of parallel physics simulation in game development

void SimulatePhysicsForChunk(int chunkID) {

// Perform physics calculations for objects in the specified chunk

}

// Create multiple threads to simulate physics for different chunks in parallel

for (int i = 0; i < numChunks; ++i) {

SDL_Thread* thread = SDL_CreateThread(SimulatePhysicsForChunk, "PhysicsThread", chunkID);

}
```

Parallel physics simulation allows for more complex and realistic physics interactions in games.

3.5.4 Load Balancing

Load balancing is crucial when distributing tasks across multiple threads. Uneven workloads can lead to underutilization of some CPU cores. Techniques like dynamic load balancing can help ensure that tasks are distributed evenly.

```
// Example of load balancing in a game engine

// Determine the number of CPU cores available

int numCores = SDL_GetCPUCount();
```

```
// Create threads and assign tasks to balance the workload across cores dynamically

for (int i = 0; i < numCores; ++i) {

SDL_Thread* thread = SDL_CreateThread(WorkerThreadFunction, "WorkerThread", data);

}
```

Load balancing ensures that all CPU cores are actively engaged in processing tasks, maximizing performance.

3.5.5 Parallel Asset Loading

Asset loading, including textures, models, and audio files, can be a bottleneck in game development. Parallel asset loading techniques allow assets to be loaded concurrently in the background, preventing the game from freezing during loading screens.

```
// Example of parallel asset loading in SDL using threads

SDL_Thread* assetLoadingThread = SDL_CreateThread(AsyncAssetLoader, "AssetLoaderThread", data);
```

Parallel asset loading maintains a responsive player experience while efficiently loading resources.

3.5.6 Profiling and Optimization

To maximize performance with parallel processing, it's crucial to profile and optimize code regularly. Profiling tools can help identify bottlenecks and areas where parallelism can be applied effectively. Additionally, optimizing algorithms and data structures for parallelism can lead to significant performance gains.

// Example of profiling and optimization in game development

// Use profiling tools to analyze thread behavior and identify performance bottlenecks.

// Optimize algorithms and data structures for parallelism.

Profiling and optimization are ongoing processes that ensure your game benefits from parallel processing to the fullest extent.

In conclusion, maximizing performance through parallel processing is a fundamental aspect of modern game development. By effectively utilizing multi-core processors, parallel rendering, physics simulation, load balancing, parallel asset loading, and continuous profiling and optimization, game developers can deliver high-quality, responsive, and visually impressive gaming experiences that fully leverage the capabilities of today's hardware.

Chapter 4: Network Engineering for Online Games

4.1 Advanced Networking Concepts in SDL

In the realm of online gaming, advanced networking concepts are essential for creating seamless multiplayer experiences. SDL (Simple DirectMedia Layer) provides robust networking capabilities to assist game developers in building efficient and reliable networked games. In this section, we will explore advanced networking concepts in SDL, including socket programming, protocols, and strategies for enhancing network performance and security.

4.1.1 Socket Programming

Socket programming forms the foundation of network communication in many online games. SDL offers support for both TCP and UDP sockets, allowing game developers to choose the appropriate communication method for their specific needs.

```
// Example of TCP socket creation in SDL

#include <SDL_net.h>

IPaddress serverIP;

TCPsocket clientSocket;

if (SDLNet_ResolveHost(&serverIP, "example.com", 12345) == 0)
{

clientSocket = SDLNet_TCP_Open(&serverIP);

if (clientSocket != NULL) {

// Successfully opened a TCP connection

}
```

```
}
```

This code demonstrates how to create a TCP socket connection to a remote server using SDL. Similar functions are available for UDP socket creation.

4.1.2 Protocols and Serialization

Efficient network communication requires well-defined protocols and serialization methods to encode and decode data. SDL allows developers to define their network protocols and provides functions for serializing and deserializing data efficiently.

```
// Example of data serialization in SDL

SDL_RWops* packetBuffer = SDL_RWFromMem(NULL, 0);

int data = 42;

// Serialize data into the packet buffer

SDL_WriteBE32(packetBuffer, data);

// Deserialize data from the packet buffer

SDL_RWseek(packetBuffer, 0, RW_SEEK_SET);

int receivedData = SDL_ReadBE32(packetBuffer);
```

By using SDL's serialization functions, you can ensure data consistency and efficient communication between game clients and servers.

4.1.3 Latency Compensation

Online games often face challenges related to network latency, which can result in delays between player actions and their effects in the game world. Implementing latency compensation techniques, such as client-side prediction and server reconciliation, can mitigate the impact of latency on gameplay.

```
// Example of client-side prediction and server reconciliation in online games

// Client-side prediction: Simulate player input on the client and predict the game state

void SimulatePlayerInput() {

// Predict the player's movement

}

// Server reconciliation: Adjust the client's prediction based on the authoritative server's response

void ReconcileWithServer() {

// Adjust the game state based on the server's authoritative response

}
```

These techniques allow players to experience smooth gameplay despite network latency.

4.1.4 Network Security Best Practices

Security is paramount in online games to protect player data and ensure a fair gaming environment. SDL provides features like secure sockets (SSL/TLS) and encryption for secure communication. Implementing secure authentication and authorization mechanisms is vital to prevent cheating and unauthorized access.

```
// Example of using SSL/TLS for secure network communication in SDL
```

```
#include <SDL_net.h>

// Initialize SSL/TLS subsystem

SDLNet_Init();

SDLNet_SetupSSL();

// Create an SSL/TLS socket

IPaddress serverIP;

SDL_TLSclient* secureSocket = SDLNet_AllocSSLClient(0);

// Securely connect to the server

if (SDLNet_ResolveHost(&serverIP, "secure.example.com", 443)
== 0) {

if (SDLNet_TCP_Open(&serverIP) != NULL) {

SDLNet_SetSSLClient(secureSocket,
SDLNet_TCP_Open(&serverIP));

// Secure connection established

}

}
```

Utilizing secure communication channels helps protect sensitive player data and game integrity.

4.1.5 Efficient Data Transmission Techniques

Efficiency is crucial in online gaming to minimize bandwidth usage and reduce latency. Techniques like data compression, delta encoding, and prioritizing critical data can help optimize data transmission.

```
// Example of data compression in SDL network communication

// Compress data before sending

SDL_RWops* compressedData = SDL_RWFromMem(NULL, 0);

SDL_Zip(compressedData, originalData);

// Decompress received data

SDL_RWseek(compressedData, 0, RW_SEEK_SET);

SDL_Unzip(compressedData, receivedData);
```

By compressing and optimizing data transmission, online games can maintain responsiveness even in low-bandwidth environments.

In summary, advanced networking concepts in SDL provide game developers with the tools and techniques needed to create online multiplayer experiences. From socket programming to network protocols, latency compensation, network security, and efficient data transmission, SDL empowers developers to build robust and high-performance networked games. Understanding and implementing these concepts is essential for creating immersive and reliable online gaming experiences.

4.2 Building Scalable Multiplayer Servers

Scalable multiplayer servers are the backbone of online games, ensuring that games can support a large number of players simultaneously while maintaining performance and responsiveness. In this section, we will delve into the intricacies of building scalable multiplayer servers using SDL and explore various strategies and considerations to meet the demands of modern online gaming.

4.2.1 Server Architecture

Choosing the right server architecture is fundamental to scalability. Two common architectures are used in online games:

- **Dedicated Servers**: Dedicated servers are standalone machines that host game sessions. They offer better control over game logic and can handle a significant number of players.
- **Peer-to-Peer (P2P)**: P2P architecture relies on players' devices to host game sessions. While suitable for small games, P2P can be challenging to scale for larger player bases.

```
// Example of setting up a dedicated game server in SDL

#include <SDL_net.h>

// Initialize SDL_net

if (SDLNet_Init() != 0) {

// Handle initialization error

}
```

```
// Create a socket for the game server

IPaddress serverIP;

TCPsocket serverSocket;

if (SDLNet_ResolveHost(&serverIP, NULL, 12345) == 0) {

serverSocket = SDLNet_TCP_Open(&serverIP);

if (serverSocket != NULL) {

// Server socket created successfully

}

}
```

4.2.2 Load Balancing and Sharding

Load balancing ensures that player connections are distributed evenly across multiple server instances. This prevents any single server from becoming a bottleneck and helps maintain performance as the player base grows. Sharding involves dividing players into smaller groups or shards, each managed by a separate server instance.

```
// Example of load balancing and sharding in a game server cluster

// Distribute player connections across server instances

void DistributePlayerConnection(TCPsocket playerSocket) {

// Assign the player to an available server instance or shard

}

// Create multiple server instances or shards in a cluster

for (int i = 0; i < numShards; ++i) {
```

```
StartServerInstance(i);

}
```

Load balancing and sharding are essential strategies for building scalable multiplayer servers.

4.2.3 State Management and Replication

Managing game state and replicating it across multiple servers is crucial for consistency in multiplayer games. Game servers must synchronize player actions, objects, and events to ensure that all players experience the same game world.

```
// Example of game state replication in a multiplayer server

// Synchronize player actions and events across server instances

void SynchronizeGameState(int shardID) {

// Replicate game state changes to other server instances

}
```

Efficient state management and replication mechanisms are key to delivering a seamless multiplayer experience.

4.2.4 Database Integration

Integrating databases into multiplayer servers is essential for storing player profiles, game progress, and other persistent data. Databases provide a central storage solution that can be accessed by all server instances.

```
// Example of database integration in a multiplayer server

#include <sqlite3.h>
```

```
sqlite3* database;

// Connect to the database

if (sqlite3_open("game_database.db", &database) == SQLITE_OK) {

// Database connection successful

}
```

Databases help maintain player data consistency and persistence across game sessions.

4.2.5 Scalability Testing

Scalability testing is a critical step in ensuring that a multiplayer server can handle the expected load. Load testing tools and stress tests can help identify bottlenecks and performance issues before the game goes live.

```
// Example of load testing in a multiplayer server

// Simulate a large number of player connections to stress test the server

void StressTestServer() {

// Simulate player connections and interactions

// Collect performance metrics and identify bottlenecks

}
```

Regular scalability testing allows developers to fine-tune server configurations and optimize performance.

In summary, building scalable multiplayer servers is a complex but essential aspect of online game development. From choosing the right server architecture to implementing load balancing, sharding, state management, database integration, and scalability testing, SDL provides the tools and frameworks needed to create robust and high-performance multiplayer server solutions. Building scalable servers ensures that players can enjoy smooth and responsive gameplay experiences, even with large player bases, ultimately contributing to the success of online games.

4.3 Network Security Best Practices

Network security is a paramount concern in online games, as it not only protects player data but also ensures fair play and a positive gaming experience. In this section, we will delve into the best practices and strategies for implementing network security in online games using SDL and related technologies.

4.3.1 Secure Sockets (SSL/TLS)

One of the fundamental security measures is implementing secure sockets using protocols like SSL/TLS. SDL provides support for secure communication, allowing game servers and clients to encrypt data exchanged over the network.

```
// Example of setting up SSL/TLS for secure network communication in SDL

#include <SDL_net.h>

// Initialize SDL_net and SSL/TLS subsystems

if (SDLNet_Init() != 0) {

// Handle initialization error

}

if (SDLNet_SetupSSL() != 0) {

// Handle SSL/TLS setup error

}

// Create a secure SSL/TLS socket for the game server
```

```
IPaddress serverIP;

SDL_TLSserver* secureServerSocket;

if (SDLNet_ResolveHost(&serverIP, "secure.example.com", 443) == 0) {

secureServerSocket = SDLNet_AllocSSLServer(0);

if (SDLNet_TCP_Open(&serverIP) != NULL) {

SDLNet_SetSSLServer(secureServerSocket, SDLNet_TCP_Open(&serverIP));

// Secure server socket created successfully

}

}
```

By implementing secure sockets, you can protect sensitive player data and ensure that communication is not intercepted or tampered with.

4.3.2 Authentication and Authorization

Implementing robust authentication and authorization mechanisms is essential to verify the identity of players and grant access to game resources and features. SDL provides tools to manage user accounts and permissions securely.

```
// Example of user authentication and authorization in SDL

#include <SDL_net.h>

// Authenticate user credentials

bool AuthenticateUser(const char* username, const char* password) {
```

```
// Verify user credentials against a secure database

if (UserDatabase::VerifyCredentials(username, password)) {

return true;

}

return false;

}

// Authorize access to game resources based on user permissions

bool AuthorizeAccess(User* user, const char* resource) {

// Check user permissions and resource access rights

if (UserPermissions::HasAccess(user, resource)) {

return true;

}

return false;

}
```

Authentication ensures that players are who they claim to be, while authorization controls what they can do within the game.

4.3.3 Data Encryption and Privacy

Protecting player privacy is crucial in online games. Ensure that sensitive data, such as personal information and login credentials, is encrypted before transmission and securely stored.

```
// Example of data encryption in SDL network communication
```

```
// Encrypt sensitive data before sending

SDL_RWops* encryptedData = SDL_RWFromMem(NULL, 0);

SDL_Encrypt(encryptedData, sensitiveData);

// Decrypt received data

SDL_RWseek(encryptedData, 0, RW_SEEK_SET);

SDL_Decrypt(encryptedData, receivedData);
```

Data encryption safeguards player data from potential eavesdropping and breaches.

4.3.4 Anti-Cheating Measures

Online games are susceptible to cheating, which can ruin the experience for legitimate players. Implementing anti-cheating measures, such as server-side validation of player actions and behavior analysis, helps maintain fair play.

```
// Example of server-side validation in an online game

// Validate player actions to prevent cheating

void ValidatePlayerAction(Player* player, Action* action) {

// Check if the action is valid based on server rules and game state

if (ServerRules::IsActionValid(player, action)) {

// Execute the action

}

}
```

Anti-cheating measures ensure that players cannot gain unfair advantages through unauthorized actions or modifications.

4.3.5 Regular Security Audits

Regular security audits and penetration testing are essential to identify vulnerabilities and weaknesses in your game's network security. Conducting these tests can help you stay ahead of potential threats and address security issues proactively.

```
// Example of conducting security audits in an online game

// Engage third-party security experts for penetration testing

void ConductSecurityAudit() {

// Identify and address vulnerabilities in the game's network security

}
```

Security audits should be part of your ongoing development and maintenance processes to ensure that your game remains secure.

In conclusion, network security is a critical aspect of online games, and SDL offers the tools and capabilities needed to implement robust security measures. By focusing on secure sockets, authentication, authorization, data encryption, anti-cheating measures, and regular security audits, game developers can create a safe and fair gaming environment while protecting player data and privacy. Prioritizing network security is essential for building player trust and ensuring the long-term success of online games.

4.4 Efficient Data Transmission Techniques

Efficient data transmission is crucial for maintaining low latency and optimal performance in online games. In this section, we will explore various techniques and strategies for optimizing data transmission in online games using SDL and related technologies.

4.4.1 Data Compression

Data compression is a common technique used to reduce the size of data before transmission. Compressed data requires less bandwidth and can be transmitted more quickly, resulting in lower latency.

```
// Example of data compression in SDL network communication

// Compress data before sending

SDL_RWops* compressedData = SDL_RWFromMem(NULL, 0);

SDL_Zip(compressedData, originalData);

// Decompress received data

SDL_RWseek(compressedData, 0, RW_SEEK_SET);

SDL_Unzip(compressedData, receivedData);
```

By compressing data before sending it over the network, you can reduce the amount of data that needs to be transmitted, resulting in improved network performance.

4.4.2 Delta Encoding

Delta encoding is a technique that transmits only the changes or differences between two sets of data instead of sending the entire data set. This is particularly useful for transmitting updates to the game state or objects.

```
// Example of delta encoding in online game data transmission

// Calculate and transmit only the changes in game state

void TransmitDeltaState(GameState* previousState, GameState* currentState) {

DeltaState delta = CalculateDelta(previousState, currentState);

Transmit(delta);

}
```

Delta encoding minimizes the amount of data transmitted and reduces network overhead, leading to lower latency and smoother gameplay.

4.4.3 Prioritization and Rate Limiting

Prioritizing data packets and implementing rate limiting mechanisms can help ensure that critical game data is transmitted promptly, while less critical data can be delayed or sent at a lower rate.

```
// Example of prioritizing and rate limiting data packets in online games

// Prioritize and send critical gameplay data immediately

void SendCriticalGameData(GameData* data) {

// Transmit the data with high priority

}
```

```
// Rate limit non-critical data to avoid congestion

void SendNonCriticalData(GameData* data) {

// Transmit the data with lower priority and rate limit

}
```

By prioritizing and rate limiting data packets, you can allocate network resources efficiently and maintain a responsive gaming experience.

4.4.4 UDP for Real-Time Data

While TCP is reliable for data transmission, it introduces some latency due to its error-checking mechanisms. In contrast, UDP (User Datagram Protocol) is less reliable but offers lower latency, making it suitable for real-time data transmission in online games, such as player positions and actions.

```
// Example of using UDP for real-time data transmission in SDL

#include <SDL_net.h>

UDPsocket udpSocket;

// Create a UDP socket

udpSocket = SDLNet_UDP_Open(0);

// Send real-time game data via UDP

UDPpacket* packet = SDLNet_AllocPacket(512);

SDLNet_UDP_Send(udpSocket, -1, packet);
```

Utilizing UDP for real-time data ensures minimal latency and a more responsive gaming experience.

4.4.5 Data Packet Size Optimization

Optimizing data packet sizes can reduce the overhead associated with network transmission. Smaller packets result in faster transmission and lower latency.

```
// Example of data packet size optimization in online games

// Minimize packet size by packing data efficiently

void PackGameData(GameData* data, char* packetBuffer) {

// Pack game data into a compact binary format

}

// Unpack data efficiently on the receiving end

void UnpackGameData(char* packetBuffer, GameData* data) {

// Unpack binary data to reconstruct game data

}
```

By carefully designing the structure of data packets and minimizing unnecessary overhead, you can improve data transmission efficiency.

In conclusion, efficient data transmission is vital for delivering a smooth and responsive online gaming experience. By implementing data compression, delta encoding, prioritization, rate limiting, choosing the appropriate protocol (UDP for real-time data), and optimizing data packet sizes, game developers can ensure that the network does not become a bottleneck and that players enjoy low-latency gameplay. These techniques are essential for creating engaging and competitive online games where split-second decisions matter.

4.5 Creating Seamless Online Experiences

Creating seamless online experiences in games is a multifaceted task that involves various aspects of game development, from network connectivity to gameplay design and user interface. In this section, we will explore strategies and best practices to ensure that online multiplayer games using SDL provide players with a smooth and immersive gaming experience.

4.5.1 Latency Mitigation

Reducing latency is critical to delivering a seamless online experience. Latency can lead to delays in player actions and reactions, affecting gameplay quality. To mitigate latency, game developers can employ techniques like client-side prediction, server reconciliation, and network optimization.

```
// Example of client-side prediction and server reconciliation in online games

// Client-side prediction: Simulate player input on the client and predict the game state

void SimulatePlayerInput() {

// Predict the player's movement

}

// Server reconciliation: Adjust the client's prediction based on the authoritative server's response

void ReconcileWithServer() {

// Adjust the game state based on the server's authoritative response
```

```
}
```

These techniques help compensate for network latency, ensuring that players experience smooth and responsive gameplay.

4.5.2 Lag Compensation

Lag compensation is essential in online games to ensure that players with varying network conditions can still enjoy a fair and balanced gaming experience. Techniques like lag prediction and hit detection can help compensate for player lag and ensure that actions are registered accurately.

```
// Example of lag compensation in online game hit detection

// Predict player positions based on network latency

void PredictPlayerPosition(Player* player) {

// Estimate the player's position based on latency

}

// Accurate hit detection considering player positions and latency

bool PerformHitDetection(Player* shooter, Player* target) {

// Check if the shot hits the target accurately

// Considering both players' positions and latency

}
```

By accounting for network latency and compensating for lag, developers can provide a more enjoyable experience for all players.

4.5.3 Dynamic Game Scaling

Dynamic game scaling involves adjusting the game's difficulty and complexity based on the number and skill levels of players. This ensures that both casual and experienced players can enjoy the game without feeling overwhelmed or bored.

```
// Example of dynamic game scaling based on player skills and numbers

// Adjust the number and difficulty of enemies in response to player performance

void ScaleGameDifficulty(int playerCount, PlayerSkillLevel skillLevel) {

// Dynamically change game parameters to match player demographics

}
```

Dynamic game scaling enhances the online experience by catering to the specific needs and preferences of the player group.

4.5.4 Robust Networking

Robust networking infrastructure is crucial for creating seamless online experiences. Implementing dedicated servers, load balancing, and server redundancy can ensure that games remain accessible even during peak player activity.

```
// Example of implementing robust networking for online games

// Use dedicated servers to host game sessions

void HostDedicatedServer() {

// Set up a dedicated server to host game sessions

}

// Implement load balancing to distribute player connections evenly
```

```
void ImplementLoadBalancing() {
// Distribute player connections across multiple server instances
}
```

Robust networking ensures that players can connect and play without disruption, enhancing the overall experience.

4.5.5 User Interface and Feedback

A user-friendly and informative user interface (UI) is essential for guiding players in online games. Providing feedback on network status, server availability, and match progress helps players understand the state of the game.

```
// Example of UI elements for network status and server feedback
// Display network connection status in the UI
void DisplayNetworkStatus(bool isConnected) {
// Update the UI to show the network status
}
// Provide feedback on server availability and match progress
void ShowServerStatus(ServerStatus status) {
// Inform players about server availability and match progress
}
```

A well-designed UI keeps players informed and engaged, contributing to a seamless online experience.

In conclusion, creating seamless online experiences in games requires a holistic approach that considers network optimization, latency mitigation, lag compensation, dynamic game scaling, robust networking, and user interface design. By focusing on these aspects, game developers can ensure that players enjoy a smooth and immersive multiplayer experience, fostering player engagement and satisfaction. Ultimately, delivering a seamless online experience is essential for the success of multiplayer games using SDL.

Chapter 5: Advanced AI and Simulation

5.1 Complex AI Algorithms for Games

In modern game development, creating immersive and challenging experiences relies heavily on advanced Artificial Intelligence (AI) algorithms. These algorithms empower NPCs (Non-Player Characters) and enemies to exhibit realistic behaviors, adapt to player actions, and contribute to the overall depth of the game world. In this section, we will explore the intricacies of implementing complex AI algorithms in games using SDL and related technologies.

5.1.1 Decision-Making Algorithms

Decision-making is at the core of AI in games. NPCs and entities need to make intelligent choices based on their current situation and objectives. One common approach is using Behavior Trees, which consist of nodes representing actions, conditions, and composite behaviors.

```
// Example of a simple Behavior Tree node in an AI system

class BehaviorNode {

public:

virtual BehaviorStatus Execute() = 0;

};

class ActionNode : public BehaviorNode {

public:

virtual BehaviorStatus Execute() override {

// Perform an action
```

```
return BehaviorStatus::Success;

}

};

class ConditionNode : public BehaviorNode {

public:

virtual BehaviorStatus Execute() override {

// Check a condition

return ConditionIsMet() ? BehaviorStatus::Success : BehaviorStatus::Failure;

}

};
```

By designing complex Behavior Trees, game developers can create AI behaviors that are both responsive and adaptable.

5.1.2 Pathfinding Algorithms

Pathfinding is crucial for AI-controlled entities to navigate the game world effectively. Algorithms like A* and Dijkstra's algorithm help NPCs find the shortest path from their current position to their destination while avoiding obstacles.

```
// Example of pathfinding using the A* algorithm in a game

class AStarPathfinder {

public:

std::vector<Node> FindPath(Node start, Node goal) {
```

```
// Implement A* pathfinding algorithm

// Return a sequence of nodes representing the path

}

};
```

Efficient pathfinding algorithms contribute to realistic and dynamic AI movement.

5.1.3 Finite State Machines (FSM)

Finite State Machines are essential for managing AI behaviors and transitions. They allow NPCs to switch between different states based on conditions, making it possible to represent complex decision-making processes.

```
// Example of a simple Finite State Machine (FSM) for AI

enum class AIState {

Idle,

Patrolling,

Chasing,

Attacking,

Fleeing

};

class AICharacter {

public:

AIState GetCurrentState() {
```

```
return currentState;
}
void Update() {
// Handle state transitions and AI logic
switch (currentState) {
case AIState::Idle:
// Handle behavior for the Idle state
break;
case AIState::Patrolling:
// Handle behavior for the Patrolling state
break;
// ... other states ...
}
}
private:
AIState currentState = AIState::Idle;
};
```

FSMs provide a structured way to model AI behaviors and make them respond to in-game events and player actions.

5.1.4 Machine Learning and Neural Networks

Machine learning techniques, including neural networks, are increasingly used in game AI. These techniques enable NPCs to learn and adapt from player interactions, providing a more dynamic and challenging experience.

```
# Example of using a neural network for AI decision-making in a game

import tensorflow as tf

# Create a neural network model

model = tf.keras.Sequential([

tf.keras.layers.Dense(64, activation='relu', input_shape=(input_size,)),

tf.keras.layers.Dense(32, activation='relu'),

tf.keras.layers.Dense(output_size, activation='softmax')

])

# Train the model using game data and player interactions

model.compile(optimizer='adam', loss='categorical_crossentropy')

model.fit(training_data, target_data, epochs=100)
```

By leveraging machine learning, game developers can create AI that learns and adapts, making each playthrough unique.

5.1.5 Sensor and Perception Systems

To make informed decisions, AI entities in games often rely on sensor and perception systems. These systems allow AI to sense their surroundings, detect player actions, and react accordingly.

```
// Example of a basic sensor system for AI perception
```

```
class Sensor {

public:

virtual bool DetectPlayer() = 0;

};

class VisualSensor : public Sensor {

public:

virtual bool DetectPlayer() override {

// Implement visual perception logic

return PlayerIsVisible();

}

};
```

Sensor and perception systems enable AI to react realistically to the player's presence and actions, enhancing immersion.

In summary, complex AI algorithms play a crucial role in creating engaging and challenging gameplay experiences. By implementing decision-making algorithms, pathfinding techniques, Finite State Machines, machine learning, and sensor systems, game developers using SDL can breathe life into their game worlds. These advanced AI techniques make NPCs and entities more dynamic, adaptive, and intelligent, ultimately enhancing the overall gaming experience for players.

5.2 Simulating Realistic Behaviors and Environments

In the realm of game development, simulating realistic behaviors and environments is a key aspect of creating immersive and engaging gameplay experiences. In this section, we will delve into various techniques and strategies for simulating realism in games using SDL and related technologies.

5.2.1 Physics Simulation

Physics simulation plays a pivotal role in creating lifelike game environments. Implementing accurate physics allows objects to move, collide, and interact with each other realistically. SDL provides physics libraries and integration options to make this task easier.

```
// Example of physics simulation using SDL libraries

#include <SDL2/SDL.h>

#include <SDL2/SDL_physics.h>

// Create a physics world

SDL_PhysicsWorld* physicsWorld = SDL_CreatePhysicsWorld();

// Create physical objects

SDL_PhysicsObject* object1 = SDL_CreatePhysicsObject(physicsWorld);

SDL_PhysicsObject* object2 = SDL_CreatePhysicsObject(physicsWorld);

// Apply forces and simulate physics
```

```
SDL_ApplyForce(object1, 10.0, 0.0);

SDL_SimulatePhysics(physicsWorld, 1.0); // Simulate 1 second of physics
```

Accurate physics simulation makes movements, collisions, and interactions in the game world feel natural, enhancing player immersion.

5.2.2 Environmental Effects

To create rich and immersive game environments, developers often incorporate various environmental effects. These effects include dynamic weather, lighting, and day-night cycles, which add depth and realism to the game world.

```
// Example of implementing dynamic weather effects in a game

// Create a weather system

WeatherSystem weatherSystem;

// Simulate weather changes

weatherSystem.SimulateWeatherChange();
```

Dynamic environmental effects create a dynamic and ever-changing game world that responds to player actions and decisions.

5.2.3 AI Behavior Simulation

Simulating realistic AI behavior is essential for making NPCs and entities in the game world feel lifelike. This involves modeling AI decision-making, learning, and adaptation to create challenging opponents or cooperative companions.

```
// Example of simulating realistic AI behavior in a combat game
```

```
// Create an AI opponent with complex behavior

AICharacter opponent;

opponent.Initialize();

// Simulate AI decision-making and combat tactics

opponent.ThinkAndAct();
```

Realistic AI behavior adds depth to the game and provides players with more engaging challenges.

5.2.4 Environmental Interactions

Allowing players to interact with the game environment in meaningful ways enhances realism and immersion. Implementing environmental interactions, such as destructible objects, interactive props, and physics-based puzzles, enables players to influence the game world.

```
// Example of implementing environmental interactions in a puzzle game

// Create a physics-based puzzle object

PhysicsPuzzle puzzle;

puzzle.Initialize();

// Allow players to interact with the puzzle

puzzle.InteractWithPlayer();
```

Environmental interactions create a sense of agency and enable players to explore the game world actively.

5.2.5 Audio and Sound Simulation

Sound and audio simulation are often underestimated but contribute significantly to realism. Implementing spatial audio, dynamic soundscapes, and realistic sound effects immerse players in the game world.

// Example of spatial audio simulation in a first-person shooter

// Play gunshot sound with spatial information

PlaySpatialSound("gunshot.wav", playerPosition, enemyPosition);

Sound simulation enhances the player's perception of the game environment and adds layers of immersion.

In conclusion, simulating realistic behaviors and environments is vital for creating immersive and engaging gameplay experiences. By focusing on physics simulation, environmental effects, AI behavior, environmental interactions, and audio simulation, game developers using SDL can craft worlds that feel dynamic, responsive, and alive. These techniques contribute to player immersion and elevate the overall quality of the gaming experience, making it more memorable and enjoyable.

5.3 AI in Large-Scale World Dynamics

Large-scale world dynamics present a unique challenge in game development. To maintain realism and engagement in expansive game worlds, it's essential to implement AI systems that can handle the complexity of such environments. In this section, we will explore the role of AI in managing large-scale world dynamics using SDL and related technologies.

5.3.1 Population Simulation

In open-world games and simulations, managing the behavior and movement of a large population of AI entities, such as NPCs or wildlife, is a common task. SDL provides tools for managing and simulating the behavior of a vast number of AI agents.

// Example of population simulation in an open-world game using SDL

// Create and manage a population of AI entities

PopulationManager populationManager;

// Simulate the behavior of AI entities in the open world

populationManager.SimulatePopulationBehavior();

Population simulation is essential for creating bustling and dynamic game worlds where AI entities exhibit diverse behaviors and interactions.

5.3.2 Distributed AI Systems

In large-scale game worlds, distributing AI processing across multiple cores or even networked servers becomes necessary to maintain performance and responsiveness. This approach, known as distributed AI, enables AI agents to collaborate, synchronize, and react to events efficiently.

```
// Example of distributed AI architecture for a large-scale game world

// Set up a distributed AI system with multiple AI agents

DistributedAISystem aiSystem;

// Distribute AI tasks across available processing units

aiSystem.AssignTasksToAgents();
```

Distributed AI ensures that AI entities across the game world can operate independently while still collaborating when necessary.

5.3.3 Dynamic World Events

Large-scale game worlds often feature dynamic events, such as weather changes, ecosystem shifts, or large-scale battles. AI systems are responsible for orchestrating these events and ensuring that they unfold realistically.

```
// Example of an AI-driven dynamic world event in a large-scale game

// Create a dynamic world event manager

DynamicEventManager eventManager;

// Simulate the progression of dynamic world events

eventManager.SimulateEvents();
```

Dynamic world events add depth and unpredictability to the game world, enhancing the player's sense of immersion and agency.

5.3.4 Global AI Planning

In a large-scale game world, global AI planning is crucial for coordinating AI behaviors across different regions and ensuring that the world's state remains consistent. Techniques like Goal-Oriented Action Planning (GOAP) are used to plan and execute complex AI actions.

```
// Example of global AI planning using GOAP in a large-scale game world

// Create a global AI planner

GlobalAIPlanner planner;

// Plan and execute actions for AI entities across the world

planner.PlanAndExecuteGlobalActions();
```

Global AI planning allows for cohesive storytelling and gameplay experiences across the entire game world.

5.3.5 Procedural Content Generation

To create vast and diverse game worlds efficiently, procedural content generation is often employed. AI algorithms can generate terrain, populate regions, and create quests dynamically, ensuring that the game world remains rich and engaging.

```
// Example of procedural world generation using AI-driven algorithms

// Generate a procedurally generated game world

ProceduralWorldGenerator worldGenerator;

// Create a unique and expansive game world on-the-fly

worldGenerator.GenerateWorld();
```

Procedural content generation leverages AI to produce diverse and realistic game environments without manual authoring.

In summary, AI plays a vital role in managing the dynamics of large-scale game worlds. Whether it's simulating populations, distributing AI tasks, orchestrating dynamic events, planning global actions, or generating procedural content, AI systems using SDL enable developers to create expansive and immersive game worlds that captivate players. These AI-driven techniques are essential for the success of open-world and sandbox-style games where players expect a vast and vibrant virtual playground to explore.

5.4 Integrating Machine Learning in Games

Integrating machine learning (ML) into games has become an exciting avenue for enhancing gameplay and AI-driven experiences. In this section, we will explore the incorporation of machine learning techniques in games using SDL and related technologies.

5.4.1 Player Behavior Prediction

One of the prominent uses of machine learning in games is predicting player behavior. By analyzing player actions and preferences, machine learning models can anticipate player decisions, making the gameplay more dynamic and challenging.

```
# Example of player behavior prediction using machine learning in a strategy game

import scikit-learn as sklearn

# Create a machine learning model to predict player actions

model = sklearn.DecisionTreeClassifier()

# Train the model on player data

model.fit(training_data, labels)

# Predict the player's next move based on the current game state

predicted_action = model.predict(current_game_state)
```

Player behavior prediction allows AI to adapt to individual player styles, creating a personalized gaming experience.

5.4.2 Procedural Content Generation

Machine learning can assist in procedural content generation by learning from existing game content and generating new levels, quests, or assets that match the player's preferences and playstyle.

```
# Example of procedural content generation using machine learning

import tensorflow as tf

# Train a neural network to generate game levels

generator = tf.keras.Sequential([

tf.keras.layers.Dense(64, activation='relu', input_shape=(input_size,)),

tf.keras.layers.Dense(32, activation='relu'),

tf.keras.layers.Dense(output_size, activation='softmax')

])

# Generate new game levels based on player preferences

generated_level = generator.predict(player_preferences)
```

Procedural content generation powered by machine learning can provide endless variations and keep the game world fresh.

5.4.3 AI Behavior Enhancement

Machine learning can improve AI behavior by allowing AI entities to learn from player interactions. Reinforcement learning is a common technique where AI agents receive rewards for desirable actions and penalties for undesirable ones, enabling them to optimize their behavior over time.

```
# Example of AI behavior enhancement using reinforcement learning
```

```
import TensorFlow as tf

# Create a reinforcement learning agent

agent = tf.keras.models.Sequential([

tf.keras.layers.Dense(128, activation='relu', input_shape=(input_size,)),

tf.keras.layers.Dense(output_size, activation='softmax')

])

# Train the agent using reward signals from player interactions

agent.compile(optimizer='adam', loss='categorical_crossentropy')

agent.fit(training_data, rewards, epochs=100)
```

By integrating reinforcement learning, AI entities can adapt and improve their strategies as they interact with players.

5.4.4 Natural Language Processing (NLP)

Natural language processing is employed for enhancing dialogue systems and providing more immersive storytelling experiences. Machine learning models can understand and generate natural language, enabling interactive and dynamic conversations with NPCs.

```
# Example of natural language processing for dialogue systems in games

import spaCy

# Use a spaCy model for understanding player input and generating NPC responses

nlp = spaCy.load("en_core_web_sm")
```

```
# Process player input

player_input = nlp("Tell me about your quest.")

# Generate NPC response based on player input

npc_response = generate_npc_response(player_input)
```

NLP-driven dialogue systems make interactions with NPCs more engaging and lifelike.

5.4.5 Personalized Game Recommendations

Machine learning can provide personalized game recommendations based on player preferences and behavior. This enhances player retention and ensures that players discover content tailored to their interests.

```
# Example of personalized game recommendations using machine learning

import sklearn

# Train a recommendation system model on player data

recommendation_model = sklearn.neighbors.NearestNeighbors()

recommendation_model.fit(player_preferences)

# Provide game recommendations for the player

recommended_games =
recommendation_model.find_nearest_games(player_preferences)
```

Personalized recommendations keep players engaged and satisfied by suggesting games they are likely to enjoy.

In conclusion, integrating machine learning in games opens up exciting possibilities for enhancing player experiences. Whether it's predicting player behavior, generating procedural content, improving AI behavior, enabling natural language interactions, or offering personalized recommendations, machine learning empowers game developers to create more dynamic, engaging, and immersive gaming worlds. SDL, with its flexibility and capabilities, provides a solid foundation for incorporating machine learning into games and taking them to new heights.

5.5 Challenges in Balancing and AI Design

Balancing gameplay and designing AI systems that provide both challenge and fairness to players is a complex task in game development. In this section, we will explore the challenges involved in achieving a balanced AI design using SDL and related technologies.

5.5.1 Difficulty Levels

One of the challenges in AI design is catering to players of varying skill levels. Game developers must create AI systems that adapt to different player skill levels, providing an enjoyable experience for both beginners and experts.

```
// Example of implementing difficulty levels in an AI system

// Define different AI behaviors for easy, medium, and hard difficulty levels

AIBehavior easyBehavior;

AIBehavior mediumBehavior;

AIBehavior hardBehavior;

// Choose the appropriate AI behavior based on the player's selected difficulty level

AIBehavior selectedBehavior = GetSelectedBehavior(playerDifficulty);
```

Balancing difficulty levels ensures that players of all skill levels can enjoy the game without feeling overwhelmed or bored.

5.5.2 Fairness and Challenge

Achieving the right balance between providing a challenging experience and maintaining fairness is a constant concern. AI systems should challenge players without resorting to unfair advantages, such as cheating or excessively difficult scenarios.

```
// Example of balancing fairness and challenge in AI design

// Implement a dynamic difficulty adjustment system

if (playerIsStruggling) {

IncreaseAIChallenge();

} else if (playerIsDominating) {

DecreaseAIChallenge();

}
```

Balancing fairness and challenge requires continuous monitoring of player performance and adjusting AI behavior accordingly.

5.5.3 Player Adaptation

AI systems must be designed to adapt to player actions and strategies. The AI should learn and respond to the player's tactics to keep the gameplay engaging.

```
// Example of player adaptation in AI behavior

// Analyze player tactics and adjust AI behavior accordingly

if (playerPrefers StealthApproach()) {

AdjustAIForStealth();

} else {
```

```
AdjustAIForAggression();
}
```

Player adaptation ensures that the AI remains responsive to player decisions and keeps the experience fresh.

5.5.4 Playtesting and Feedback

Balancing AI design often requires extensive playtesting and feedback from players. Developers must analyze player experiences, gather feedback, and make adjustments to the AI system accordingly.

```
// Example of collecting player feedback for AI improvement
// Implement a feedback system for players to report AI-related issues
if (playerReportsAIChallengeIssue()) {
AnalyzeFeedbackAndMakeAdjustments();
}
```

Player feedback is invaluable in identifying areas where AI balance can be improved.

5.5.5 Ethical Considerations

Balancing AI design also extends to ethical considerations. Developers must ensure that AI behaviors and challenges do not promote harmful or offensive content and adhere to ethical standards.

```
// Example of ethical considerations in AI design
// Implement content filters and moderation systems to prevent offensive AI behavior
```

```
if (contentIsDetectedAsOffensive()) {

ApplyContentFilter();

}
```

Ethical considerations are essential to create a safe and inclusive gaming environment.

5.5.6 Emergent Behavior

In complex AI systems, emergent behavior can be challenging to predict and control. AI entities may exhibit unexpected behavior due to interactions with the game world and other AI entities.

```
// Example of emergent behavior in AI design

// Monitor and analyze unexpected AI behavior

if (emergentBehaviorIsDetected()) {

InvestigateAndFine-TuneAIParameters();

}
```

Managing emergent behavior requires thorough testing and fine-tuning of AI parameters.

In summary, balancing AI design in games is a multifaceted challenge that involves catering to different player skill levels, maintaining fairness, adapting to player actions, collecting feedback, addressing ethical concerns, and managing emergent behavior. SDL provides the tools and flexibility to implement AI systems that strike the right balance, offering players engaging and enjoyable experiences while ensuring fairness and ethical standards are upheld. Balancing AI design is an ongoing process that requires careful consideration and continuous refinement to create memorable and enjoyable games.

Chapter 6: Physics and Real-Time Interactions

6.1. Realistic Physics for Game Dynamics

In the world of game development, realistic physics simulation is a crucial element that can greatly enhance the player's immersion and overall gaming experience. Whether it's the way objects collide, how characters move, or the behavior of projectiles, realistic physics can make a game feel more lifelike. In this section, we will explore the importance of implementing realistic physics in your game and discuss various techniques and libraries that can help you achieve this.

Why Realistic Physics Matter

Realistic physics add depth and authenticity to your game world. When objects behave as they would in the real world, players can better predict and understand the outcomes of their actions. This leads to a more satisfying and immersive gameplay experience.

Imagine a car racing game where vehicles slide and drift on icy roads, or a platformer where the protagonist's jumps and landings are affected by gravity. These realistic physics interactions make the game more engaging and enjoyable.

Physics Engines

To implement realistic physics in your game, you'll often rely on physics engines. These engines are specialized libraries or systems designed to handle complex physics calculations efficiently. Popular physics engines like **Box2D** and **PhysX** provide a wide range of tools and functions for simulating realistic physics interactions.

Here's a basic example of using Box2D to simulate physics in a game:

```
import Box2D

# Create a world with gravity

world = Box2D.b2World(gravity=(0, -9.81))

# Create a dynamic body (e.g., a falling object)

body = world.CreateDynamicBody(position=(0, 10))

shape = body.CreateCircleFixture(radius=1, density=1)
```

In this example, we create a Box2D world with gravity and a dynamic body representing an object. The object will fall under the influence of gravity, and its collision interactions are simulated realistically.

Collision Detection and Response

Realistic physics also involve accurate collision detection and response. When two objects collide, their behavior should follow the laws of physics. For example, if a ball collides with a wall, it should bounce off with an appropriate angle and speed, taking into account factors like friction.

Physics engines handle collision detection and response for you, but you need to configure materials and properties to achieve the desired behavior. Here's a simplified example:

```
# Set up materials for collision
```

```
ball_fixture = ball.CreateCircleFixture(radius=1, density=1, friction=0.3)

wall_fixture = wall.CreateEdgeFixture(vertices=[(-10, 0), (10, 0)], friction=0.5)

# Configure restitution (bounciness) for the ball

ball_fixture.restitution = 0.8
```

In this code, we configure materials for the ball and the wall, including their friction. We also set the restitution to control how bouncy the ball is when it collides with the wall.

Integrating Real-Time Interactions

Realistic physics should seamlessly integrate with your game's real-time interactions. Whether it's controlling a character, handling user input, or responding to dynamic events, the physics simulation should be an integral part of your game loop.

To achieve this, you'll update the physics simulation within your game loop and synchronize it with other game elements. This ensures that everything, from character movements to environmental interactions, aligns with the physics simulation.

```
# Game loop

while running:

# Handle user input and game events

handle_input_and_events()

# Update physics simulation
```

```
world.Step(time_step, velocity_iterations, position_iterations)

# Update game objects based on physics

update_game_objects()

# Render the game

render_game()
```

In this simplified game loop, the physics simulation is updated using world.Step(), and game objects are updated accordingly. This synchronization ensures that the game's visuals and interactions align with the physics simulation.

Summary

Realistic physics simulation is a crucial component of modern games, enhancing player immersion and interaction. Using physics engines like Box2D or PhysX, configuring materials, handling collision detection, and synchronizing real-time interactions are key steps in implementing realistic physics in your game. As you explore the possibilities of physics in game development, you'll find creative ways to make your virtual worlds come alive.

6.2. Implementing Advanced Collision Detection

In the realm of physics and real-time interactions, advanced collision detection is a critical aspect of game development. Collision detection allows you to determine when and where objects in your game world intersect or come into contact with each other. Implementing advanced collision detection techniques can significantly enhance the realism and complexity of your game's interactions.

Basic Collision Detection

Before delving into advanced techniques, let's briefly review basic collision detection. At its core, collision detection involves checking whether two objects, such as player characters, enemies, or projectiles, are overlapping or in close proximity.

AABB Collision Detection

One common technique for basic collision detection is Axis-Aligned Bounding Box (AABB) collision detection. It involves creating a bounding box (rectangle) around each object and checking if these bounding boxes intersect.

Here's a simplified example in Python:

 # Define AABBs for two objects

object1 = AABB(x1, y1, width1, height1)

object2 = AABB(x2, y2, width2, height2)

 # Check for collision

```
if object1.intersects(object2):
# Handle collision
resolve_collision(object1, object2)
```

In this code, AABB represents an Axis-Aligned Bounding Box, and the intersects function checks if two AABBs overlap. If a collision is detected, you can then resolve it based on your game's rules.

Circle-Circle Collision Detection

Another basic technique is Circle-Circle collision detection, which checks whether two circular objects intersect. This method is often used for games involving circular entities, such as projectiles or planets.

```
# Define circles for two objects
object1 = Circle(x1, y1, radius1)
object2 = Circle(x2, y2, radius2)
# Check for collision
if object1.intersects(object2):
# Handle collision
resolve_collision(object1, object2)
```

Advanced Collision Detection Techniques

While basic collision detection serves many purposes, advanced collision detection techniques can handle complex scenarios and irregularly shaped objects. Here are some advanced techniques:

Polygon Collision Detection

Polygon collision detection is used when objects have irregular shapes defined by vertices. You can implement the Separating Axis Theorem (SAT) to determine if two convex polygons intersect.

Continuous Collision Detection

Continuous collision detection is essential for fast-moving objects. It ensures that you detect collisions even if objects move too quickly to be captured by discrete collision detection methods. One common approach is to use swept AABBs or swept circles to check for collisions along the objects' path.

Collision Response

Handling collisions involves more than just detection; you must also respond appropriately. This may include updating object velocities, applying forces, or triggering specific game events. The response depends on your game's physics and mechanics.

Collision Layers and Filtering

In complex game worlds, you often need to manage which objects can collide with each other. Collision layers and filtering mechanisms allow you to control which objects interact and which do not. This is crucial for optimizing performance and managing complex interactions.

Performance Considerations

Implementing advanced collision detection can be computationally expensive, especially when dealing with a large number of objects. To optimize performance:

- Use spatial partitioning techniques like quad-trees or grid-based systems to reduce the number of collision checks.

- Consider using optimized libraries or engines that provide efficient collision detection algorithms.

- Profile your game to identify performance bottlenecks and optimize collision detection as needed.

In summary, advanced collision detection techniques are essential for creating engaging and realistic game interactions. Understanding and implementing these techniques can take your game's physics and real-time interactions to the next level, enhancing both gameplay and player immersion.

6.3. Fluid and Soft Body Dynamics

In the realm of physics simulation for games, fluid and soft body dynamics represent advanced topics that can greatly enhance the realism and interactivity of virtual worlds. These dynamics extend beyond rigid objects and introduce flexible and fluid-like behaviors into your game environments. In this section, we will explore the concepts and techniques behind fluid and soft body dynamics.

Fluid Dynamics

Fluid dynamics simulates the behavior of liquids, gases, and other fluids in a game environment. This can include effects like water flow, splashes, and ripples. Implementing fluid dynamics in your game can create stunning visual effects and add depth to aquatic environments, weather simulations, and more.

Particle-Based Fluid Simulation

One common approach to simulating fluid dynamics in games is through particle-based methods. In these simulations, fluid is represented by a large number of individual particles that interact with each other. These particles can simulate the movement and behavior of fluid in a dynamic way.

Here's a simplified example of particle-based fluid simulation in pseudocode:

```
# Initialize fluid particles

particles = initialize_particles()

# Simulation loop
```

```
while running:

# Update particle positions based on fluid dynamics equations

update_particle_positions(particles)

# Render particles to create the fluid's appearance

render_particles(particles)
```

In this code, the simulation loop updates the positions of fluid particles based on fluid dynamics equations. These equations consider factors like particle velocity, pressure, and interactions between neighboring particles.

Real-Time Fluid Rendering

Creating realistic fluid visuals goes hand-in-hand with fluid dynamics. Real-time fluid rendering techniques, such as shader-based approaches, are used to produce visually convincing representations of fluids. These techniques can simulate the reflective and refractive properties of water, as well as dynamic surface effects like waves and foam.

Soft Body Dynamics

Soft body dynamics involve the simulation of deformable and flexible objects. Unlike rigid bodies, soft bodies can bend, stretch, and deform realistically in response to forces and interactions. This is particularly useful for simulating materials like cloth, rubber, or even the human body.

Cloth Simulation

One common application of soft body dynamics is cloth simulation. Cloth can be modeled as a grid of particles connected by springs. These springs enforce the cloth's structural integrity while allowing it to deform naturally when subjected to external forces like wind or gravity.

```
# Initialize cloth simulation with particles and springs

cloth_particles, springs = initialize_cloth()

# Simulation loop

while running:

# Update cloth particle positions based on forces and springs

update_cloth_particles(cloth_particles, springs)

# Render the deforming cloth

render_cloth(cloth_particles)
```

In this example, the simulation loop updates the positions of cloth particles based on forces and spring connections, creating the illusion of a flexible and deformable cloth.

Soft Body Physics for Characters

Soft body dynamics can also be applied to character animations. When simulating characters, soft body physics can provide realistic secondary motion, such as jiggling clothing, swaying hair, or muscle deformation during movements.

Performance Considerations

Implementing fluid and soft body dynamics can be computationally intensive due to the complex calculations involved. To ensure smooth gameplay:

- Use optimized algorithms and data structures.
- Employ level-of-detail (LOD) techniques to reduce the complexity of simulations when objects are distant from the camera.
- Utilize hardware acceleration and GPU-based computations for real-time fluid and soft body rendering.
- Profile and optimize your code to identify performance bottlenecks.

In conclusion, fluid and soft body dynamics are advanced techniques that can add a new dimension of realism and interactivity to your game world. Whether you're simulating flowing water, deformable cloth, or realistic character animations, mastering these dynamics can elevate your game's visual appeal and immersion.

6.4. Real-Time Environmental Effects

Real-time environmental effects play a crucial role in creating immersive and visually stunning game worlds. These effects are responsible for simulating various natural phenomena and environmental interactions, enhancing the realism and depth of the in-game environment. In this section, we will explore different real-time environmental effects and techniques for their implementation.

Weather Simulation

Weather simulation is a common environmental effect used to depict changing weather conditions like rain, snow, fog, and storms. Implementing weather systems adds complexity and dynamism to your game world.

Rain and Snow

To simulate rain or snow, you can employ particle systems or shader-based techniques. Particle systems emit raindrop or snowflake particles, which move downward under gravity. Additionally, shaders can add distortion effects to create the appearance of rain hitting surfaces or accumulating as snow.

```
// Sample shader code for raindrop distortion

float2 distortion = ComputeRainDistortion(screenPosition);

float2 uvOffset = distortion * rainIntensity;
```

Fog

Fog can add depth to your game's environment and enhance atmosphere. Implementing fog can be achieved using distance-based fog equations or by applying fog volumes to specific areas within the game world. Fog volumes control the density and appearance of fog in designated regions.

```
// Sample distance-based fog in a shader

float fogDensity = ComputeFogDensity(viewDistance);

float3 finalColor = lerp(fogColor, objectColor, exp(-fogDensity * fogFactor));
```

Day-Night Cycle

A day-night cycle is another environmental effect that can significantly impact the ambiance of your game. It simulates the changing lighting conditions throughout the day, including sunrise, daytime, sunset, and nighttime.

To implement a day-night cycle, you can manipulate the position and intensity of the sun and moonlight sources. You can also adjust the colors and intensities of ambient lighting to create different moods during various times of the day.

```
// Sample code to adjust sun position and lighting intensity

float dayTime = CalculateDayTime(); // 0.0 for night, 0.5 for noon, 1.0 for night

float sunAngle = Lerp(-PI, PI, dayTime);

sunLight.position = Vector3(cos(sunAngle), sin(sunAngle), 0.0);
```

sunLight.intensity = Lerp(sunriseIntensity, noonIntensity, dayTime);

Dynamic Wind and Vegetation

Simulating wind and its effects on vegetation and other objects in the game world can enhance realism and immersion. Dynamic wind can cause trees to sway, grass to ripple, and flags to flutter realistically.

Wind simulation often involves creating a wind field that affects objects within its range. You can use techniques like vertex displacement shaders to animate vegetation in response to the wind field's properties.

// Sample vertex shader for simulating wind on vegetation

float3 windDirection = ComputeWindDirection();

float windStrength = ComputeWindStrength(position);

position += windDirection * windStrength * vertexNormal;

Performance Considerations

Implementing real-time environmental effects can be computationally demanding, particularly in open-world games with large, detailed environments. To ensure good performance:

- Use level-of-detail (LOD) techniques to optimize the rendering of distant objects and reduce computational load.

- Employ occlusion culling to avoid rendering objects that are not visible to the camera.

- Utilize modern graphics APIs and hardware acceleration for efficient rendering of complex environmental effects.

- Profile and optimize your code to identify and address performance bottlenecks.

In summary, real-time environmental effects are essential for creating captivating and immersive game worlds. Whether it's simulating weather, day-night cycles, or dynamic wind, mastering these effects can significantly enhance your game's visual appeal and player engagement.

6.5. Integrating Physics with Game Logic

Integrating physics into the game logic is a fundamental aspect of game development, as it allows objects to interact with the virtual world in a realistic and dynamic manner. This integration enables you to create engaging and immersive gameplay experiences. In this section, we will explore how to effectively integrate physics into your game's logic.

Physics Engines

Physics engines are software libraries or frameworks designed to simulate physical interactions within a game world. These engines handle complex calculations for collision detection, rigid body dynamics, and more, allowing you to focus on game-specific logic.

Integration Steps

To integrate a physics engine into your game, follow these general steps:

1. **Initialization:** Initialize the physics engine and set up the world with parameters such as gravity and collision settings.

```
// Example initialization of a physics engine

PhysicsEngine physics;

physics.Initialize();

physics.SetGravity(Vector3(0.0f, -9.81f, 0.0f));
```

1. **Create Objects:** Define game objects that require physics

simulations, such as characters, vehicles, or environmental objects.

```
// Example object creation and physics representation

GameObject player = CreatePlayerObject();

PhysicsObject playerPhysics = physics.CreateRigidBody(player);
```

1. **Update Physics:** In your game's update loop, update the physics engine to advance the simulation.

```
// Example physics update within the game loop

while (running) {

physics.Update(deltaTime);

// Other game logic and rendering

}
```

1. **Collision Handling:** Detect and handle collisions between objects to trigger events or gameplay responses.

```
// Example collision detection and response

if (physics.CheckCollision(playerPhysics, enemyPhysics)) {

HandleCollision(player, enemy);

}
```

1. **Cleanup:** Properly release resources when the game is finished to avoid memory leaks.

```
// Example cleanup of physics engine
```

```
physics.Cleanup();
```

Physics and Gameplay Interaction

Integrating physics with gameplay logic opens up various possibilities:

Realistic Movements

Physics-driven movements can provide a sense of realism to characters and objects. For instance, a physics-based character controller can accurately simulate walking, jumping, and falling.

```
// Example physics-based character movement

Vector3 playerInput = GetPlayerInput();

playerPhysics.ApplyForce(playerInput * moveSpeed);
```

Puzzles and Challenges

Physics can be used to create puzzles and challenges in your game. Leveraging physics for puzzles involving switches, moving platforms, or object manipulation can add depth and engagement.

```
// Example physics-based puzzle interaction

if (physics.CheckCollision(switchPhysics, doorPhysics)) {

OpenDoor(door);

}
```

Dynamic Environments

Physics-driven environments can react to player actions. For example, destructible objects can crumble realistically when hit, adding immersion to combat scenarios.

```
// Example destructible object physics

if (isHit) {

physics.ApplyImpulse(objectPhysics, hitDirection * impactForce);

}
```

Performance Considerations

Efficiently integrating physics with gameplay logic is crucial for maintaining a smooth gaming experience:

- Implement efficient collision detection algorithms to minimize computational load.
- Use simplified collision shapes for objects when possible to reduce complexity.
- Employ physics LOD techniques to optimize physics calculations for objects that are far from the player's viewpoint.
- Utilize multi-threading or parallel processing for physics calculations, especially in games with numerous physics interactions.

In conclusion, integrating physics into your game's logic is essential for creating dynamic and engaging gameplay experiences. By following best practices and leveraging physics engines, you can achieve realistic movements, create challenging puzzles, and design interactive environments that enhance player immersion.

7.1. Spatial Audio and 3D Soundscapes

Spatial audio and 3D soundscapes are crucial elements in game development that enhance immersion and create a more immersive audio experience for players. These techniques allow sounds to be positioned in three-dimensional space, providing a sense of direction and depth. In this section, we will delve into the concepts of spatial audio and 3D soundscapes in game development.

The Importance of Spatial Audio

Spatial audio plays a vital role in simulating the auditory aspects of the game world. It enables players to locate and identify sounds based on their position, creating a more realistic and engaging environment. Here are some key aspects of spatial audio:

Sound Positioning

Spatial audio allows you to specify the 3D position of sounds within the game world. This positioning is crucial for delivering information to players about the location of objects, characters, or events. For example, the sound of footsteps can reveal an approaching enemy's direction.

```
// Example code to set the position of a sound source

SoundSource footstepSound;

footstepSound.SetPosition(Vector3(x, y, z));
```

Sound Attenuation

Sound attenuation refers to the decrease in volume as the distance between the listener and the sound source increases. In the real world, sounds become quieter as they move farther away. Spatial audio models this effect to create a natural auditory experience.

```
// Example code to simulate sound attenuation

float distance = CalculateDistance(listenerPosition, soundPosition);

float volume = CalculateAttenuation(distance, maxAudibleDistance);
```

soundSource.SetVolume(volume);

Doppler Effect

The Doppler effect simulates the change in pitch of a sound as the source and listener move relative to each other. For instance, as a car approaches and passes a player in a racing game, the engine noise's pitch changes realistically.

// Example code to simulate the Doppler effect

float relativeSpeed = CalculateRelativeSpeed(soundSource, listener);

float pitch = CalculateDopplerPitch(relativeSpeed, soundSpeed);

soundSource.SetPitch(pitch);

Implementing Spatial Audio

To implement spatial audio in your game, you'll need an audio engine or library that supports 3D sound positioning and effects. Many game engines and audio middleware solutions offer these features, making it easier to integrate spatial audio into your project.

Listener and Sound Source

In spatial audio, you typically have a listener representing the player's position and orientation and multiple sound sources representing in-game sounds. You update the positions of sound sources based on their in-game positions, and the audio engine handles the rest.

```
// Example code to update sound source positions

SoundListener listener;

listener.SetPosition(playerPosition);

footstepSound.SetPosition(enemyPosition);
```

Environmental Effects

Spatial audio can also model environmental effects such as reverb and occlusion. Reverb simulates the reflection of sound waves in different environments (e.g., a cave or a room), while occlusion models the blocking of sound by objects or obstacles.

```
// Example code to apply environmental effects

footstepSound.SetReverb(RoomReverb);

footstepSound.SetOcclusionStatus(isBlockedByWall);
```

Real-Time Calculations

To achieve realistic spatial audio, you often perform real-time calculations based on the positions of the listener, sound sources, and environmental factors. These calculations ensure that audio reflects changes in the game world accurately.

```
// Example code to calculate real-time spatial audio effects

float distance = CalculateDistance(listenerPosition, soundPosition);

float volume = CalculateAttenuation(distance, maxAudibleDistance);

float relativeSpeed = CalculateRelativeSpeed(soundSource, listener);

float pitch = CalculateDopplerPitch(relativeSpeed, soundSpeed);
```

Performance Considerations

Efficiently implementing spatial audio is essential for maintaining good game performance. Here are some performance considerations:

- **Audio Streaming**: Use audio streaming for large soundscapes or music tracks to reduce memory usage.
- **Object Pooling**: Implement object pooling for sound sources to minimize overhead when creating and destroying sources frequently.
- **Spatialization Techniques**: Choose appropriate spatialization techniques (e.g., HRTF, panning, or channel-based) based on your game's needs and platform capabilities.
- **Optimized Algorithms**: Use optimized algorithms for real-time calculations, especially when dealing with many sound sources.

In conclusion, spatial audio and 3D soundscapes are powerful tools for creating immersive and engaging game experiences. By accurately positioning sounds, simulating attenuation and the Doppler effect, and considering environmental effects, you can enhance your game's audio quality and player immersion.

7.2. Advanced Audio Processing Techniques

Advanced audio processing techniques are essential in game development to create immersive and dynamic soundscapes. These techniques go beyond simple playback and include effects, mixing, and manipulation of audio assets. In this section, we will explore some advanced audio processing techniques commonly used in game development.

Real-Time Effects

Real-time audio effects are a key component of game audio processing. They allow you to modify audio signals in real-time, enhancing the auditory experience. Some common real-time effects include:

- **Reverb**: Adding reverb to audio can simulate different environments, such as caves, halls, or outdoor spaces. Real-time reverb algorithms create the illusion of sound reflections and enhance the spatial aspect of audio.

```
// Example code to apply real-time reverb

AudioSource audioSource;

audioSource.SetReverb(RoomReverb);
```

- **Equalization (EQ)**: EQ can be used to adjust the frequency balance of audio, emphasizing or attenuating specific frequency bands. This is useful for fine-tuning the tonal quality of sounds.

```
// Example code to apply real-time EQ
```

```
AudioSource audioSource;

audioSource.ApplyEqualization(EQSettings);
```

- **Pitch Shifting**: Real-time pitch shifting alters the pitch of audio without changing its speed. This effect is valuable for creating variations in voice or musical elements.

```
// Example code to apply real-time pitch shifting

AudioSource audioSource;

audioSource.SetPitchShift(SemitoneChange);
```

Dynamic Mixing

Dynamic mixing involves adjusting the balance of audio sources in real-time based on in-game events and player actions. This technique ensures that the most relevant sounds are prominent while maintaining a coherent auditory experience.

- **Duckers**: Duckers are used to reduce the volume of one audio source when another source is active. For instance, background music can be ducked when a character speaks to ensure the dialog is clear.

```
// Example code for dynamic ducking

AudioSource backgroundMusic;

AudioSource characterDialog;

// When character dialog is active, reduce background music volume.

if (characterDialog.IsActive()) {

backgroundMusic.SetVolume(DuckedVolume);
```

```
} else {
backgroundMusic.SetVolume(NormalVolume);
}
```

- **Priority-Based Mixing**: Assigning priorities to audio sources allows you to dynamically adjust their volumes. Higher-priority sounds are more prominent, ensuring that important audio events are always heard.

```
// Example code for priority-based mixing
AudioSource highPrioritySound;
AudioSource lowPrioritySound;
// Adjust volumes based on priorities.
if (highPrioritySound.Priority() > lowPrioritySound.Priority()) {
highPrioritySound.SetVolume(NormalVolume);
lowPrioritySound.SetVolume(LowVolume);
} else {
highPrioritySound.SetVolume(LowVolume);
lowPrioritySound.SetVolume(NormalVolume);
}
```

Spatialized Audio

We've discussed spatial audio in the previous section, but it's worth emphasizing its importance in advanced audio processing. Spatialized audio, when combined with real-time effects and dynamic mixing, creates a highly immersive audio environment where sounds respond to the player's actions and the game world.

Interactive Music Systems

Interactive music systems adapt the game's soundtrack based on gameplay events and player actions. These systems seamlessly transition between different musical layers, intensifying or calming the music to match the game's mood.

```
// Example code for interactive music transition

MusicLayer calmLayer;

MusicLayer intenseLayer;

// Transition to intense music when a battle starts.

if (battleStarted) {

calmLayer.FadeOut();

intenseLayer.FadeIn();

}
```

Performance Optimization

Advanced audio processing can be computationally expensive, so optimization is crucial. Employ techniques such as audio asset streaming, memory management, and efficient algorithms to ensure smooth audio processing without impacting overall game performance.

In summary, advanced audio processing techniques play a significant role in enhancing the overall gaming experience. Real-time effects, dynamic mixing, spatialized audio, interactive music systems, and performance optimization are essential components of a successful audio strategy in game development. These techniques contribute to the immersion, engagement, and emotional impact of a game's audio, making it an integral part of the player's journey.

7.3. Dynamic Sound Systems in Games

Dynamic sound systems in games are essential for creating rich and immersive auditory experiences. These systems enable the game to respond dynamically to player actions, events, and the in-game environment, enhancing realism and player engagement. In this section, we will explore the key aspects of dynamic sound systems in game development.

Dynamic Sound Generation

Dynamic sound generation involves creating sounds on-the-fly based on various parameters and events within the game. This technique is particularly useful for procedural audio, where sounds are generated algorithmically to match specific in-game situations.

For example, in a racing game, tire screeching sounds can be generated based on factors such as the car's speed, the type of road surface, and the angle of the turn.

```
// Example code for dynamic tire screech sound generation

void GenerateTireScreechSound(Car car, RoadSurface road, float turnAngle) {

float screechIntensity = CalculateScreechIntensity(car.Speed, road.SurfaceType, turnAngle);

Sound screechSound = GenerateScreechSound(screechIntensity);

AudioManager.PlaySound(screechSound);

}
```

Environmental Audio

Environmental audio plays a crucial role in creating a believable game world. Dynamic sound systems allow for the integration of environmental audio, where sounds adapt to the player's location and surroundings.

In an open-world game, for instance, the sound of a flowing river should change as the player moves closer or farther away from it. Dynamic sound systems use spatial audio techniques to achieve this effect, ensuring that the sound source's position and properties influence what the player hears.

```
// Example code for environmental audio using spatial audio

void UpdateRiverSound(Player player, River river) {

float distanceToRiver = CalculateDistance(player.Position, river.Position);

float volume = CalculateVolume(distanceToRiver);

river.SetVolume(volume);

}
```

Interactive Soundscapes

Interactive soundscapes are dynamic audio environments that adapt to in-game events and player interactions. These soundscapes can include ambient sounds, music, and sound effects that change based on the game's narrative or the player's choices.

In a horror game, for instance, the soundscape can intensify as the player explores a dark and eerie environment. Interactive soundscapes heighten tension and provide audio cues that enhance the player's immersion.

```
// Example code for interactive soundscape in a horror game

void UpdateHorrorSoundscape(Player player, Environment environment) {

if (player.IsInDarkArea(environment)) {

AudioManager.PlaySound(DarkAmbience);

AudioManager.PlaySound(Whispers);

AudioManager.PlaySound(Heartbeat);

} else {

AudioManager.StopSound(DarkAmbience);

AudioManager.StopSound(Whispers);

AudioManager.StopSound(Heartbeat);

}

}
```

Player-Centric Audio

Dynamic sound systems can also be player-centric, focusing on the sounds the player's character perceives. In first-person and third-person games, the audio experience is closely tied to the character's perspective, and sounds should reflect what the character would realistically hear.

For instance, in a first-person shooter, the player's character may hear their own footsteps, the reloading of their weapon, and distant gunfire from other players. These sounds are crucial for situational awareness and gameplay immersion.

```
// Example code for player-centric audio

void UpdatePlayerCharacterSounds(PlayerCharacter playerCharacter) {

AudioManager.PlaySound(playerCharacter.FootstepSound);

if (playerCharacter.IsReloading()) {

AudioManager.PlaySound(playerCharacter.ReloadSound);

}

}
```

Performance Considerations

While dynamic sound systems enhance the gaming experience, they can be computationally intensive. Developers must optimize audio processing to ensure that the game's performance remains smooth. Techniques such as audio streaming, sound asset management, and efficient sound algorithms play a crucial role in achieving this balance.

In conclusion, dynamic sound systems are a vital component of modern game development, contributing significantly to player immersion and engagement. These systems enable the creation of interactive and responsive audio experiences, enhancing the overall quality of the game. By implementing dynamic sound generation, environmental audio, interactive soundscapes, player-centric audio, and considering performance, developers can create memorable and immersive soundscapes that complement their games.

7.4. Integrating Adaptive Music

Integrating adaptive music into games is a powerful technique that enhances the player's emotional engagement and immersion. Adaptive music systems dynamically respond to in-game events, player actions, and the game's narrative, adjusting the music to match the mood and pace of the gameplay. In this section, we will explore the key aspects of integrating adaptive music in game development.

The Role of Adaptive Music

Music has a profound impact on a player's gaming experience. It can intensify action sequences, create tension in suspenseful moments, or provide relaxation during exploration. Adaptive music systems allow composers and developers to craft soundtracks that evolve in real-time, synchronizing with the player's actions and the game's context.

Dynamic Layering

One of the fundamental techniques in adaptive music is dynamic layering. Instead of playing a single, static music track, the game's soundtrack is composed of multiple layers or stems. Each layer corresponds to a specific mood or instrument, and these layers can be combined or removed dynamically based on in-game events.

For example, in an action-packed scene, layers with intense drums and fast-paced melodies can be added to the music mix. In contrast, during a peaceful exploration phase, layers with soft strings and ambient sounds can be emphasized.

// Example code for dynamic layering in adaptive music

```
void UpdateMusicLayers(GameState gameState, MusicComposer composer) {
if (gameState.IsInActionSequence()) {
composer.AddLayer(IntenseDrums);
composer.AddLayer(FastMelody);
} else {
composer.RemoveLayer(IntenseDrums);
composer.RemoveLayer(FastMelody);
}
}
```

Interactive Crossfading

Interactive crossfading is another technique used in adaptive music systems. It allows for smooth transitions between different musical themes or variations. When the game transitions from one gameplay phase to another, crossfading ensures that the music changes gradually and seamlessly.

For instance, when a player goes from exploring a tranquil forest to encountering an enemy, the music can smoothly crossfade from a serene melody to a more intense battle theme.

```
// Example code for interactive crossfading in adaptive music
void CrossfadeMusic(MusicTheme currentTheme, MusicTheme nextTheme, float crossfadeDuration) {
```

```
AudioManager.Crossfade(currentTheme, nextTheme, crossfadeDuration);

}
```

Musical Emotion Mapping

In adaptive music, emotions play a pivotal role. Game developers and composers map specific emotions to in-game events and states. For example, victory in a battle might trigger a triumphant musical theme, while a character's death could lead to a mournful melody.

```
// Example code for emotion mapping in adaptive music

void PlayEmotionBasedMusic(GameEvent gameEvent, MusicComposer composer) {

if (gameEvent == GameEvent.Victory) {

composer.PlayTheme(TriumphantTheme);

} else if (gameEvent == GameEvent.CharacterDeath) {

composer.PlayTheme(MournfulTheme);

}

}
```

Player-Centric Music

Adaptive music systems can also be player-centric, tailoring the soundtrack to the player's actions and choices. In games with branching narratives, the player's decisions can influence the music's progression and outcome.

For example, in a role-playing game, the player's choice to ally with a particular faction can trigger music that reflects their alliance, creating a personalized musical experience.

```
// Example code for player-centric adaptive music

void UpdatePlayerAlignment(PlayerAlignment playerAlignment, MusicComposer composer) {

if (playerAlignment == PlayerAlignment.AlliedWithFactionA) {

composer.PlayTheme(FactionATheme);

} else if (playerAlignment == PlayerAlignment.AlliedWithFactionB) {

composer.PlayTheme(FactionBTheme);

}

}
```

Performance Considerations

While adaptive music greatly enhances player immersion, it can also introduce performance challenges. Developers need to optimize music transitions, layer management, and memory usage to ensure smooth gameplay. Additionally, adaptive music systems should be flexible and easily configurable to accommodate changes during development.

In conclusion, integrating adaptive music into games is a creative and technical endeavor that can significantly enhance the player's emotional connection with the game world. Dynamic layering, interactive crossfading, musical emotion mapping, player-centric music, and performance considerations are key elements in creating adaptive music systems that elevate the gaming experience. Game developers and composers should collaborate closely to craft music that not only complements the gameplay but also adapts and responds to the player's actions and choices, making each playthrough a unique and memorable journey.

7.5. Audio Optimization for Various Platforms

Audio optimization is a crucial aspect of game development, ensuring that your game's sound performance is optimized for various platforms and devices. Different platforms have different hardware capabilities and requirements, so it's essential to tailor your audio assets and processing to achieve the best possible audio experience. In this section, we will explore strategies for audio optimization across different platforms.

Platform-Specific Audio Considerations

Each gaming platform, whether it's a console, PC, mobile device, or VR headset, has unique audio capabilities and limitations. Understanding these differences is essential for audio optimization.

- **Console and PC**: These platforms often have dedicated GPU and CPU resources for audio processing. Game developers have more control over audio quality and can implement advanced audio features like surround sound and realistic spatial audio.

- **Mobile Devices**: Mobile devices have limited processing power and memory compared to consoles and PCs. Optimizing audio for mobile platforms involves using compressed audio formats, reducing the number of simultaneous audio channels, and carefully managing memory.

- **VR and AR**: Virtual reality and augmented reality devices require precise spatial audio to enhance immersion. These platforms demand low-latency audio processing to match the user's head movements accurately.

Audio Compression and Formats

Audio files can consume a significant amount of storage space, especially when dealing with high-quality samples and music. To optimize audio assets for various platforms, consider using audio compression and choosing appropriate formats.

- **Lossless vs. Lossy Compression**: Lossless compression retains the original audio quality but may not provide significant file size reduction. Lossy compression sacrifices some audio quality but results in smaller file sizes, making it suitable for mobile platforms and online games.

- **File Formats**: Different platforms support various audio file formats. Common formats include WAV, MP3, OGG, and AAC. Ensure your game uses formats compatible with the target platform and that you implement proper decoding and playback.

Audio Streaming

In open-world games or those with large, dynamic environments, audio streaming can be a powerful tool for audio optimization. Instead of loading the entire audio asset into memory, streaming loads and unloads audio data as needed, reducing memory usage.

```
// Example code for audio streaming in a game engine

void StreamAudio(AudioStream audioStream) {

if (audioStream.IsWithinHearingRange()) {
```

```
audioStream.LoadData();

audioStream.Play();

} else {

audioStream.Stop();

audioStream.UnloadData();

}

}
```

Memory Management

Efficient memory management is essential when dealing with audio assets. Loading and unloading audio data in real-time based on the game's context can significantly reduce memory usage.

Additionally, consider using asset bundling techniques to group audio files and load them on-demand, avoiding excessive memory consumption at the start of the game.

Cross-Platform Audio Middleware

To streamline audio development across multiple platforms, consider using audio middleware solutions. These middleware packages provide tools and libraries that abstract the platform-specific audio APIs, allowing developers to focus on creating and optimizing audio content.

Popular audio middleware solutions include FMOD and Wwise, which offer comprehensive audio authoring and optimization capabilities.

Platform-Specific Audio Effects

Different platforms may support platform-specific audio effects and technologies. For example, some consoles offer hardware-accelerated audio processing, while others provide specialized audio plugins. Take advantage of these platform-specific features to enhance audio quality and performance.

Testing and Quality Assurance

Thoroughly test your game's audio on each target platform to ensure that it meets the desired quality standards and performance expectations. Pay attention to audio playback, synchronization with visuals, and any platform-specific audio issues.

Implementing robust quality assurance procedures for audio, including playtesting on various devices and configurations, can help identify and resolve potential audio optimization issues.

In summary, audio optimization is a critical step in game development, especially when targeting multiple platforms. Understanding the unique audio requirements and capabilities of each platform, employing compression and streaming techniques, managing memory efficiently, utilizing cross-platform audio middleware, and leveraging platform-specific audio effects are essential strategies for achieving optimal audio performance across different devices and platforms. A thorough testing and quality assurance process ensures that your game's audio provides an immersive and enjoyable experience for players on all target platforms.

Chapter 8: Developing for Emerging Technologies

8.1. Virtual Reality (VR) Integration with SDL

Virtual Reality (VR) has rapidly evolved and gained popularity in the gaming industry, offering immersive experiences that transport players into virtual worlds. Integrating VR into your game using the Simple DirectMedia Layer (SDL) can open up new possibilities and create captivating gameplay. In this section, we will explore the integration of VR technology with SDL, providing an overview of the key considerations and steps involved.

Understanding Virtual Reality (VR)

Before diving into VR integration with SDL, it's essential to have a solid understanding of VR technology. VR provides users with a fully immersive, 3D virtual environment that responds to their movements and interactions. Key components of VR include:

- **Head-Mounted Display (HMD)**: The device worn on the head that displays the virtual world to the user. HMDs often include sensors to track head movement.

- **Motion Controllers**: Handheld controllers that allow users to interact with objects and manipulate the virtual environment.

- **Tracking Systems**: Sensors and cameras that track the position and movement of the HMD and motion controllers, enabling accurate rendering of the virtual world.

- **VR-Ready PCs or Consoles**: High-performance hardware capable of rendering VR content at a high frame rate to ensure a smooth experience.

SDL and VR Integration

SDL is a versatile library that provides functionality for window management, input handling, and multimedia, making it suitable for VR integration. When integrating VR into your SDL-based game, consider the following steps:

1. **Choose VR Platforms**: Determine which VR platforms you want to support. Popular VR platforms include Oculus Rift, HTC Vive, PlayStation VR, and Windows Mixed Reality. Each platform may require different SDKs and development environments.
2. **Install VR SDKs**: Install the necessary VR software development kits (SDKs) and tools for the chosen platforms. These SDKs provide access to VR hardware and functionality. For example, Oculus provides the Oculus SDK, while SteamVR is used for HTC Vive.
3. **Initialize SDL with VR Support**: Configure SDL to work with VR hardware. This often involves initializing SDL with additional flags and settings to enable VR mode.
4. **VR Input Handling**: Implement input handling for VR controllers and HMD tracking. SDL's input handling capabilities can be extended to accommodate VR input devices, allowing players to interact with the virtual world.
5. **Render for VR**: Modify your game's rendering pipeline to support VR. VR rendering typically involves rendering two separate views, one for each eye, with appropriate distortion correction.

```
// Example code for rendering to VR HMD using SDL

void RenderForVR(SDL_Renderer* renderer, SDL_Texture* leftEyeTexture, SDL_Texture* rightEyeTexture) {

SDL_Rect leftView = {0, 0, VR_WIDTH / 2, VR_HEIGHT};

SDL_Rect rightView = {VR_WIDTH / 2, 0, VR_WIDTH / 2, VR_HEIGHT};

SDL_RenderSetViewport(renderer, &leftView);

SDL_RenderCopy(renderer, leftEyeTexture, NULL, NULL);

SDL_RenderSetViewport(renderer, &rightView);

SDL_RenderCopy(renderer, rightEyeTexture, NULL, NULL);

// Apply distortion correction and present the frame to the HMD

}
```

1. **Stereo 3D Audio**: Enhance the immersive experience by implementing stereo 3D audio that takes into account the player's head position and orientation. SDL can be used for audio playback and spatial audio.
2. **Optimization**: Optimize your game's performance to ensure a consistent frame rate, as low frame rates can lead to motion sickness in VR. Profiling and tuning are crucial for VR experiences.
3. **Testing and QA**: Rigorously test your VR integration on the target hardware to ensure compatibility, performance, and comfort. Pay attention to factors like latency, head tracking accuracy, and frame rate.
4. **User Interface (UI) Design**: Redesign your game's UI to be VR-friendly. VR UIs should be readable, accessible, and

easy to interact with in a 3D space.

5. **Publishing and Distribution**: Prepare your VR-enabled game for distribution on the respective VR platforms. This may involve compliance testing and submission to platform-specific stores.

Conclusion

Integrating VR technology with SDL opens up exciting possibilities for immersive gaming experiences. However, it also presents unique challenges related to hardware compatibility, performance optimization, and user interface design. By following the steps outlined in this section and leveraging the capabilities of SDL, you can create engaging VR games that transport players into fantastical virtual worlds. Remember to stay updated with the latest developments in VR technology and SDKs to ensure your game remains cutting-edge in the world of virtual reality.

8.2. Augmented Reality (AR) in Game Development

Augmented Reality (AR) is a technology that superimposes digital content, such as virtual objects or information, onto the real world. Unlike Virtual Reality (VR), which creates entirely immersive environments, AR enhances the real-world experience by adding digital elements. In this section, we will explore how to incorporate Augmented Reality into your game development using the Simple DirectMedia Layer (SDL) and AR toolkits.

Understanding Augmented Reality (AR)

Before diving into AR game development with SDL, let's understand the fundamental concepts of Augmented Reality:

- **Marker-Based AR**: Marker-based AR uses physical markers or images as triggers for AR content. When a camera detects a specific marker, it overlays digital content associated with that marker onto the real-world view.

- **Markerless AR**: Markerless AR, also known as SLAM (Simultaneous Localization and Mapping), relies on computer vision and sensor data to detect and track the real-world environment. It can place AR objects in the scene without the need for markers.

- **AR Tracking**: Tracking in AR involves continuously monitoring the position and orientation of the device or camera relative to the real world. This is crucial for placing AR objects accurately and making them appear stable.

• **AR Toolkits**: AR development often involves using AR SDKs and toolkits like ARKit (iOS), ARCore (Android), Vuforia, or OpenCV. These toolkits provide the necessary APIs and functionality for AR content creation.

SDL and AR Integration

SDL can be used as the foundation for creating AR games, providing capabilities for rendering, input handling, and multimedia. Here are the key steps to integrate Augmented Reality into your SDL-based game:

1. **Choose AR Platforms**: Determine which AR platforms or toolkits you want to target. Depending on your target audience and platforms (e.g., mobile devices or smart glasses), you may select ARKit, ARCore, or other AR frameworks.
2. **Set Up SDL Environment**: Set up your SDL development environment and ensure that SDL is configured correctly. You can find SDL libraries and resources on the official SDL website.
3. **AR SDK Integration**: Integrate the chosen AR SDK or toolkit into your project. This typically involves adding the SDK to your project dependencies and configuring it to work with SDL.
4. **Camera Access**: Access the device's camera or other sensors to capture the real-world environment. SDL provides functionalities to access camera feeds and display them within your game's window.
5. **AR Object Placement**: Use the AR toolkit's tracking and detection capabilities to place virtual objects in the real world. This may involve recognizing markers or utilizing markerless tracking techniques.

6. **Rendering AR Content**: Render AR content seamlessly within your SDL-based game. You'll need to combine the camera feed with the rendered virtual objects to create the augmented view.
7. **User Interactions**: Implement user interactions with AR objects. This can include gestures, taps, or other input methods to interact with and manipulate virtual content.
8. **Performance Optimization**: Optimize your game's performance, as AR can be resource-intensive. Efficient rendering, camera processing, and frame rate management are critical for a smooth AR experience.
9. **Testing and Calibration**: Thoroughly test your AR game on the target devices and environments. Ensure that tracking and placement are accurate, and the AR elements behave as expected.
10. **AR UI and UX**: Design an intuitive and user-friendly AR user interface. Consider how users will interact with AR elements and provide clear instructions or guidance.
11. **Deployment and Distribution**: Prepare your AR-enabled game for distribution on app stores or platforms that support AR technology. Follow the guidelines and requirements of the chosen AR platform.

Conclusion

Augmented Reality offers exciting opportunities for game developers to create unique and immersive experiences that blend digital and physical worlds. By integrating AR into your SDL-based game, you can engage players in novel ways and provide them with interactive and entertaining content. Keep in mind that AR development may require specialized knowledge and tools, so be prepared to invest time in learning and experimentation to master this innovative technology.

8.3. Exploring Haptic Feedback and Sensory Inputs

Haptic feedback, also known as tactile feedback, is a technology that allows users to experience touch-like sensations in the digital world. In game development, haptic feedback enhances immersion by providing physical sensations that correspond to in-game events or interactions. This section explores the integration of haptic feedback and sensory inputs into your game using the Simple DirectMedia Layer (SDL) and related technologies.

Understanding Haptic Feedback

Haptic feedback encompasses various tactile sensations, including vibrations, force feedback, and more. It is commonly used in gaming to convey information or enhance the player's experience. Here are some key aspects of haptic feedback:

- **Vibrations**: Vibrations are the most common form of haptic feedback. They are generated by small motors or actuators in controllers, smartphones, or specialized haptic devices. Vibrations can simulate impacts, explosions, or other in-game events.

- **Force Feedback**: Force feedback provides resistance or counterforce against the player's actions. It can simulate the feel of steering a car, pulling a trigger, or interacting with objects in the game world.

- **Texture and Surface Simulation**: Advanced haptic systems can simulate the texture and surface properties of in-game objects. For example, a player might feel the difference between driving on a rough road and a smooth track.

- **Sensory Feedback**: In addition to touch sensations, haptic feedback can include sensory inputs like temperature or pressure changes. These sensations further enhance immersion by engaging multiple senses.

SDL and Haptic Feedback

SDL provides support for haptic feedback through its Haptic API. To integrate haptic feedback into your SDL-based game, follow these steps:

1. **Haptic Device Detection**: Begin by detecting available haptic devices, such as controllers or specialized haptic hardware. SDL's Haptic API allows you to enumerate and identify these devices.
2. **Initializing Haptic Devices**: Initialize the chosen haptic device, specifying its properties and capabilities. This step involves opening the haptic device and configuring its parameters.
3. **Creating Haptic Effects**: Create haptic effects that define the type and characteristics of feedback. You can design effects for various in-game events, such as collisions, weapon recoil, or environmental interactions.
4. **Triggering Haptic Feedback**: Implement logic in your game to trigger haptic feedback events. For example, when a player's character takes damage, you can trigger a vibration effect to simulate impact.
5. **Feedback Customization**: Allow players to customize haptic feedback settings in your game's options menu. This includes adjusting intensity, frequency, and duration to

match individual preferences.

6. **Synchronization with In-Game Events**: Ensure that haptic feedback is synchronized with in-game events and actions. Timing and accuracy are crucial to creating a seamless and immersive experience.
7. **Multi-Platform Considerations**: If your game targets multiple platforms, be aware that haptic feedback implementations may differ across devices and operating systems. Adjust your code accordingly.
8. **Testing and Optimization**: Thoroughly test haptic feedback on various devices to ensure consistent and enjoyable feedback. Optimize the effects and settings for performance and realism.

Sensory Inputs

In addition to haptic feedback, consider incorporating other sensory inputs into your game to enhance immersion:

- **Audio**: High-quality audio, including spatial audio and dynamic soundscapes, can significantly contribute to the sensory experience. Use SDL's audio capabilities to create immersive auditory environments.

- **Visual Effects**: Visual effects, such as particle systems, dynamic lighting, and shader effects, can complement haptic feedback by providing visual cues that align with tactile sensations.

- **VR and AR**: For virtual reality (VR) and augmented reality (AR) experiences, sensory inputs become even more critical. Utilize VR and AR hardware to engage users' visual, auditory, and haptic senses simultaneously.

Conclusion

Integrating haptic feedback and sensory inputs into your game can elevate the player experience to new heights. By leveraging SDL's Haptic API and related technologies, you can create games that not only look and sound great but also feel immersive and engaging. Remember that the key to success lies in careful design, synchronization, and optimization of haptic feedback and sensory inputs to align with your game's narrative and mechanics.

8.4. Adaptive Gaming with AI and IoT

The convergence of Artificial Intelligence (AI) and the Internet of Things (IoT) has opened up exciting opportunities in the realm of adaptive gaming. This section explores how game developers can harness the power of AI and IoT to create personalized and dynamic gaming experiences.

AI in Gaming

AI has been a game-changer in the gaming industry, enabling more intelligent NPCs (Non-Playable Characters), advanced enemy behaviors, and adaptive game mechanics. With AI, games can learn from player behavior and adapt to their preferences and skill levels. Here's how AI can be applied to create adaptive gaming experiences:

- **Player Profiling**: AI algorithms can analyze player behavior, preferences, and skill levels to create player profiles. These profiles help in tailoring the gaming experience to individual players.

- **Adaptive Difficulty**: AI can dynamically adjust the difficulty of a game based on the player's performance. If a player is struggling, the AI can make the game easier, and vice versa.

- **Personalized Content**: AI can recommend in-game content, such as quests, items, or challenges, based on a player's profile and past interactions.

- **Dynamic Storytelling**: AI-driven narratives can adapt to player choices, creating a unique storytelling experience for each player.

IoT Integration

IoT devices, such as wearables, smart home devices, and sensors, can be integrated into gaming experiences to capture real-world data and enhance immersion. Here are some ways IoT can be used in adaptive gaming:

- **Health and Biometrics**: Wearable devices can monitor a player's heart rate, body temperature, and other biometrics to influence in-game events. For example, a horror game can increase tension based on the player's physiological responses.

- **Environmental Data**: IoT sensors can collect real-world environmental data, like weather conditions or time of day, and use this information to influence in-game weather, lighting, or events.

- **Smart Objects**: Integrating IoT with physical objects can extend the gaming experience beyond the screen. For instance, a puzzle game might require players to interact with real-world objects connected to the game.

- **Location-Based Gaming**: IoT-enabled location data can create location-based gaming experiences. Players can explore the real world while interacting with virtual elements.

Challenges and Considerations

While AI and IoT offer exciting possibilities, game developers should be mindful of some challenges and considerations:

- **Data Privacy**: Collecting and using player data requires strict adherence to data privacy regulations and ethical considerations. Players must have control over their data and be informed about its usage.

- **Complexity**: Implementing AI and IoT can introduce complexity into game development. Developers need the expertise to work with these technologies effectively.

- **Connectivity**: IoT devices rely on internet connectivity, which can be inconsistent. Games must gracefully handle connectivity issues and provide a seamless experience.

- **Cost**: Developing games with AI and IoT integration may involve additional costs for hardware, data storage, and maintenance.

Examples of Adaptive Gaming

Several games have successfully incorporated AI and IoT to create adaptive experiences:

- **Horizon Zero Dawn**: This action RPG uses AI to control the behavior of robotic creatures in a dynamic open world. The creatures adapt their tactics based on the player's actions.

- **Watch Dogs 2**: This open-world game uses IoT devices in its narrative, allowing players to hack into and control various smart objects in the game world.

- **Left 4 Dead**: This cooperative multiplayer game uses an AI Director to dynamically adjust the intensity of the zombie horde based on player performance.

- **Pokemon GO**: This mobile game uses location-based data from IoT devices to create an augmented reality experience where players must explore real-world locations to catch virtual creatures.

Conclusion

AI and IoT are transforming the gaming landscape by enabling adaptive experiences that respond to individual player preferences and real-world conditions. Game developers can harness these technologies to create more engaging and immersive games that captivate players on a personal level. However, it's crucial to approach AI and IoT integration with a clear understanding of the challenges and ethical considerations involved, prioritizing player privacy and data security.

8.5. Preparing for Future Gaming Technologies

As technology continues to advance at a rapid pace, the gaming industry is poised for exciting developments and innovations. In this section, we'll explore strategies for preparing your game development efforts for future gaming technologies and staying ahead of the curve.

Embracing Emerging Trends

To thrive in the ever-evolving world of game development, it's essential to keep a close eye on emerging trends and technologies. Here are some areas to consider:

- **Virtual Reality (VR) and Augmented Reality (AR)**: VR and AR are continuously evolving, offering new possibilities for immersive gaming experiences. Consider how your games can leverage these technologies to provide unique gameplay and storytelling.

- **Cloud Gaming**: The cloud gaming market is growing, with services like Google Stadia and Microsoft's xCloud leading the way. Developers should explore cloud-based game development and streaming to reach a broader audience.

- **Artificial Intelligence (AI)**: AI-driven gameplay, procedural content generation, and dynamic storytelling are becoming more prevalent. Familiarize yourself with AI tools and techniques to enhance your games.

- **Blockchain and NFTs**: Blockchain technology is gaining traction in the gaming world, enabling ownership of in-game assets through non-fungible tokens (NFTs). Understanding blockchain integration can be valuable.

- **5G Connectivity**: The rollout of 5G networks promises faster and more reliable internet connections, opening up possibilities for real-time multiplayer experiences and reduced latency in online gaming.

Cross-Platform Development

As gaming platforms diversify, cross-platform development becomes increasingly important. Ensuring that your games can run on various devices and operating systems expands your potential player base. Tools like Unity and Unreal Engine offer robust cross-platform support.

Future-Proofing Game Assets

Invest in high-quality game assets that can withstand changes in technology and resolution. Future-proofing your assets by creating them at high resolutions and using scalable techniques ensures they remain visually appealing on next-generation hardware.

Adaptive Game Engines

Consider using adaptive game engines that can scale and adapt to different hardware capabilities. These engines can adjust graphics settings and performance dynamically, optimizing the gaming experience on various devices.

Collaboration with Research Institutions

Collaborating with research institutions or universities specializing in gaming technology can provide valuable insights into emerging technologies. These partnerships can lead to innovative projects and early access to cutting-edge tools.

Ethical Considerations

With advanced technologies come ethical responsibilities. Be mindful of how your games use player data, handle privacy concerns, and promote responsible gaming practices. Ethical game development is crucial for long-term success.

Continuous Learning

Stay curious and committed to continuous learning. Attend industry conferences, take online courses, and engage with gaming communities to stay informed about the latest advancements. A well-informed development team is better equipped to adapt to change.

Conclusion

The gaming industry's future is bright, filled with opportunities for innovation and creativity. By embracing emerging trends, prioritizing cross-platform development, future-proofing assets, and staying ethically responsible, game developers can position themselves for success in an ever-evolving landscape. Remember that adaptability, collaboration, and a commitment to learning are key factors in preparing for future gaming technologies and creating memorable gaming experiences for players worldwide.

Chapter 9: Profiling and Performance Tuning

9.1. Advanced Profiling Techniques

Profiling and performance tuning are critical aspects of game development. In this section, we'll delve into advanced profiling techniques that help you identify and optimize performance bottlenecks in your games. Profiling is the process of measuring and analyzing a program's execution to identify areas that can be optimized. Effective profiling can lead to smoother gameplay, shorter loading times, and better overall player experiences.

Profiling Tools and Frameworks

To get started with advanced profiling, you'll need the right tools and frameworks. Several profiling tools are available for different platforms and game engines. Here are some commonly used options:

- **Unity Profiler**: Unity provides a built-in profiler that offers insights into CPU and GPU usage, memory allocation, and rendering performance. It's an essential tool for Unity developers.

- **Unreal Engine Profiler**: Unreal Engine also includes a comprehensive profiler for tracking and analyzing various aspects of game performance.

- **Visual Studio Profiler**: If you're developing in C++ or C#, Visual Studio's built-in profiler can help you identify bottlenecks in your code.

- **GPU Profilers**: For GPU-intensive tasks, GPU profilers like NVIDIA Nsight or AMD Radeon GPU Profiler are invaluable. They provide detailed information about GPU utilization and bottlenecks.

CPU Profiling

CPU profiling helps you identify CPU-bound performance issues in your game. Common CPU profiling techniques include:

- **Sampling Profilers**: Sampling profilers periodically interrupt your program's execution to record the call stack. By aggregating the collected data, you can identify which functions consume the most CPU time.

- **Instrumentation Profilers**: Instrumentation profilers add code to your game to measure the execution time of specific functions or code blocks. This provides more precise performance data but may introduce some overhead.

GPU Profiling

GPU profiling is crucial for optimizing rendering performance. Here's what you can analyze with GPU profilers:

- **Draw Calls**: Identify the number of draw calls and their impact on GPU performance. Reducing unnecessary draw calls can significantly improve rendering speed.

- **Shader Performance**: GPU profilers can show you which shaders are the most expensive to execute. Optimize these shaders to improve frame rates.

- **Texture and Buffer Usage**: Analyze how textures and buffers are used during rendering. Reducing texture swaps and memory transfers can boost GPU performance.

Memory Profiling

Memory profiling helps you manage memory usage and detect memory leaks in your game. Key memory profiling tasks include:

- **Memory Allocation Tracking**: Identify where and how memory is allocated in your game. Tools like Valgrind (for C/C++) or built-in memory profilers in game engines can help.

- **Memory Leak Detection**: Track memory allocations and deallocations to find potential memory leaks. Fixing memory leaks is crucial for long-term stability.

Multi-Threading Profiling

In modern game development, multi-threading is common for improved performance. However, it can also introduce synchronization issues and bottlenecks. Profiling multi-threaded code is essential for finding and resolving such issues.

Automated Testing and Continuous Integration

Integrate profiling into your automated testing and continuous integration pipelines. Profiling should be part of your regular testing process to catch performance regressions early.

Conclusion

Advanced profiling techniques are invaluable for game developers looking to create high-performance, responsive games. By using the right tools and frameworks, analyzing CPU and GPU performance, tracking memory usage, and addressing multi-threading issues, you can optimize your games for a smoother player experience. Remember that profiling should be an ongoing process throughout your game development cycle, helping you maintain and improve performance over time.

9.2. Identifying and Solving Performance Bottlenecks

Identifying and solving performance bottlenecks is a crucial step in optimizing your game's performance. Performance bottlenecks are specific areas of your code or game systems that are causing slowdowns or resource inefficiencies. In this section, we will explore common performance bottlenecks and strategies to address them.

Common Performance Bottlenecks

1. **CPU Bound Code**: If your game logic or physics simulations are taking up a significant portion of CPU time, it can lead to frame rate drops. Identify computationally expensive code and optimize it.
2. **Excessive Draw Calls**: High numbers of draw calls, especially in 3D games, can strain the GPU. Reducing draw calls through batching and culling techniques can improve rendering performance.
3. **Inefficient Memory Usage**: Memory allocation and deallocation can be a bottleneck, especially if you have frequent allocations and deallocations during gameplay. Use memory pools and minimize unnecessary memory copying.
4. **Texture and Asset Loading**: Loading textures and assets from disk can cause frame rate hitches. Implement asynchronous asset loading and use streaming to load assets dynamically.
5. **Poorly Optimized Shaders**: Complex shaders can be expensive to execute on the GPU. Optimize your shaders by reducing unnecessary calculations and texture fetches.
6. **Network Latency**: In online multiplayer games, network

latency can lead to lag. Implement predictive networking and client-side interpolation to hide the effects of latency.

7. **Inefficient AI**: Complex AI behaviors can consume CPU resources. Use techniques like behavior trees and state machines to optimize AI processing.
8. **I/O Operations**: Reading and writing data to storage devices can introduce delays. Use background loading and caching to minimize the impact of I/O operations.

Profiling and Analysis

Profiling tools, as mentioned in the previous section, are essential for identifying performance bottlenecks. Use these tools to measure CPU and GPU usage, memory allocation patterns, and frame rendering times. Profilers can pinpoint areas of your code that need optimization.

Optimization Strategies

Once you've identified bottlenecks, consider these optimization strategies:

- **Parallelization**: Make use of multi-threading to distribute CPU-intensive tasks across multiple cores. Be cautious about thread synchronization overhead.

- **Batching**: Combine similar rendering tasks into batches to reduce the number of draw calls.

- **Level of Detail (LOD)**: Implement LOD techniques for objects and terrain to reduce rendering complexity at a distance.

• **Caching**: Cache frequently used data to avoid redundant calculations or I/O operations.

• **Streaming**: Implement streaming systems to load assets dynamically as needed, reducing memory usage.

• **Data Compression**: Compress data when transmitting it over the network or when storing it on disk to reduce transfer times.

• **Algorithmic Optimization**: Optimize algorithms and data structures to reduce computational complexity.

• **GPU Optimization**: Profile and optimize shaders to reduce GPU load, and consider using GPU instancing for rendering multiple identical objects.

• **Memory Pooling**: Use memory pooling techniques to reduce memory fragmentation and allocation overhead.

• **Asynchronous Processing**: Implement asynchronous operations for tasks that don't require immediate results, such as asset loading.

• **Hardware Acceleration**: Take advantage of hardware acceleration, such as using the GPU for physics simulations (GPU physics) or AI (GPU AI).

Continuous Testing and Optimization

Optimization is an ongoing process. Continuously test and profile your game as you make changes to ensure that new code or content additions don't introduce performance regressions. Regularly monitor your game's performance across different platforms and hardware configurations to ensure a smooth player experience.

In conclusion, identifying and addressing performance bottlenecks is crucial for delivering a high-quality gaming experience. Profiling tools, optimization strategies, and ongoing testing are your allies in achieving optimal performance for your game. Remember that optimization should be a consideration from the early stages of development and should be revisited throughout the project's lifecycle.

9.3. Memory Management and Leak Detection

Effective memory management is critical for game performance and stability. In this section, we'll discuss memory management techniques and how to detect and prevent memory leaks in your game.

Memory Management Techniques

1. Manual Memory Management:

- In some game engines and programming languages, you may need to manually allocate and deallocate memory using functions like malloc and free. Be cautious when using manual memory management, as it can lead to memory leaks and crashes if not handled correctly.

2. Automatic Memory Management:

- Many modern game engines and languages provide automatic memory management through features like garbage collection or reference counting. These mechanisms automatically reclaim memory that is no longer in use, reducing the risk of memory leaks.

3. Smart Pointers:

- Smart pointers are a type of data structure that automatically manage memory for you. They ensure that memory is deallocated when it's no longer needed.

Examples include std::shared_ptr and std::unique_ptr in C++.

4. Memory Pools:

- Memory pools allocate a large block of memory upfront and manage smaller memory allocations from within that block. They reduce memory fragmentation and allocation overhead.

5. Resource Management Systems:

- Use resource management systems to load and unload assets efficiently. These systems handle the loading and unloading of textures, models, and other assets, ensuring that resources are released when they're no longer needed.

Detecting Memory Leaks

Memory leaks occur when your game allocates memory but fails to deallocate it, leading to a gradual increase in memory usage over time. Detecting and fixing memory leaks is crucial for maintaining the stability of your game. Here's how to detect memory leaks:

1. Profiling Tools:

- Use memory profiling tools that are available for your game engine or programming language. These tools can identify memory leaks and provide detailed reports on memory usage.

2. Manual Inspection:

- Review your code and look for places where memory is allocated but not properly deallocated. Pay close attention to functions and classes responsible for memory management.

3. Unit Testing:

- Implement unit tests that check for memory leaks. These tests can allocate and deallocate memory in controlled scenarios and verify that memory is being released correctly.

4. Third-Party Tools:

- Consider using third-party memory analysis tools like Valgrind, Purify, or AddressSanitizer. These tools can detect memory errors and leaks during runtime.

Preventing Memory Leaks

Preventing memory leaks is as important as detecting them. Here are some best practices for preventing memory leaks in your game:

1. Follow Ownership Rules:

- Clearly define ownership and responsibility for memory management. Ensure that every allocated resource has a clear owner responsible for releasing it.

2. Use Smart Pointers:

- Whenever possible, use smart pointers or automatic memory management mechanisms provided by your programming language or game engine.

3. Resource Cleanup:

- Implement resource cleanup routines that are called when resources are no longer needed. For example, release textures, models, and other assets when they're no longer in use.

4. Testing and Profiling:

- Regularly test and profile your game to catch memory leaks early in development. Make memory leak detection a part of your testing and QA processes.

5. Code Reviews:

- Conduct code reviews with a focus on memory management. Peer reviews can help identify potential memory leaks before they become a problem.

6. Static Analysis:

- Use static code analysis tools that can detect potential memory leaks at compile-time.

By implementing these memory management techniques and being vigilant about detecting and preventing memory leaks, you can ensure that your game runs smoothly and doesn't suffer from performance and stability issues related to memory usage.

9.4. Cross-Platform Performance Considerations

Cross-platform game development has become increasingly prevalent, with games targeting various platforms such as Windows, macOS, Linux, consoles, mobile devices, and more. While it offers a broader audience for your game, it also brings unique challenges in terms of performance considerations. In this section, we will explore key aspects to consider when optimizing your game for cross-platform development.

1. Hardware Variability

Different platforms have varying hardware capabilities, including CPU power, GPU capabilities, memory size, and storage speed. To ensure your game performs well across platforms:

- **Profiling**: Use profiling tools to identify performance bottlenecks on each platform. Optimize code, assets, and settings accordingly for each target platform.

- **Scalability**: Implement scalable graphics and rendering options. Allow users to adjust settings like graphics quality, resolution, and frame rate to match their device's capabilities.

2. Input Methods

Cross-platform games may need to support a wide range of input methods, such as keyboard and mouse, gamepad, touchscreen, and motion controls. Consider the following:

- **Input Abstraction**: Implement an input abstraction layer that handles various input methods. This allows your game to adapt to different platforms seamlessly.

- **Customization**: Allow players to customize input mappings and sensitivity to cater to their preferred input devices.

3. Operating System Differences

Different platforms may use distinct operating systems, resulting in variations in system APIs and behaviors. Address these differences:

- **Platform Abstraction**: Develop platform-agnostic code by abstracting platform-specific functionalities. Use libraries or frameworks that provide cross-platform support.

- **Testing**: Thoroughly test your game on each target platform to identify and resolve issues related to OS-specific behaviors and dependencies.

4. Screen Resolutions and Aspect Ratios

Different devices have various screen resolutions and aspect ratios. Ensure your game looks good and functions correctly on various screens:

- **Responsive UI**: Design a responsive user interface that adapts to different screen sizes and orientations.

- **Resolution Scaling**: Implement resolution scaling techniques to adjust the game's rendering to fit the screen without distortion or loss of detail.

5. Performance Optimization

Optimizing performance is crucial for cross-platform games to run smoothly on a wide range of devices:

- **Asset Compression**: Use appropriate asset compression techniques to reduce storage and memory usage without sacrificing visual quality.

- **Dynamic Level of Detail (LOD)**: Implement dynamic LOD systems to adjust the level of detail in assets based on the player's proximity to them, saving GPU and memory resources.

- **Asynchronous Loading**: Use asynchronous loading of assets to prevent frame rate drops when loading large resources.

6. Battery Life and Resource Management

On mobile devices and laptops, battery life is a significant concern. Ensure your game is energy-efficient:

- **Resource Monitoring**: Monitor CPU and GPU usage to prevent excessive resource consumption that can drain battery life quickly.

- **Background Processes**: Suspend or reduce resource-intensive processes when the game is in the background to conserve battery life.

7. Cross-Platform Testing

Rigorous testing across all target platforms is essential to ensure a consistent and enjoyable gaming experience:

- **Device Farm**: Use device farms or cloud-based testing services to test your game on a wide range of devices and platforms.

- **User Feedback**: Gather feedback from players on different platforms and address platform-specific issues promptly.

8. Updates and Patches

Cross-platform development often involves managing multiple versions of your game. Consider the following for updates and patches:

- **Version Control**: Implement a version control system to manage different platform-specific code branches and assets.

- **Patch Delivery**: Plan how patches and updates will be delivered to players on various platforms to ensure a seamless experience.

By addressing these cross-platform performance considerations, you can create a successful game that provides a consistent and enjoyable experience across a diverse range of devices and platforms. Adapting to the unique challenges of cross-platform development can lead to broader market reach and increased player satisfaction.

9.5. Tuning Games for Optimal Performance

Performance tuning is a critical aspect of game development, ensuring that your game runs smoothly and efficiently on players' devices. In this section, we will explore various techniques and best practices for tuning games to achieve optimal performance.

1. Profiling and Benchmarking

Profiling and benchmarking your game is the first step in identifying performance bottlenecks. Consider using profiling tools to analyze CPU and GPU usage, memory usage, and frame rates. Common profiling tools include:

- **CPU Profilers**: Tools like Intel VTune, AMD CodeXL, and Xcode Instruments help you identify CPU-bound performance issues.

- **GPU Profilers**: Graphics profilers like NVIDIA Nsight and AMD GPU PerfStudio are essential for optimizing GPU performance.

- **Memory Profilers**: Tools like Valgrind and Visual Studio Memory Profiler assist in detecting memory leaks and excessive memory usage.

Once you identify performance bottlenecks, focus on optimizing the critical areas of your game.

2. Code Optimization

Optimizing your game's code can significantly improve performance. Consider the following code optimization techniques:

- **Loop Unrolling**: Manually unroll loops in critical code sections to reduce loop overhead.

- **Data-Oriented Design**: Organize data for cache coherency to minimize memory access times.

- **SIMD Instructions**: Utilize Single Instruction, Multiple Data (SIMD) instructions for parallel processing when appropriate.

- **Avoid Global Variables**: Minimize the use of global variables, as they can lead to cache thrashing and reduced performance.

- **Culling and Occlusion**: Implement object culling and occlusion techniques to reduce rendering overhead.

3. Asset Optimization

Optimizing game assets is crucial for improving load times and reducing memory usage:

- **Texture Compression**: Use texture compression formats like DXT, ETC, and ASTC to reduce memory usage without sacrificing visual quality.

- **Level of Detail (LOD)**: Implement LOD systems for 3D models to reduce the complexity of distant objects.

- **Streaming Assets**: Load assets dynamically as needed to reduce initial loading times and memory overhead.

4. Threading and Parallelism

Leverage multithreading and parallelism to distribute work across multiple CPU cores:

- **Task-Based Threading**: Use task-based threading libraries like Intel TBB or C++11's std::async to parallelize CPU-intensive tasks.

- **GPU Parallelism**: Offload compute-intensive tasks to the GPU using compute shaders and GPU parallel computing APIs.

- **Job Systems**: Implement a job system to manage parallel tasks efficiently, especially in systems with multiple cores.

5. Memory Management

Efficient memory management is crucial for preventing memory leaks and reducing runtime overhead:

- **Object Pooling**: Use object pooling to reuse game objects and reduce memory allocation overhead.

- **Memory Pools**: Implement custom memory allocators or memory pools for frequently allocated data structures.

- **Resource Cleanup**: Ensure proper resource cleanup to prevent memory leaks and unnecessary memory usage.

6. Render Batching and Draw Calls

Minimize the number of draw calls and render state changes to optimize rendering performance:

- **Batching**: Combine multiple similar objects into a single draw call to reduce overhead.

- **Instancing**: Use GPU instancing to render multiple instances of the same object with a single draw call.

- **Material Shaders**: Optimize shaders by reducing unnecessary calculations and minimizing branching.

7. Runtime Optimization

Optimize your game's performance during runtime by considering the following:

- **Streaming and Loading**: Implement background loading and streaming to load assets seamlessly during gameplay.

- **Dynamic Quality Settings**: Adjust game settings dynamically based on the player's hardware capabilities.

- **Prefetching**: Predict and load assets that are likely to be needed in the near future to reduce lag.

8. Cross-Platform Considerations

If you are targeting multiple platforms, be aware of platform-specific performance considerations. Each platform may have different hardware capabilities and limitations.

9. Player Feedback

Gather player feedback to identify performance issues specific to certain configurations. Encourage players to report performance problems, and consider using telemetry tools to monitor game performance in the wild.

10. Testing and Optimization Iteration

Regularly test your game on various devices and configurations to ensure optimal performance. Conduct performance tests, gather metrics, and address any issues that arise. Performance optimization is an iterative process that continues throughout the development lifecycle.

By implementing these performance tuning techniques and continuously monitoring and optimizing your game, you can provide players with a smooth and enjoyable gaming experience on a wide range of hardware configurations.

Chapter 10: Scalable Game Server Architecture

10.1. Designing High-Availability Game Servers

Scalability and high availability are critical considerations when designing game server architecture. In this section, we will explore the principles and strategies for designing high-availability game servers that can handle large concurrent player bases while ensuring uninterrupted gameplay experiences.

1. Redundancy and Failover

One key aspect of high availability is redundancy. Redundant game server instances are essential to mitigate the risk of server failures. Consider the following strategies:

- **Load Balancing**: Implement load balancers to distribute incoming player connections evenly across multiple server instances. This ensures that no single server is overwhelmed with traffic.

- **Failover Mechanisms**: Set up failover mechanisms that automatically switch player connections to healthy servers in case of server failures. This can involve monitoring server health and reallocating players as needed.

- **Data Replication**: Replicate game state and player data across multiple servers to ensure that even if one server goes down, players can seamlessly reconnect to another server without losing progress.

2. Scalability Strategies

Scalability is crucial to accommodate growing player bases. Here are some strategies to achieve scalability in your game server architecture:

- **Horizontal Scaling**: Design your game servers to be horizontally scalable, meaning you can add more server instances as needed to handle increased player loads. Use containerization technologies like Docker to simplify server deployment.

- **Elastic Scaling**: Implement auto-scaling solutions that automatically add or remove server instances based on demand. Cloud providers like AWS, Azure, and Google Cloud offer tools for elastic scaling.

- **Sharding**: Divide your player base into smaller shards or instances, each with its dedicated set of game servers. This distributes the load and allows for more granular scaling.

3. Data Persistence and Backup

Ensure the persistence of critical game data and perform regular backups:

- **Database Replication**: If your game relies on a database, set up database replication to maintain redundant copies of game data. This prevents data loss in case of database server failures.

- **Regular Backups**: Schedule regular backups of game data, configurations, and server state. Store backups in geographically diverse locations to protect against data center failures.

- **Data Integrity**: Implement data integrity checks and validation mechanisms to detect and correct data inconsistencies that may arise during server failures or crashes.

4. Monitoring and Alerting

Implement robust monitoring and alerting systems to proactively identify and respond to issues:

- **Health Checks**: Continuously monitor server health, including CPU usage, memory consumption, network latency, and player connections. Set up health checks that trigger alerts when thresholds are exceeded.

- **Log Analysis**: Collect and analyze server logs to identify performance bottlenecks, errors, and anomalies. Utilize log aggregation tools like ELK Stack or Splunk for centralized log management.

- **Automated Alerts**: Configure automated alerting systems that notify your operations team or administrators in real-time when critical issues occur. Consider using tools like Prometheus and Grafana for monitoring and alerting.

5. Geographic Distribution

For global multiplayer games, consider distributing your game servers geographically:

- **Content Delivery Networks (CDNs)**: Use CDNs to distribute static game assets like images, videos, and downloadable content to reduce latency and ensure fast content delivery to players worldwide.

- **Edge Locations**: Deploy game servers in edge locations or data centers closer to players to minimize network latency. This enhances the overall player experience by reducing lag.

- **Global Load Balancing**: Implement global load balancing to route player connections to the nearest available game servers, ensuring low-latency gameplay.

6. Security and DDoS Mitigation

High-availability game servers are attractive targets for DDoS attacks and malicious activities. Implement security measures to protect your infrastructure:

- **DDoS Mitigation**: Use DDoS protection services and solutions to detect and mitigate DDoS attacks in real-time. These services often employ traffic scrubbing and rate limiting.

- **Firewalls and Access Controls**: Set up firewalls and access controls to restrict unauthorized access to your game servers and databases. Implement role-based access control (RBAC) to manage user permissions.

- **Regular Security Audits**: Conduct regular security audits and penetration testing to identify vulnerabilities and address them proactively.

7. Disaster Recovery Planning

Develop a comprehensive disaster recovery plan to ensure business continuity:

- **Backup Data Centers**: Establish backup data centers or server locations in different geographic regions to maintain service availability in the event of catastrophic failures.

- **Data Center Redundancy**: Use data centers with high levels of redundancy, including redundant power sources, network connections, and cooling systems.

- **Failover Testing**: Regularly test failover and disaster recovery procedures to ensure they function as expected in a real emergency.

By implementing these high-availability strategies, you can design a robust game server architecture that can scale to meet player demands while maintaining uninterrupted gameplay experiences, even in the face of server failures and unexpected challenges.

10.2. Load Balancing and Resource Allocation

Load balancing and resource allocation are critical aspects of designing a scalable game server architecture. In this section, we will delve into the principles and strategies for load balancing player connections and efficiently allocating server resources to ensure optimal performance and player experience.

1. Load Balancing Strategies

Load balancing is the process of distributing incoming player connections and game requests across multiple game server instances. Proper load balancing ensures that no single server becomes a bottleneck and that player requests are evenly distributed. Consider the following load balancing strategies:

- **Round Robin**: The simplest load balancing technique is round-robin, where incoming requests are distributed sequentially to each available server in a circular manner. While straightforward, it may not account for server health or player loads.

- **Dynamic Load Balancing**: Implement dynamic load balancing algorithms that consider factors like server health, CPU utilization, memory usage, and player loads. Popular algorithms include weighted round-robin and least-connections.

- **Session Affinity (Sticky Sessions)**: In some cases, it's essential to maintain session affinity, also known as sticky sessions. This ensures that a player's requests are always directed to the same server instance, which is crucial for maintaining session state in some games.

- **Content-Based Routing**: For more advanced scenarios, consider content-based routing, where requests are routed based on the type of content or service required. This can be beneficial for separating gameplay and non-gameplay services.

2. Elastic Scaling and Auto-Scaling

Elastic scaling allows your game server infrastructure to automatically adapt to changing player loads. Cloud providers offer auto-scaling solutions that can add or remove server instances based on demand. Here's how to leverage this capability:

- **Auto-Scaling Groups**: Create auto-scaling groups in cloud environments like AWS, Azure, or Google Cloud. Define scaling policies based on metrics like CPU utilization or player connections.

- **Resource Allocation Policies**: Define resource allocation policies that specify the minimum and maximum number of game server instances and the criteria for scaling up or down. This ensures efficient resource usage.

- **Load-Based Scaling**: Implement load-based scaling, where new server instances are added when player loads increase, and instances are terminated during low traffic periods to save costs.

3. Resource Allocation and Game Instances

Efficient resource allocation is crucial for maximizing the utilization of your game server infrastructure. Here are some resource allocation strategies to consider:

- **CPU and Memory Management**: Monitor CPU and memory usage across server instances. Allocate resources dynamically based on the actual workload, ensuring that no server is over-provisioned or under-provisioned.

- **Instance Types**: Use cloud-specific instance types optimized for gaming workloads. Some cloud providers offer specialized gaming instances with enhanced CPU and GPU capabilities for game servers.

- **Containerization**: Consider containerization technologies like Docker and Kubernetes to encapsulate game server processes. This allows for better resource isolation and efficient scaling.

- **Resource Pools**: Create resource pools or clusters of game servers with similar resource requirements. This simplifies resource allocation and ensures that servers with similar characteristics are grouped together.

4. Monitoring and Performance Metrics

Continuous monitoring and performance metrics are essential for making informed decisions regarding load balancing and resource allocation. Implement the following practices:

- **Real-Time Metrics**: Collect real-time metrics on server performance, player connections, and resource utilization. Use monitoring tools to visualize these metrics and set up alerts for threshold breaches.

- **Game-Specific Metrics**: Define game-specific metrics that are relevant to your gameplay. This might include tracking the number of in-game transactions, active players, or match duration.

- **Performance Profiling**: Periodically profile your game server code to identify performance bottlenecks. Optimize critical code paths to ensure efficient resource usage.

- **Capacity Planning**: Based on historical data and performance metrics, perform capacity planning to anticipate future resource requirements and ensure that you can scale proactively.

By implementing effective load balancing and resource allocation strategies, you can create a game server architecture that not only scales to accommodate player loads but also optimizes resource usage for cost-efficiency and optimal player experiences.

10.3. Server Scaling Strategies

Server scaling strategies are essential for managing and expanding your game server infrastructure to meet the demands of a growing player base. In this section, we will explore various server scaling strategies, including horizontal scaling, vertical scaling, and hybrid approaches, to ensure your game servers can handle increased traffic and deliver a seamless gaming experience.

1. Horizontal Scaling

Horizontal scaling, also known as scaling out, involves adding more server instances to your infrastructure to distribute the load. This approach is well-suited for stateless services and can be implemented as follows:

- **Load Balancers**: Employ load balancers to evenly distribute incoming player connections and requests among multiple server instances. This ensures that the load is distributed efficiently.

- **Stateless Services**: Design your game server architecture to be stateless, meaning that no server instance stores critical game state. Instead, the game state is stored externally, such as in a database or distributed cache.

- **Auto-Scaling**: Implement auto-scaling policies that automatically add or remove server instances based on predefined criteria like CPU utilization, player load, or response times.

 # Example auto-scaling policy using AWS Auto Scaling

```
if CPU_utilization > 80%:

add_game_server_instances(5) # Add 5 more game servers

elif CPU_utilization < 30%:

remove_game_server_instances(3) # Remove 3 game servers
```

- **Containerization**: Consider containerization technologies like Docker and Kubernetes to simplify the deployment and management of game server instances. Containers can be easily scaled up or down as needed.

2. Vertical Scaling

Vertical scaling, also known as scaling up, involves increasing the resources (CPU, memory, etc.) of existing server instances to handle increased loads. This approach is suitable for stateful services and can be implemented as follows:

- **Vertical Scaling Tools**: Cloud providers often offer tools for vertically scaling server instances. For example, AWS provides instance types with varying CPU and memory specifications.

- **Database Optimization**: If your game server relies heavily on a database, optimize the database performance by increasing the provisioned IOPS or choosing a larger database instance type.

- **Performance Monitoring**: Continuously monitor the performance of your server instances, and trigger vertical scaling actions when predefined thresholds are exceeded.

```
# Example vertical scaling trigger based on memory usage
```

if memory_usage > 90%:

increase_memory(2**x**) *# Double the memory capacity*

- **Stateful Services**: Vertical scaling is suitable for stateful services where migrating game state between instances is challenging. Ensure that your server architecture can gracefully handle the increased resource capacity.

3. Hybrid Approaches

In some cases, a combination of horizontal and vertical scaling may be the most effective strategy. Here are a few scenarios where hybrid approaches are beneficial:

- **Auto-Scaling with Vertical Scaling**: Use auto-scaling to add or remove server instances horizontally while simultaneously adjusting the resources allocated to each instance vertically based on performance metrics.

- **Stateful Components**: Identify specific stateful components of your game server architecture that can benefit from vertical scaling, while keeping other components horizontally scalable.

- **Resource Pools**: Create resource pools with different instance types to accommodate varying resource requirements. Allocate game server instances to resource pools based on their needs.

 # Example hybrid approach: Distributing instances across resource pools

if player_count < 1000:

```
allocate_to_low_resource_pool()
elif player_count < 5000:
allocate_to_medium_resource_pool()
else:
allocate_to_high_resource_pool()
```

Effective server scaling strategies depend on the nature of your game, player behaviors, and resource constraints. By carefully planning and implementing these strategies, you can ensure that your game servers remain responsive, reliable, and cost-efficient as your player base grows.

10.4. Handling Massive Concurrent Player Bases

Handling massive concurrent player bases is a challenge that arises when your game gains popularity and attracts a large number of players. This section discusses strategies and techniques to manage and optimize game servers for such scenarios.

1. Load Balancing

Load balancing is crucial when dealing with a massive player base. Distribute incoming player connections and requests evenly across multiple game server instances to avoid overloading any single server. Some considerations for load balancing include:

- **Round Robin**: Use a round-robin algorithm to distribute player connections among available game servers. This simple method ensures an even distribution of players.

- **Session Affinity**: Implement session affinity (also known as sticky sessions) to route a player's requests consistently to the same game server, preserving their game state and progress.

```
# Example session affinity using a player's unique ID

if player_id not in session_dict:

session_dict[player_id] = select_game_server()

route_request_to_server(session_dict[player_id])
```

- **Health Checks**: Continuously monitor the health of game server instances and remove unhealthy servers from the load balancing pool to ensure players are routed to healthy servers.

2. Caching and Data Optimization

Efficiently manage and cache frequently accessed data to reduce database and server load. Some optimization techniques include:

- **Content Delivery Networks (CDNs)**: Use CDNs to cache and distribute static assets like images, audio, and video to reduce the load on your game servers.

- **In-Memory Caches**: Implement in-memory caching solutions like Redis or Memcached to store frequently accessed game data, reducing the need for repeated database queries.

```
# Example caching with Redis

if data_key not in cache:

data = fetch_data_from_database(data_key)

cache.set(data_key, data, expire_time)

return cache.get(data_key)
```

- **Data Sharding**: Divide your game data into smaller shards and distribute them across multiple database instances to parallelize database queries.

3. Asynchronous Processing

Leverage asynchronous processing to offload time-consuming tasks and maintain responsiveness. Common asynchronous techniques include:

- **Message Queues**: Use message queues like RabbitMQ or Apache Kafka to handle background tasks such as sending notifications, processing analytics, or performing resource-intensive calculations.

```
# Example of adding a task to a message queue

queue.add_task(process_notification, notification_data)
```

- **Worker Pools**: Create worker pools to process asynchronous tasks concurrently. Ensure that worker pools are properly configured to handle varying workloads.

4. Database Scaling

Scaling your database is critical to accommodate a massive player base. Consider the following database scaling strategies:

- **Read Replicas**: Implement read replicas to offload read operations from the primary database, allowing it to focus on write operations.

- **Database Sharding**: Shard your database to horizontally partition data across multiple database instances. This helps distribute the database load evenly.

- **Database Indexing**: Optimize your database queries by creating appropriate indexes to speed up data retrieval.

5. Real-Time Monitoring and Scaling

Implement real-time monitoring and scaling solutions to ensure your game servers can adapt to changing player loads. Some aspects to consider include:

- **Automated Scaling**: Set up automated scaling policies that dynamically adjust the number of game server instances based on predefined performance metrics.

- **Performance Monitoring**: Continuously monitor server performance, player activity, and server resource utilization to identify and resolve issues promptly.

```
# Example monitoring and scaling based on player count
if player_count > max_threshold:
scale_out_game_servers(5) # Add more game servers
elif player_count < min_threshold:
scale_in_game_servers(3) # Remove excess game servers
```

- **Incident Response**: Have a well-defined incident response plan in place to address unexpected server issues or spikes in player activity.

Handling massive concurrent player bases is a complex task that requires careful planning, monitoring, and optimization. By implementing the strategies mentioned in this section, you can ensure a smooth and enjoyable gaming experience for your players, even as your player base grows significantly.

10.5. Cloud-Based Solutions and Integrations

Cloud-based solutions have become increasingly popular in the gaming industry due to their scalability, flexibility, and cost-effectiveness. This section explores the benefits of using cloud services and how to integrate them into your game development process.

1. Benefits of Cloud-Based Solutions

Scalability

Cloud platforms like Amazon Web Services (AWS), Microsoft Azure, and Google Cloud provide on-demand scalability, allowing you to quickly adapt to changes in player demand. You can easily add or remove resources as needed, ensuring a smooth gaming experience during peak times.

Cost Efficiency

Cloud services offer a pay-as-you-go model, eliminating the need for large upfront investments in infrastructure. This cost-effective approach allows you to allocate resources efficiently and only pay for what you use.

Global Reach

Cloud providers have data centers located worldwide, enabling you to deploy your game closer to players in various regions. This reduces latency and ensures a consistent gaming experience for players worldwide.

Security and Compliance

Cloud providers invest heavily in security measures and compliance certifications. By leveraging their expertise, you can enhance the security of your game and meet industry-specific regulatory requirements.

2. Cloud-Based Game Servers

Serverless Computing

Serverless computing platforms like AWS Lambda and Azure Functions allow you to run code in response to events without managing servers. This is ideal for handling specific game functions, such as processing player requests or running background tasks.

```
# Example AWS Lambda function for processing player requests

def lambda_handler(event, context):

# Process player request here

return {

'statusCode': 200,

'body': 'Request processed successfully.'

}
```

Managed Game Servers

Cloud providers offer managed game server solutions that simplify server management tasks. Services like AWS GameLift and Google

Cloud Game Servers provide automated scaling, matchmaking, and player session management.

3. Cloud-Based Databases

Database as a Service (DBaaS)

Cloud-based databases, such as Amazon RDS, Azure SQL Database, and Google Cloud SQL, offer managed database solutions. They handle tasks like backups, patching, and scaling, allowing you to focus on game development.

```
# Example code for connecting to a cloud-based database

import psycopg2

conn = psycopg2.connect(

host="database-instance.cxyz12345678.us-east-1.rds.amazonaws.com",

database="game_database",

user="db_user",

password="db_password"

)
```

NoSQL Databases

Cloud providers also offer NoSQL database services like Amazon DynamoDB and Azure Cosmos DB. These databases are suitable for storing player profiles, game state, and other unstructured data.

4. Cloud-Based Game Analytics

Analytics Services

Leverage cloud-based analytics services, such as AWS Kinesis Analytics and Google Analytics for Firebase, to gain insights into player behavior. Monitor player engagement, track in-game events, and make data-driven decisions to improve your game.

```
# Example of using AWS Kinesis Analytics for real-time analytics

import boto3

# Configure the Kinesis client

client = boto3.client('kinesisanalytics')

# Create an application and configure analytics

response = client.create_application(

ApplicationName='GameAnalyticsApp',

ApplicationCode="""\

CREATE OR REPLACE STREAM "DESTINATION_SQL_STREAM" AS

SELECT STREAM *

FROM "SOURCE_SQL_STREAM_001"

WHERE ...

"""

)
```

5. Cloud-Based Asset Storage

Object Storage

Store game assets, such as images, audio files, and 3D models, in cloud-based object storage services like Amazon S3, Azure Blob Storage, or Google Cloud Storage. These services provide high availability and low-latency access to your assets.

```
# Example code for uploading assets to Amazon S3

import boto3

# Create an S3 client

s3 = boto3.client('s3')

# Upload an asset to a bucket

s3.upload_file('game_asset.jpg', 'my-game-bucket', 'assets/game_asset.jpg')
```

6. Continuous Integration and Deployment (CI/CD)

Integrate cloud-based CI/CD pipelines using services like AWS CodePipeline or Azure DevOps to automate the build, testing, and deployment of your game. This ensures a streamlined development process and allows for rapid updates.

```
# Example CI/CD pipeline configuration using AWS CodePipeline

stages:

- name: Build

actions:
```

- name: BuildAction

actionTypeId:

category: Build

owner: AWS

provider: CodeBuild

configuration:

ProjectName: MyGameBuildProject

runOrder: 1

7. Multi-Platform Support

Cloud-based solutions facilitate multi-platform support by providing cross-platform development tools and resources. You can target various platforms, including PC, console, mobile, and even emerging technologies like VR and AR.

8. Data Backups and Disaster Recovery

Cloud providers offer data backup and disaster recovery solutions to safeguard your game data against unforeseen events. Implement automated backups and replication to ensure data availability and business continuity.

Integrating cloud-based solutions into your game development process can significantly enhance your game's scalability, performance, and cost efficiency. Whether you're developing a small indie game or a large-scale multiplayer title, cloud services provide the flexibility and resources needed to succeed in the ever-evolving gaming industry.

Chapter 11: Advanced Shader and Visual Effects

Section 11.1: Writing Custom Shader Programs

In modern game development, achieving stunning visuals often relies on the effective use of shader programs. Shaders are small programs executed on the GPU (Graphics Processing Unit) that enable developers to control how graphics are rendered, allowing for a wide range of visual effects. In this section, we will explore the fundamentals of writing custom shader programs, a crucial skill for enhancing the visual appeal of your games.

Understanding Shaders

Shaders are an integral part of the rendering pipeline, influencing how light interacts with objects in your game world. There are two primary types of shaders:

1. **Vertex Shaders:** These shaders manipulate the position and attributes of vertices (points) in 3D space. They are responsible for transforming 3D models into 2D screen space.
2. **Fragment Shaders (Pixel Shaders):** Fragment shaders determine the color and other properties of individual pixels on the screen. They are crucial for adding details such as lighting, shadows, and textures.

Shader Languages

Shaders are typically written in specialized shader languages. The most commonly used shader languages are:

- **GLSL (OpenGL Shading Language):** Used in OpenGL and WebGL.

- **HLSL (High-Level Shading Language):** Used in DirectX.
- **ShaderLab:** Unity's shader language.

While the syntax and capabilities of these languages may vary, the underlying concepts remain similar. In this section, we'll focus on GLSL as it's widely used and provides a good foundation for understanding shaders.

Anatomy of a Shader

A shader program consists of two main parts: the vertex shader and the fragment shader. Let's take a closer look at each:

Vertex Shader:

The vertex shader processes each vertex of a 3D model. It typically performs transformations like scaling, rotation, and translation to position the vertices correctly on the screen. Here's a simplified example of a basic vertex shader in GLSL:

```
#version 330 core

layout(location = 0) in vec3 inPosition;

uniform mat4 model;

uniform mat4 view;

uniform mat4 projection;

void main()

{
```

```
gl_Position = projection * view * model * vec4(inPosition, 1.0);

}
```

In this example, inPosition represents the input vertex position, and model, view, and projection are transformation matrices.

Fragment Shader (Pixel Shader):

The fragment shader is responsible for determining the final color of each pixel. It can apply textures, calculate lighting, and create various visual effects. Here's a simple fragment shader that colors all pixels red:

```
#version 330 core

out vec4 FragColor;

void main()

{

FragColor = vec4(1.0, 0.0, 0.0, 1.0); // Red

}
```

Creating Visual Effects

Custom shaders allow you to create a wide range of visual effects, including:

- **Realistic Lighting:** Implementing advanced lighting models like Phong or PBR (Physically Based Rendering) for realistic reflections and shading.

- **Post-Processing Effects:** Applying effects like motion blur, depth of field, and bloom to enhance the visuals.
- **Textures and Materials:** Combining textures to create detailed materials for objects in the game world.
- **Particle Systems:** Simulating dynamic effects like fire, smoke, or sparks using shaders.
- **Visual Filters:** Applying filters for grayscale, sepia, or other visual styles to achieve a unique look.
- **Water Simulation:** Creating realistic water surfaces with reflections, refractions, and wave simulations.

Writing custom shaders requires a good understanding of linear algebra, as you'll work extensively with matrices and vectors. Additionally, experimenting and iterating are essential for achieving the desired visual effects.

In the following sections, we will delve deeper into specific shader techniques and their implementations. Custom shaders open up a world of possibilities for creating visually stunning games, making them a valuable tool in your game development toolkit.

Section 11.2: Real-Time Lighting and Shadow Techniques

Real-time lighting and shadows play a crucial role in creating immersive and visually appealing game environments. In this section, we will explore the fundamental concepts and techniques used to achieve realistic lighting and shadows in modern game development.

Lighting Models

Realistic lighting starts with understanding lighting models, which simulate how light interacts with surfaces in your game world. Here are a few common lighting models:

1. **Ambient Lighting:** Represents the overall light level in a scene, providing a base level of illumination regardless of the light sources. It's often used to simulate indirect or global illumination.
2. **Diffuse Lighting:** Models the way light scatters evenly in all directions when it hits a surface. It's essential for determining the base color of objects.
3. **Specular Lighting:** Simulates the reflection of light off shiny surfaces, creating highlights. Specular lighting is critical for achieving a glossy appearance.
4. **Emissive Lighting:** Represents materials that emit light, such as glowing objects or emissive textures.

Types of Light Sources

To create realistic lighting, you'll work with various types of light sources:

1. **Point Lights:** Represent light sources with a specific

position and emit light uniformly in all directions. They are used for simulating light bulbs and small light sources.

2. **Directional Lights:** Model light sources that emit parallel light rays from a distant source. These lights are typically used to simulate sunlight.
3. **Spotlights:** Simulate focused light beams with a specific direction and angle. Spotlights are often used for flashlights and car headlights.
4. **Area Lights:** Represent light sources with an extended surface area, such as fluorescent tubes. They emit light from a defined surface rather than a single point.

Shadow Mapping

Shadows are essential for creating depth and realism in a scene. Shadow mapping is a popular technique used to render shadows in real-time. Here's how it works:

1. **Depth Map Generation:** A depth map, also known as a shadow map, is created from the perspective of the light source. This map stores depth information of the scene from the light's point of view.
2. **Shadow Testing:** During the rendering process, each pixel on a surface is compared to the values in the shadow map. If the pixel is farther from the light source than the corresponding depth value in the shadow map, it's in shadow.
3. **Soft Shadows:** To achieve soft shadows, developers can use techniques like Percentage Closer Filtering (PCF) or Variance Shadow Mapping (VSM). These methods introduce smooth transitions between light and shadow.

Global Illumination

Global Illumination (GI) is a technique used to simulate indirect lighting, such as reflections, refractions, and bounced light. Real-time GI algorithms like Screen Space Global Illumination (SSGI) and Real-Time Ray Tracing can greatly enhance the realism of a scene by considering how light bounces off surfaces and affects nearby objects.

Light Probes

Light probes are used to approximate global illumination in real-time. They capture lighting information from the environment and provide it to objects within their influence. Light probes are particularly useful for achieving consistent lighting across objects in a scene.

Deferred Rendering

Deferred rendering is a rendering technique that separates the rendering process into multiple passes, allowing for advanced lighting and shading effects. It's commonly used in modern game engines to efficiently handle complex lighting and shading calculations.

Post-Processing Effects

Post-processing effects, such as bloom, HDR (High Dynamic Range), and lens flares, can further enhance the visual quality of lighting in a game. These effects simulate the way light interacts with the camera and the player's viewpoint.

Real-time lighting and shadow techniques continue to evolve, with advancements in hardware and software enabling ever more realistic visual experiences. As a game developer, understanding and mastering these techniques is essential for creating visually stunning and immersive game worlds.

Section 11.3: Special Effects with Particle Systems

Particle systems are a fundamental tool for creating a wide range of special effects in games. These effects can include explosions, fire, smoke, rain, snow, sparks, and much more. In this section, we'll delve into the world of particle systems, exploring how they work and how you can use them to add dynamic and visually engaging elements to your games.

What Are Particle Systems?

A particle system is a technique used in computer graphics and game development to simulate and render a large number of small, individual objects (particles) that collectively create complex visual effects. These particles are typically lightweight and don't require much processing power, making them ideal for real-time rendering.

Basic Components of a Particle System

A typical particle system consists of the following components:

1. **Emitter:** The emitter is the source of particles. It defines where and how particles are spawned into the scene. Emitters can be static or moving, and they determine the initial properties of particles.
2. **Particles:** These are the individual objects that make up the effect. Particles have properties like position, velocity, color, size, and lifetime. They move and change over time according to predefined rules.
3. **Behaviors:** Behaviors, also known as forces or modifiers, affect how particles evolve. For example, gravity can pull particles downward, wind can blow them in a certain

direction, and turbulence can add randomness to their movement.

4. **Renderer:** The renderer is responsible for drawing particles. It defines how particles are displayed, including their shape, texture, and blending mode. Different renderers can create various visual effects.

Particle System Workflow

Creating a particle system involves the following steps:

1. **Initialization:** Define the initial state of the particle system, including the emitter's position, particle properties, and any initial behaviors.
2. **Simulation:** In this step, particles are updated over time. The simulation loop computes the new positions, velocities, colors, and sizes of particles based on their behaviors.
3. **Rendering:** Once particles are updated, they are rendered to the screen. The renderer takes care of drawing particles with the specified visual properties.
4. **Lifetime Management:** Particles have a finite lifetime. When a particle's lifetime expires, it is either removed from the system, recycled, or replaced with a new particle.

Particle Effects Examples

Here are some common examples of particle effects:

- **Explosions:** Simulate fiery explosions with particles for flames and sparks. The emitter is usually placed at the explosion's point of origin.

• **Fire and Smoke:** Create realistic fire and smoke effects by using particle systems with heat distortion and rising smoke particles.

• **Rain and Snow:** Simulate raindrops or snowflakes falling from the sky. Particle systems allow you to control the density, size, and speed of the precipitation.

• **Magical Effects:** Design magical spells and effects with glowing particles that follow intricate paths or patterns.

• **Water Splashes:** Capture the dynamics of water splashes when objects hit a liquid surface.

• **Dust and Debris:** Create dust clouds and debris when objects collide or structures collapse.

Optimization and Performance

Efficiently handling large numbers of particles is crucial for maintaining good performance. Techniques such as particle pooling (reusing particles instead of creating and destroying them) and level-of-detail (LOD) for particles can help manage performance.

Particle systems offer a versatile and creative way to add life and dynamism to your game environments. Whether you want to create explosive action sequences or subtle atmospheric effects, mastering particle systems is an essential skill for game developers looking to craft visually engaging and immersive experiences.

Section 11.4: Advanced Rendering Techniques for Realism

In the world of game development, achieving realism in graphics has been a long-standing goal. Realistic graphics not only enhance the immersive experience but also set a high standard for modern games. In this section, we'll explore advanced rendering techniques that can bring a new level of realism to your games.

Physically Based Rendering (PBR)

Physically Based Rendering is a rendering technique that aims to simulate the behavior of light in the real world. It takes into account the physical properties of materials, such as reflectivity, roughness, and metallicity, to produce highly realistic and consistent visuals.

PBR shaders use complex mathematical models to calculate how light interacts with a surface. These shaders are widely used in modern game engines to create lifelike materials like metals, plastics, and fabrics. They provide a more accurate representation of how light bounces off different surfaces, resulting in stunning visual fidelity.

Global Illumination (GI)

Global Illumination is a rendering technique used to simulate indirect lighting in a scene. It accounts for how light bounces off surfaces and indirectly illuminates other parts of the environment. GI techniques, such as Radiosity and Ray Tracing, can significantly enhance the realism of your game's lighting.

Ray Tracing, in particular, has gained popularity due to its ability to simulate realistic reflections, refractions, and soft shadows. It accurately traces the paths of rays of light as they interact with objects in the scene, leading to photorealistic visuals. Ray Tracing is often used for real-time ray tracing in high-end gaming hardware.

High Dynamic Range (HDR) Rendering

High Dynamic Range Rendering is a technique that extends the range of luminance values in a scene beyond what traditional displays can reproduce. HDR rendering allows for more realistic and visually striking lighting effects, including bright highlights and deep shadows.

To implement HDR rendering, you'll need to use floating-point color formats and tone mapping techniques to map the high dynamic range values to the limited range of a display. This ensures that bright areas don't get clipped and that subtle details are preserved in both dark and bright regions of the image.

Screen-Space Reflections (SSR)

Screen-Space Reflections is a rendering technique used to simulate accurate reflections on surfaces. SSR analyzes the depth buffer and screen-space information to calculate reflections dynamically based on what's visible on the screen. This technique is often used to create realistic water surfaces, glossy materials, and reflective objects.

While SSR is efficient and suitable for many scenarios, it may have limitations in handling off-screen or non-visible reflections. In such cases, a combination of SSR with other techniques like Cubemap Reflections or Ray Tracing can produce even more realistic results.

Post-Processing Effects

Post-processing effects are applied to the rendered image after the main rendering passes. These effects can significantly impact the visual quality and realism of your game. Some common post-processing effects include:

- **Bloom:** Adds a glowing effect to bright areas, enhancing the sense of brightness and realism.
- **Depth of Field (DOF):** Simulates the camera's focus, blurring objects in the foreground or background to create cinematic effects.
- **Motion Blur:** Mimics the motion blur of fast-moving objects or camera panning, contributing to a more immersive experience.
- **Anti-Aliasing:** Reduces the appearance of jagged edges and stair-stepping artifacts, resulting in smoother and more realistic visuals.

By combining these post-processing effects with advanced rendering techniques like PBR, GI, HDR, and SSR, you can achieve a level of realism that was once reserved for pre-rendered cinematic sequences. These techniques collectively contribute to the breathtaking visual quality seen in modern AAA games.

Performance Considerations

While advanced rendering techniques offer unparalleled realism, they can be computationally expensive. It's essential to optimize your game's performance by implementing level-of-detail (LOD) systems, occlusion culling, and efficient shaders to ensure that these techniques run smoothly, even on lower-end hardware.

In conclusion, achieving realism in game graphics requires a deep understanding of advanced rendering techniques. By integrating

Physically Based Rendering, Global Illumination, High Dynamic Range Rendering, Screen-Space Reflections, and Post-Processing Effects, you can create visually stunning and immersive game worlds that captivate players and set new standards for the gaming industry.

Section 11.5: Shader Optimization and GPU Resources

Optimizing shaders and managing GPU resources are crucial aspects of game development, especially when aiming for high-performance and realism. In this section, we'll explore techniques and best practices for shader optimization and efficient utilization of GPU resources.

Shader Optimization

Shaders are fundamental components of modern graphics rendering pipelines, responsible for defining how objects are rendered and lit. Optimizing shaders ensures that they run efficiently on the GPU, minimizing bottlenecks and improving overall performance.

1. Minimize Branching:

Branching in shaders can be costly, as it can lead to divergence in GPU threads, impacting parallelism. Minimize conditional statements in your shaders and prefer using simpler arithmetic operations where possible.

```
// Avoid branching like this

if (condition) {

// Complex operations

} else {

// Complex operations

}
```

```
// Prefer this

result = (condition) ? operation1 : operation2;
```

2. Use Shader Constants:

Use uniform variables for constant values that don't change per vertex or fragment. This reduces the need for calculations in shaders, as constants are set once and reused across multiple shader invocations.

```
// In your shader

uniform float PI = 3.14159;

// In the application code

glUniform1f(glGetUniformLocation(shaderProgram, "PI"), 3.14159);
```

3. Texture Sampling Optimization:

Texture sampling can be a shader performance bottleneck. Use texture atlases to reduce the number of texture lookups, and employ mipmapping for efficient texture sampling at various distances.

```
// Enable mipmapping

glTexParameteri(GL_TEXTURE_2D, GL_TEXTURE_MIN_FILTER, GL_LINEAR_MIPMAP_LINEAR);

glGenerateMipmap(GL_TEXTURE_2D);
```

GPU Resource Management

Efficiently managing GPU resources like textures, buffers, and shader programs is essential for maintaining good performance and avoiding resource-related bottlenecks.

1. Texture Compression:

Utilize texture compression formats like DXT, BC, or ETC to reduce memory bandwidth and storage requirements for textures. This reduces the data transferred between CPU and GPU.

2. Resource Pooling:

Implement resource pooling for frequently used GPU resources like vertex buffers, framebuffers, and shader programs. Reusing resources reduces the overhead of creating and destroying them.

3. Resource Streaming:

For open-world or large-scale games, implement resource streaming to load textures, models, and shaders on-demand. This minimizes initial loading times and optimizes memory usage.

4. Occlusion Culling:

Use occlusion culling techniques to avoid rendering objects that are not visible to the camera. This reduces the GPU workload and improves frame rates.

5. Shader Program Variation:

Avoid creating a multitude of shader programs with minor variations. Instead, use shader preprocessor directives (#define) or uniform variables to control shader behavior dynamically.

```
// In your shader

#ifdef USE_SPECULAR

// Specular calculations

#endif
```

Optimizing shaders and managing GPU resources are ongoing tasks throughout game development. Profiling tools, like GPU profilers, are invaluable for identifying performance bottlenecks and areas that require optimization. By adhering to best practices and continuously refining your shaders and GPU resource management, you can deliver visually impressive and high-performance games to players.

Chapter 12: Cross-Platform Development Challenges

Cross-platform game development presents unique challenges and considerations, particularly when targeting multiple operating systems, consoles, and devices. In this chapter, we will explore these challenges and discuss strategies for effectively addressing them.

Section 12.1: Managing Platform-Specific Features

When developing games for multiple platforms, it's common to encounter platform-specific features and capabilities. These features can range from unique hardware functionalities to specific input methods and APIs. Managing these differences efficiently is essential for a successful cross-platform project.

1. Abstraction Layers:

One approach to managing platform-specific features is to use abstraction layers or middleware that provide a consistent interface across platforms. Game engines like Unity or Unreal Engine offer such abstraction, allowing developers to write code once and deploy it on various platforms.

```
// Unity example: Input handling

if (Input.GetKey(KeyCode.Space)) {

// Perform an action

}
```

2. Conditional Compilation:

Conditional compilation directives in your code can help isolate platform-specific code segments. By using #ifdef and #ifndef directives, you can include or exclude sections of code based on the target platform.

```
// Conditional compilation for platform-specific code
#ifdef PLATFORM_WINDOWS
// Windows-specific code
#elif PLATFORM_MAC
// macOS-specific code
#else
// Default code for other platforms
#endif
```

3. Feature Detection:

Instead of relying on preprocessor directives, you can use runtime feature detection to determine the capabilities of the current platform. This allows your game to adapt dynamically to the platform it's running on.

```
// Feature detection for touch input
if (PlatformSupportsTouchInput()) {
// Enable touch controls
}
```

4. Asset Management:

Managing platform-specific assets, such as textures, sounds, and models, can be challenging. Consider using a resource management system that loads the appropriate assets for the current platform at runtime.

5. User Interface (UI) Adaptation:

User interfaces often require significant adaptation for different platforms. Ensure that your UI elements are designed to accommodate various screen sizes, resolutions, and input methods.

6. Testing and Quality Assurance:

Thoroughly test your game on each target platform to identify and resolve platform-specific issues. Invest in quality assurance (QA) processes to ensure a consistent and polished player experience across all platforms.

7. Documentation:

Maintain clear and up-to-date documentation that outlines platform-specific considerations, requirements, and best practices. This documentation can be valuable for both current and future team members.

8. Platform-Specific Releases:

Consider staggered or platform-specific release schedules if necessary. This allows you to focus on optimizing and polishing each platform's version individually.

Managing platform-specific features in cross-platform development is a balancing act between code reuse and platform optimization. By implementing these strategies and staying vigilant about platform-specific challenges, you can create games that run seamlessly on a variety of devices and operating systems.

Section 12.2: Strategy for Universal Input Handling

One of the fundamental challenges in cross-platform game development is handling input from various devices and input methods. Different platforms may have distinct input mechanisms, including keyboards, mice, game controllers, touchscreens, and motion sensors. Creating a unified input handling system that works seamlessly across platforms is essential for delivering a consistent player experience.

Here are some strategies and considerations for implementing universal input handling in your cross-platform game:

1. **Abstraction Layer for Input**:

   Create an input abstraction layer that provides a unified interface for handling input events. This layer should abstract away the platform-specific details and expose a consistent set of input actions, such as "jump," "fire," or "move."

   // Input abstraction layer example

   if (InputManager.GetButtonDown("Jump")) {

   player.Jump();

   }

1. **Input Mapping**:

Use input mapping to associate physical input devices and buttons with in-game actions. This allows players to customize their input preferences while ensuring a consistent mapping of actions.

```
// Input mapping configuration
{
"Jump": {
"Keyboard": "Space",
"Gamepad": "ButtonA",
"Touchscreen": "Tap"
},
"Fire": {
"Keyboard": "MouseLeft",
"Gamepad": "RightTrigger"
}
}
```

1. **Input Profiles**:

Implement input profiles that are specific to each platform or device type. This allows you to fine-tune input settings to match the characteristics of each platform while maintaining a unified input handling codebase.

1. **Fallback Mechanisms**:

Consider implementing fallback mechanisms for platforms that lack certain input capabilities. For example, if a platform doesn't support gamepad input, provide alternative control schemes using the available input methods.

1. **Responsive Touch and Gesture Handling**:

If your game targets touchscreen devices, ensure that touch and gesture interactions are intuitive and responsive. Implement features like multitouch support and gesture recognition for gestures like swipes and pinches.

1. **Support for Accelerometers and Gyroscopes**:

For platforms with motion sensors, such as smartphones and some game consoles, incorporate support for accelerometers and gyroscopes to enable motion-based controls and gameplay mechanics.

1. **Accessibility Features**:

Consider accessibility features that accommodate players with disabilities. Implement customizable key bindings, haptic feedback, and options for adjusting input sensitivity.

1. **Testing and Calibration**:

Rigorous testing is crucial to ensure that input handling works as expected on all target platforms. Test your game on various devices and adjust sensitivity settings and dead zones as needed.

1. **User Feedback**:

Collect user feedback regarding input issues and preferences. Listen to your player community and make necessary adjustments in patches or updates to improve the input experience.

1. **Documentation and Tutorials**:

Provide clear documentation and tutorials for players on how to configure and customize their input settings. Ensure that players understand how to remap controls and access input-related options.

Implementing universal input handling requires careful planning and consideration of the diverse input landscape across different platforms. By creating a flexible and adaptable input system, you can offer a consistent and enjoyable gaming experience to players on various devices and operating systems.

Section 12.3: Ensuring Consistent Performance Across Platforms

Cross-platform game development often involves targeting a wide range of hardware configurations and operating systems. Ensuring consistent performance across these platforms is essential for delivering a satisfying gaming experience to players. In this section, we will explore strategies and best practices to achieve performance consistency in your cross-platform games.

1. **Performance Profiling**:

Begin by profiling your game on each target platform to identify performance bottlenecks and hardware-specific challenges. Tools like profilers and performance monitoring software can help you pinpoint areas that need optimization.

1. **Graphics and Rendering**:

Graphics rendering is a significant factor in game performance. Optimize rendering pipelines, use efficient shaders, and implement level-of-detail (LOD) systems to manage graphical complexity based on the platform's capabilities.

1. **Resolution and Quality Settings**:

Provide options for players to adjust resolution and graphics quality settings. Lower-end devices may benefit from reduced graphical fidelity, while high-end platforms can handle more demanding visuals.

1. **Frame Rate Targeting**:

Consider targeting a consistent frame rate across platforms, such as 30 or 60 frames per second (FPS). Maintaining a stable frame rate contributes to smoother gameplay and a more enjoyable experience.

1. **Asset Optimization**:

Compress and optimize game assets, including textures, models, and audio files. Use platform-specific asset pipelines to generate optimized versions of assets for different platforms.

1. **Platform-Specific Code**:

Utilize platform-specific code optimizations when necessary. Some platforms may require unique solutions for performance, so modularize your code to accommodate platform-specific implementations.

1. **Memory Management**:

Efficient memory management is critical. Avoid memory leaks, implement garbage collection or reference counting, and minimize memory fragmentation to ensure stable performance.

1. **Background Processes**:

Account for background processes and interruptions on mobile and console platforms. Suspend and resume game states gracefully when the game is paused or interrupted.

1. **Load Times**:

Optimize loading times, especially on devices with slower storage. Implement loading screens or interactive elements to keep players engaged during loading sequences.

1. **Testing on Target Devices**:

Regularly test your game on all target devices and hardware configurations. Performance issues may arise on specific devices or operating system versions that are not apparent during development on more powerful machines.

1. **Updates and Patches**:

Be prepared to release updates and patches to address performance issues discovered after the game's initial launch. Player feedback can be invaluable for identifying and resolving performance-related issues.

1. **Thermal and Battery Considerations**:

On mobile devices, consider thermal and battery limitations. Prolonged intensive gameplay can cause devices to heat up and drain battery quickly. Implement power-saving modes if applicable.

1. **Cross-Platform APIs and Libraries**:

Utilize cross-platform game engines, libraries, and APIs that abstract hardware-specific details. These tools can simplify development and ensure a degree of performance consistency.

1. **Player Feedback**:

   Encourage players to provide feedback on performance issues. Their insights can help you identify and address performance problems on specific devices or configurations.

Balancing performance across different platforms is a continuous process that requires ongoing monitoring and optimization. By following these strategies and staying attuned to player feedback, you can achieve a high level of performance consistency, resulting in a more enjoyable gaming experience for players on various devices and platforms.

Section 12.4: Automated Testing for Multi-Platform Support

Automated testing is an essential part of cross-platform game development. It helps ensure that your game functions correctly and consistently across different platforms and configurations. In this section, we'll explore the importance of automated testing and discuss strategies for implementing it effectively in your development pipeline.

1. **Testing Scope**:

Define the scope of your automated tests. You should cover a range of devices, operating systems, and hardware configurations relevant to your target platforms. This may include different PC setups, mobile devices, and consoles.

1. **Unit Tests**:

Start with unit tests to evaluate individual components of your game code. These tests help catch bugs and ensure that core functionalities work as expected. For example, you might have unit tests for physics calculations, AI behavior, or network communication.

1. **Integration Tests**:

Integration tests assess how different parts of your game interact with each other. They can help identify issues that arise when various systems or modules work together. For instance, you might test how physics interacts with rendering or how AI interacts with player input.

1. **Functional Tests**:

Functional tests focus on high-level game features and behaviors. They ensure that gameplay mechanics, user interfaces, and overall game functionality work correctly on each platform. For example, you might test level progression, character abilities, or user interface navigation.

1. **Regression Testing**:

Implement regression testing to catch unintended side effects when making changes or updates to your game. Automated tests can quickly identify if a new feature or bug fix has introduced issues in existing functionality.

1. **Continuous Integration (CI)**:

Integrate automated testing into your CI/CD (Continuous Integration/Continuous Deployment) pipeline. CI tools like Jenkins, Travis CI, or GitHub Actions can automatically run tests whenever code changes are pushed to the repository.

1. **Emulators and Simulators**:

Utilize emulators and simulators to test your game on different platforms without the need for physical devices. These tools can help you cover a wide range of configurations efficiently.

1. **Real Device Testing**:

While emulators are useful, real device testing is crucial to ensure accurate results. Acquire the actual devices you plan to support and regularly test your game on them.

1. **Test Automation Frameworks**:

Consider using test automation frameworks such as Appium, Espresso, or XCTest for mobile platforms, and tools like Selenium for web-based games. These frameworks provide structures for creating and running tests.

1. **Test Reporting**:

Set up a robust reporting system for your tests. Detailed reports should include information on test cases, platforms, and the specific configurations tested. This helps in diagnosing and fixing issues more efficiently.

1. **Test Environments**:

Maintain consistent test environments for reproducibility. Docker containers or virtual machines can help create isolated and reproducible testing setups.

1. **Load and Performance Testing**:

Conduct load and performance testing to ensure your game can handle the expected user load and stress tests to identify potential bottlenecks under heavy usage.

1. **Accessibility Testing**:

Don't forget accessibility testing to ensure your game is inclusive and usable by players with disabilities. Automated accessibility testing tools can help identify issues related to screen readers, keyboard navigation, and more.

1. **Localization Testing**:

If your game is internationalized, include tests to verify that translations and localized content appear correctly on different language settings and character encodings.

1. **Usability Testing**:

While automated tests can catch many technical issues, consider complementing them with usability testing to gather feedback on the player experience.

Automated testing significantly reduces the risk of platform-specific bugs and compatibility issues. It helps maintain a high level of quality and consistency across different platforms, ultimately leading to a more successful and enjoyable gaming experience for your players.

Section 12.5: Navigating Different Distribution Models

When it comes to distributing your game to players, there are various models to consider. The distribution model you choose can have a significant impact on your game's reach, monetization strategy, and player engagement. In this section, we will explore different distribution models and discuss how to navigate them effectively.

1. **Retail Distribution**:

Retail distribution involves selling physical copies of your game through brick-and-mortar stores or online retailers. This model is less common in the digital age but is still relevant for console games and collectors' editions. When pursuing retail distribution, consider production, packaging, and distribution logistics.

1. **Digital Storefronts**:

Digital distribution is the most prevalent model for PC and mobile games. Platforms like Steam, Epic Games Store, Google Play Store, and Apple App Store offer direct access to a vast player base. Ensure your game complies with each platform's requirements, including content guidelines and technical specifications.

1. **Subscription Services**:

Subscription-based distribution models, such as Xbox Game Pass, PlayStation Now, and Apple Arcade, offer players access to a library of games for a recurring fee.

Participating in these services can provide steady revenue and increased exposure, but it may require adapting your monetization strategy.

1. **Free-to-Play (F2P)**:

F2P games are free to download and play, with monetization coming from in-game purchases, ads, or premium content. Implementing F2P requires careful consideration of monetization mechanics, balancing player engagement, and providing value to paying players.

1. **Premium/Pay-to-Play**:

Premium games require an upfront purchase, providing access to the full game experience. This model often appeals to players who prefer a one-time payment without in-game purchases. Price your game appropriately and offer post-launch support to maintain player satisfaction.

1. **Ad-Supported**:

Ad-supported games offer free gameplay, with revenue generated from ads displayed within the game. Effective ad placement and ad mediation can optimize earnings in this model. Balancing ad frequency without disrupting the player experience is crucial.

1. **Crowdfunding and Early Access**:

Crowdfunding platforms like Kickstarter and early access programs on platforms like Steam allow developers to secure funding and gather player feedback before the full release. Manage expectations and deliver regular updates to keep backers engaged.

1. **Cross-Platform Considerations**:

If your game targets multiple platforms, ensure a consistent user experience. Implement cross-platform play and progression where possible to allow players to switch between devices seamlessly.

1. **Local Regulations**:

Be aware of local regulations and content restrictions, especially if distributing your game internationally. Some regions may have specific guidelines or rating requirements.

1. **User Reviews and Feedback**:

Encourage players to leave reviews and provide feedback on digital storefronts. Positive reviews can boost visibility, while constructive criticism can help improve your game.

1. **Marketing and Promotion**:

Regardless of the distribution model, effective marketing and promotion are essential. Create a marketing plan tailored to your target audience and platforms. Utilize social media, influencers, and press coverage to generate buzz.

1. **Monetization Optimization**:

Continuously analyze and optimize your chosen monetization model. Understand player behavior and adapt your strategy to improve player retention and monetization rates.

1. **Legal Considerations**:

Ensure your distribution model complies with legal requirements, including copyright, licensing, and taxation. Consult legal experts if necessary, especially when dealing with international distribution.

1. **Post-Launch Support**:

Commit to post-launch support, including bug fixes, updates, and new content. Maintaining a positive player experience after release is crucial for player retention and long-term success.

Choosing the right distribution model for your game depends on your target audience, game type, and monetization goals. Flexibility and adaptability are key as the gaming industry evolves, and new distribution models emerge. Stay informed about industry trends and player preferences to make informed decisions and maximize the reach and profitability of your game.

Chapter 13: Advanced User Interface and HUD Design

Section 13.1: Designing Intuitive and Dynamic UIs

User Interface (UI) design is a critical aspect of game development. A well-designed UI can enhance the player's experience, making the game more enjoyable and accessible. In this section, we'll focus on designing intuitive and dynamic UIs that cater to the needs of your players.

1. **Player-Centric Design**:

When designing your game's UI, always keep the player in mind. Consider their preferences, expectations, and playstyle. Conduct user testing to gather feedback and iterate on your design.

1. **Consistency and Familiarity**:

Maintain a consistent design language throughout your game. Use familiar icons, fonts, and color schemes to create a cohesive and recognizable UI. Consistency helps players navigate your game more easily.

1. **Minimalism and Clarity**:

Strive for a clean and uncluttered UI. Avoid unnecessary elements that can overwhelm players. Use visual hierarchy to emphasize essential information and actions.

1. **Responsive Design**:

Design your UI to be responsive to different screen sizes and resolutions. Ensure that it scales gracefully on various devices, from smartphones to large monitors.

1. **Accessibility**:

Make your UI accessible to all players, including those with disabilities. Provide options for text size, color schemes, and input methods. Use alt text for images and ensure proper keyboard and controller support.

1. **Intuitive Navigation**:

Create a logical flow for your UI. Use clear labels, buttons, and menus that guide players through your game's features and settings. Minimize the number of clicks or gestures required to perform common actions.

1. **Interactive Elements**:

Design interactive elements that respond to player input. Buttons should provide visual feedback when pressed. Consider adding animations and transitions to make your UI feel dynamic.

1. **HUD Design**:

The Heads-Up Display (HUD) should convey crucial information without obstructing the gameplay. Balance the amount of information displayed and provide options for players to customize the HUD's visibility.

1. **Localization**:

If your game targets international audiences, plan for localization from the start. Allow space for text expansion in your UI elements and use a localization system that can handle multiple languages.

1. **Testing and Iteration**:

Test your UI with real players and gather their feedback. Pay attention to how they interact with the UI and make improvements based on their input. Iteration is essential for refining your UI design.

1. **Scalability**:

Consider how your UI design can scale as you add new features or content to your game. Ensure that the UI remains intuitive and organized as the complexity of your game grows.

1. **Dynamic Elements**:

Implement dynamic UI elements that respond to in-game events. For example, display a health bar that depletes as the player takes damage or show an objective marker that updates based on the player's progress.

1. **Feedback and Confirmation**:

Provide feedback to players when they perform actions, such as button presses or menu selections. Confirmation dialogs can prevent accidental actions that could disrupt the player's experience.

1. **Player-Customizable UI**:

Consider allowing players to customize aspects of the UI, such as repositioning elements, adjusting transparency, or choosing which information to display.

1. **Documentation**:

Create documentation for your UI design guidelines. This helps ensure consistency, especially when multiple team members are working on different aspects of the UI.

1. **Collaboration**:

Collaboration between UI designers, artists, and developers is crucial. Regular communication and feedback loops can result in a more polished and effective UI.

Remember that UI design is an ongoing process. As your game evolves and receives updates, continue to refine and optimize the UI to provide the best possible experience for your players.

Section 13.2: Customizable and Scalable HUD Systems

In this section, we'll delve into the design and implementation of customizable and scalable Heads-Up Display (HUD) systems for your games. HUD elements are essential for providing players with real-time information while minimizing distractions. Creating a HUD that players can customize to their preferences can greatly enhance their gaming experience.

1. **Modular HUD Design**:

   Start by designing your HUD in a modular way. Divide it into distinct elements, such as health bars, minimaps, objective trackers, and notifications. Each of these elements should be self-contained and easily rearranged.

1. **HUD Customization Options**:

   Provide players with customization options for their HUD layout. Allow them to reposition, resize, and enable/disable specific HUD elements based on their preferences. Implement a user-friendly interface for making these adjustments.

1. **Presets:**

   Consider including predefined HUD layout presets that cater to different playstyles or preferences (e.g., "Minimalist," "Immersive," "Competitive"). Players can choose from these presets or create their own custom layouts.

1. **Anchoring System**:

Implement an anchoring system that allows HUD elements to be attached to specific corners or edges of the screen. This system should snap elements into place when players drag them, ensuring precise positioning.

1. **Transparency and Opacity**:

Enable players to adjust the transparency or opacity of HUD elements. This feature ensures that critical information remains visible while minimizing visual clutter.

1. **Scaling and Resolution Independence**:

Design your HUD to scale gracefully across different screen sizes and resolutions. Ensure that text and icons remain legible and that elements don't overlap or become too small on high-resolution displays.

1. **HUD Editor**:

Consider including an in-game HUD editor that provides a visual representation of the HUD layout. Players can use this editor to drag and drop elements, adjust sizes, and customize colors.

1. **Keybinds and Hotkeys**:

Allow players to assign hotkeys or keybinds to HUD actions, such as toggling specific elements or changing the layout. This can streamline interactions and cater to players who prefer keyboard shortcuts.

1. **Contextual Information**:

Implement a system that dynamically displays contextual information. For example, the HUD might show a weapon's ammo count only when the player is using that weapon.

1. **Visibility Modes**:

Create different visibility modes for the HUD, such as a "Combat Mode" that shows essential combat-related information or a "Exploration Mode" that focuses on exploration and quest-tracking elements.

1. **HUD Animations**:

Add subtle animations to HUD elements to make them feel dynamic and responsive. For instance, health bars can smoothly fill or deplete when health changes.

1. **Performance Optimization**:

Ensure that the customizable HUD doesn't negatively impact game performance. Implement efficient rendering and update logic to minimize resource usage.

1. **Testing and Feedback**:

Test the customizable HUD extensively with players to gather feedback on usability and intuitiveness. Use this feedback to refine the HUD customization features.

1. **Accessibility**:

   Make sure that HUD customization options are accessible to all players, including those with disabilities. Provide alternative methods of customization for players who may have difficulty using traditional input devices.

1. **Saving and Loading Layouts**:

   Allow players to save multiple HUD layouts and switch between them easily. This feature can be particularly useful for players who enjoy different playstyles or roles within the game.

1. **Documentation and Tutorials**:

   Provide clear documentation or in-game tutorials explaining how to use the HUD customization features. Ensure that players can quickly learn how to personalize their HUD.

Customizable and scalable HUD systems not only enhance player immersion but also improve usability and accessibility. By offering players control over their gaming experience, you can cater to a broader audience and create a more engaging gameplay environment.

Section 13.3: Implementing Touch and Gesture Controls

In this section, we'll explore the implementation of touch and gesture controls for your game's user interface (UI) on touch-enabled devices like smartphones and tablets. Touch controls are essential for providing an intuitive and responsive gaming experience on these platforms. We'll cover various aspects of designing and integrating touch and gesture controls effectively.

1. **Detecting Touch Input**:

Begin by setting up touch input detection. Most game development frameworks provide built-in functions or events to capture touch events, such as tapping, swiping, and multi-touch gestures.

1. **Virtual Joysticks and Buttons**:

Implement virtual joysticks and buttons that overlay the game screen. These elements allow players to control character movement, actions, and interactions by tapping or dragging on the screen.

1. **Gesture Recognition**:

Recognize common gestures like tapping, double-tapping, swiping, pinching, and rotating. Assign specific actions or commands to these gestures based on context.

1. **Multi-Touch Support**:

Ensure that your game can handle multiple simultaneous touch inputs. This capability is crucial for complex interactions and multi-finger gestures.

1. **Responsive UI Elements**:

Design UI elements, such as buttons and sliders, to be touch-friendly. Ensure that they have adequate spacing, size, and visual feedback to accommodate touch interactions accurately.

1. **Drag-and-Drop Mechanics**:

If your game involves inventory management, item dragging, or puzzle-solving, implement drag-and-drop mechanics. Allow players to drag objects or UI elements intuitively.

1. **Contextual Interaction**:

Use touch controls to provide context-aware interactions. For example, tapping on a character in an adventure game might initiate a conversation, while tapping an item could trigger a pick-up action.

1. **Double-Tap to Zoom**:

If your game features zoomable maps or scenes, enable double-tap gestures to zoom in or out. Implement smooth transitions to enhance the user experience.

1. **Pinch-to-Zoom**:

For detailed views or maps, support pinch-to-zoom gestures. Ensure that the zoom level is limited to prevent unintended extreme zooming.

1. **Rotate Gestures**:

If your game benefits from screen rotation or orientation changes, implement rotate gestures to allow players to manipulate objects or the camera's view.

1. **Swipe Navigation**:

Enable swipe gestures for navigation purposes, such as scrolling through menus, changing camera angles, or navigating between in-game screens.

1. **Feedback and Animation**:

Provide visual and audio feedback for touch interactions. Elements should respond to touches with animations, changes in appearance, or sound effects to confirm actions.

1. **Customizable Controls**:

Consider allowing players to customize touch controls by repositioning buttons or adjusting sensitivity settings. This customization can improve comfort and accessibility.

1. **Testing on Different Devices**:

Test touch and gesture controls on various devices with different screen sizes and aspect ratios to ensure consistent functionality and responsiveness.

1. **Accessibility Considerations**:

Make sure that touch controls are accessible to players with disabilities. Provide alternatives, such as voice commands or simplified touch interactions, if necessary.

1. **Performance Optimization**:

Optimize touch input processing for efficiency, especially in graphics-intensive games. Minimize input lag and ensure smooth gameplay.

1. **Documentation and Tutorials**:

Include clear instructions or in-game tutorials that explain how touch and gesture controls work. New players should quickly understand how to interact with the game.

By effectively implementing touch and gesture controls, you can create a seamless and engaging gaming experience on touch-enabled devices. These controls should feel intuitive and responsive, allowing players to immerse themselves fully in your game without the need for physical controllers.

Section 13.4: Accessibility and Universal Design Principles

Ensuring that your game is accessible to a wide range of players, including those with disabilities, is not only a moral imperative but also makes good business sense. By following universal design principles, you can create a more inclusive gaming experience that welcomes players with diverse needs and abilities. In this section, we'll explore key considerations for making your game accessible.

1. **Keyboard and Controller Support**:

Besides touch controls, ensure that your game supports keyboards and various controllers. Many players, including those with mobility impairments, rely on these input methods.

1. **Customizable Controls**:

Allow players to customize controls to suit their preferences. Provide options for remapping keys or buttons, adjusting sensitivity, and accommodating different control schemes.

1. **Text and Language Support**:

Make in-game text accessible by using readable fonts, adjustable text sizes, and high contrast between text and backgrounds. Support multiple languages and offer subtitles or captions for spoken content.

1. **Audio Cues and Visual Alerts**:

Ensure that your game provides both audio and visual cues for important events and information. Some players may have hearing impairments and rely on visual alerts or subtitles.

1. **Colorblind-Friendly Design**:

Design your game with colorblind players in mind. Avoid relying solely on color coding, and use patterns or symbols to convey information. Provide colorblind mode options if necessary.

1. **Adjustable Difficulty**:

Implement scalable difficulty levels so that players of all skill levels can enjoy your game. Some players may need easier challenges, while others seek more advanced gameplay.

1. **Assistive Technologies Compatibility**:

Test your game with assistive technologies like screen readers and voice commands to ensure compatibility. Provide clear labels and descriptions for UI elements.

1. **Feedback and Confirmation**:

Offer feedback and confirmation prompts for important actions. This helps players with cognitive disabilities who may need additional time to process information.

1. **Skip and Pause Options**:

Allow players to skip non-essential content, such as cutscenes or tutorials, and pause the game at any time. This supports players who may need to take breaks or have interruptions.

1. **Testing with Diverse Users**:

Conduct playtesting with individuals who have different abilities and disabilities. Gather feedback and iterate on your game's accessibility features based on their experiences.

1. **Accessibility Settings Menu**:

Create a dedicated accessibility settings menu where players can adjust various options to meet their needs. Document these features in your game's instructions or help menu.

1. **Ethical Considerations**:

Respect players' privacy and data when implementing accessibility features. Ensure that any data collected for accessibility purposes is used responsibly and transparently.

1. **Community Engagement**:

Engage with your player community to learn about specific accessibility needs and gather feedback. Players can provide valuable insights into improving your game's accessibility.

1. **Legal Compliance**:

   Familiarize yourself with accessibility laws and guidelines in your region or target markets. Comply with these regulations to avoid legal issues.

1. **Continuous Improvement**:

   Commit to ongoing accessibility improvements in your game. Regularly update and refine your accessibility features based on feedback and evolving best practices.

By embracing accessibility and universal design principles, you can create a more inclusive and enjoyable gaming experience for all players. Making your game accessible not only expands your potential player base but also demonstrates a commitment to creating a welcoming and diverse gaming community.

Section 13.5: UI Animation and Interaction Techniques

User Interface (UI) elements play a crucial role in shaping the overall gaming experience. In this section, we'll explore UI animation and interaction techniques that can enhance the usability, engagement, and visual appeal of your game's interface.

1. **Transitions and Animations**:

Implement smooth transitions and subtle animations for UI elements. Transitions can include fade-ins, slide-ins, or scaling effects when menus or windows appear/disappear. Animations can make UI elements more engaging, such as buttons with subtle hover effects.

1. **Visual Feedback**:

Use animation to provide visual feedback for user actions. For example, when a button is pressed, it can briefly change color or size to indicate the action was registered. Visual feedback helps users understand their interactions with the UI.

1. **Microinteractions**:

Microinteractions are small, focused animations that respond to user input. They can be used to communicate information, guide users, or simply add delight. Examples include icon changes, loading spinners, or interactive tooltips.

1. **Progress Indicators**:

When loading content or performing background tasks, use progress indicators to keep users informed. Progress bars, spinners, or percentage-based animations can indicate that something is happening.

1. **Transitions Between Screens**:

Make transitioning between different game screens or menus visually appealing. Use animations like screen fades, sliding panels, or 3D rotations to create a seamless experience.

1. **Gesture-Based UI**:

If your game supports touch or gesture controls, use animations to respond to gestures. For example, swiping between menu screens can trigger smooth sliding animations.

1. **Contextual Menus**:

When context menus appear, use animations to draw attention to them. This can include subtle bouncing or popping animations to indicate their availability.

1. **Hover Effects**:

For desktop or web-based games, add hover effects to UI elements. When users hover their mouse over a button, it can change color, grow in size, or display additional information.

1. **Button Press Animations**:

When a button is pressed, create a visual effect to simulate a physical button press. This can include a slight depression or shadow effect to make the button feel tactile.

1. **Loading Screens**:

Use loading animations and progress bars during loading screens to entertain users and manage their expectations. Consider adding interactive elements like mini-games to keep users engaged.

1. **Tutorial and Guidance**:

Guide players through tutorials and instructions with animations that highlight the relevant UI elements. Use arrows, pulsating effects, or tooltips to draw attention.

1. **Accessibility Considerations**:

Ensure that UI animations do not hinder accessibility. Provide options to disable or reduce animations for players with motion sensitivity or cognitive disabilities.

1. **Performance Optimization**:

Optimize your animations to ensure they run smoothly across different devices and platforms. Consider using hardware acceleration for complex animations.

1. **User Testing**:

Test UI animations with real users to gather feedback on their effectiveness and potential improvements. Pay attention to how animations impact user satisfaction and comprehension.

1. **Consistency**:

Maintain consistency in your UI animations throughout the game. Use a common set of animations and transitions to create a cohesive user experience.

1. **Documentation**:

Document your UI animation guidelines and best practices for your development team. This ensures that animations are applied consistently during the game's development.

UI animation and interaction techniques can elevate your game's overall quality and user experience. When used thoughtfully and purposefully, animations can guide, inform, and engage players, making your game more enjoyable and intuitive to navigate.

Chapter 14: In-depth Analytics and Player Tracking

Section 14.1: Implementing Game Analytics Tools

Implementing game analytics tools is crucial for gaining insights into player behavior and preferences. These tools provide valuable data that can inform game design decisions, monetization strategies, and post-launch updates. In this section, we'll explore the importance of implementing game analytics and discuss various aspects of integrating analytics tools into your game development process.

1. **Understanding Player Behavior**:

   Game analytics tools allow you to collect data on how players interact with your game. This includes tracking which levels they play, how long they spend in the game, and the actions they take. Understanding player behavior helps you identify areas for improvement and optimization.

1. **Feature Usage Analysis**:

   Analyze which game features are most and least popular among players. By tracking feature usage, you can determine which aspects of your game are engaging and which may need enhancement or refinement.

1. **Monetization Insights**:

   Game analytics can provide insights into your game's monetization strategy. Track in-game purchases, ad revenue, and virtual currency transactions. Understand the conversion rates and spending patterns of your player base.

1. **Level Difficulty and Progression**:

Analyze how players progress through your game's levels or content. Identify bottlenecks or overly challenging sections that may frustrate players. Use data to balance the difficulty curve.

1. **Player Retention**:

Analyze player retention rates to determine how many players return to your game over time. High retention rates are often indicative of a successful game, while low retention may signal issues that need addressing.

1. **A/B Testing**:

Game analytics tools enable you to perform A/B testing to compare different game versions or features. Test variations of in-game elements, such as user interfaces, tutorials, or reward systems, to determine which performs better with players.

1. **Custom Events**:

Many analytics tools allow you to define custom events to track specific in-game actions or behaviors. This flexibility lets you gather data on unique aspects of your game that are important for your design goals.

1. **Player Segmentation**:

Segment your player base based on various criteria like spending habits, playtime, or skill level. This segmentation can help tailor game experiences and marketing strategies to different player groups.

1. **Real-Time Analytics**:

Some analytics tools offer real-time data, allowing you to monitor player activity as it happens. Real-time insights are valuable for making immediate adjustments or responding to emerging trends.

1. **Data Privacy and Compliance**:

When implementing game analytics, ensure that you comply with privacy regulations and protect player data. Inform players about data collection and give them options to opt out if desired.

1. **Third-Party Analytics Providers**:

Consider using established third-party analytics providers like Google Analytics for Firebase, Unity Analytics, or custom solutions tailored to your game's needs.

1. **Data Visualization**:

Use data visualization tools to create graphs, charts, and dashboards that make it easier to interpret and communicate the insights gained from analytics data.

1. **Iterative Development**:

Game analytics should be an integral part of your iterative development process. Continuously gather and analyze data to inform updates and improvements.

1. **Balancing Data and Intuition**:

While analytics provide valuable insights, it's essential to balance data-driven decisions with creative intuition and player feedback. Data alone may not capture the full player experience.

1. **Post-Launch Support**:

After the game's release, use analytics to monitor performance, track player sentiment, and guide post-launch updates and content releases.

1. **Ethical Considerations**:

Handle player data ethically and transparently. Be mindful of players' privacy and use data for the betterment of the game and player experience.

Implementing game analytics tools is an ongoing process that should be integrated into your game development pipeline from the early stages. By leveraging analytics data effectively, you can make informed decisions that enhance your game's quality, engagement, and financial success.

Section 14.2: Analyzing Player Behavior and Preferences

Analyzing player behavior and preferences is a core aspect of utilizing game analytics tools effectively. By diving deeper into this data, you can gain valuable insights that inform game design decisions, player engagement strategies, and content updates. In this section, we'll explore various techniques and considerations for analyzing player behavior and preferences through analytics.

1. **Player Journey Mapping**:

   Create player journey maps to visualize how different player segments progress through your game. Identify common paths and drop-off points to improve the overall player experience.

1. **Funnel Analysis**:

   Funnel analysis involves tracking the steps players take to complete specific actions or goals, such as making an in-game purchase. Analyze where players drop out of these funnels to optimize conversion rates.

1. **Cohort Analysis**:

   Group players into cohorts based on similar characteristics, such as acquisition date or spending habits. Compare how different cohorts engage with your game to tailor retention and monetization strategies.

1. **Heatmaps**:

Heatmaps visually represent player interactions within your game. Use heatmaps to identify which areas of your game's user interface are most engaging or confusing for players.

1. **Session Analysis**:

Study player sessions to understand playtime patterns and session length. Are players spending more time in specific game modes or during certain times of day?

1. **Player Surveys**:

Implement in-game surveys to gather direct feedback from players. Use surveys to understand player preferences, pain points, and suggestions for improvement.

1. **A/B Testing Results**:

Analyze the results of A/B tests to determine which variations of your game elements are preferred by players. Use this information to refine your game's design.

1. **User Segmentation**:

Segment players based on various criteria, such as skill level, spending habits, or geographic location. Tailor gameplay experiences, offers, and marketing campaigns for each segment.

1. **Social Interactions**:

Analyze player interactions within social features of your game, such as chat or guilds. Understand how social engagement impacts player retention and enjoyment.

1. **Player Feedback Sentiment**:

Use sentiment analysis to assess player feedback sentiment. Are players generally satisfied, frustrated, or neutral about specific aspects of your game?

1. **Content Engagement**:

Analyze how players engage with different game content, such as levels, quests, or events. Identify content that resonates most with your player base.

1. **Churn Prediction**:

Implement machine learning models to predict player churn. By identifying players at risk of leaving your game, you can take proactive steps to retain them.

1. **Purchase Behavior**:

Examine players' spending behavior, including the frequency and types of in-game purchases. Optimize your in-game store and pricing strategies accordingly.

1. **Community Insights**:

Monitor player activity on community forums, social media, and review platforms. Understand player sentiment outside of the game itself.

1. **Custom Analytics Events**:

Utilize custom events to track specific in-game actions or behaviors that are relevant to your game's design and objectives.

1. **Iterative Design**:

Use analytics insights to inform iterative game design. Regularly update your game based on what the data reveals about player preferences and behavior.

1. **Privacy and Data Security**:

Ensure that player data is handled securely and ethically throughout the analysis process. Comply with data protection regulations and respect player privacy.

1. **Communication and Transparency**:

Communicate key findings and changes to your player community transparently. Show players that their feedback and data are valued.

Analyzing player behavior and preferences is an ongoing process that evolves as your game matures. By consistently evaluating analytics data and adjusting your game accordingly, you can create a more engaging and satisfying experience for your player base.

Section 14.3: Utilizing Data for Game Improvements

Once you've gathered and analyzed player behavior and preference data, the next crucial step is to utilize this information for game improvements. The insights you gain from analytics can guide your decision-making process, ultimately leading to a better player experience and increased engagement. In this section, we'll explore how to effectively leverage data for game enhancements.

1. **Iterative Game Updates**:

Use analytics to identify areas of your game that require attention. Implement regular updates and improvements based on player feedback and data-driven insights. This iterative approach keeps your game fresh and engaging.

1. **Balancing Gameplay**:

Data can help you fine-tune game balance by revealing which aspects are overpowered or underutilized. Adjust character abilities, weapon stats, or level difficulties to create a more enjoyable experience.

1. **Content Creation**:

Develop new content based on player preferences and engagement metrics. Analytics can highlight which types of levels, quests, or challenges resonate with your audience, allowing you to focus your content creation efforts effectively.

1. **Monetization Strategies**:

Optimize your in-game store, pricing, and monetization strategies using data on player spending behavior. Implement targeted offers and discounts to increase conversion rates.

1. **Retention Tactics**:

Identify player churn patterns and implement retention tactics. For example, reward loyal players with incentives, events, or special content to keep them engaged.

1. **User Interface (UI) Enhancements**:

Improve the user interface based on player feedback and heatmaps. Ensure that players can easily navigate menus, access important features, and understand in-game information.

1. **Bug Fixes**:

Prioritize and address bugs and issues that affect the player experience. Analyze error reports and runtime data to identify and resolve critical problems.

1. **Performance Optimization**:

Use analytics to pinpoint performance bottlenecks, such as frame rate drops or memory leaks. Optimize your game's performance to ensure a smooth and enjoyable gameplay experience.

1. **Community Engagement**:

Foster a sense of community by addressing player feedback and suggestions. Encourage player-driven initiatives, such as fan art or user-generated content, to create a more engaged player base.

1. **Player-Centric Features**:

Develop new features that align with player desires and preferences. For example, if data shows that players enjoy cooperative gameplay, consider adding more co-op modes or features.

1. **Event Planning**:

Plan in-game events and updates based on data indicating peak player activity times. Timing events to coincide with player availability can maximize participation.

1. **Localization and Regionalization**:

Utilize analytics to identify regions with high player engagement. Consider localizing your game or tailoring content for specific regions to cater to a broader audience.

1. **Testing and Prototyping**:

Experiment with new gameplay mechanics or features and use analytics to assess their impact. Prototyping allows you to gauge player interest before committing to full development.

1. **Data-Driven Decision-Making**:

Incorporate data into your decision-making process at all levels of game development, from design to marketing. Encourage a data-driven culture within your development team.

1. **Ethical Considerations**:

While utilizing data for game improvements, ensure that your actions align with ethical standards. Avoid manipulative practices and prioritize player satisfaction and fairness.

1. **Communication with Players**:

Keep players informed about upcoming improvements and changes. Share insights about how player feedback and data have influenced these decisions to foster transparency.

1. **Long-Term Planning**:

Develop a long-term roadmap for your game's evolution based on analytics insights. Plan for the sustained growth and success of your game in a competitive market.

Remember that player preferences and trends may change over time, so ongoing data analysis is essential. By continuously leveraging data for game improvements, you can create a more engaging and satisfying experience that keeps players coming back for more.

Section 14.4: Ethical Considerations in Player Data Usage

As game developers increasingly rely on player data for improving their games and making informed decisions, it's essential to address ethical considerations surrounding the collection and usage of this data. Players entrust developers with their data, and respecting their privacy and ensuring ethical practices is of utmost importance. In this section, we'll explore the ethical considerations associated with player data usage in game development.

1. **Informed Consent**:

Ensure that players provide informed consent before collecting any personal data. This consent should be clear, easy to understand, and specific to the types of data being collected.

1. **Transparency**:

Be transparent about the data you collect and how it will be used. Provide a privacy policy or disclosure that explains the purpose and scope of data collection.

1. **Data Minimization**:

Collect only the data necessary for game functionality and improvement. Avoid unnecessary data collection, especially sensitive information.

1. **Anonymization and Aggregation**:

When analyzing player data, use techniques like anonymization and aggregation to protect individual identities. Ensure that the data cannot be used to personally identify players.

1. **Data Security**:

Implement robust security measures to protect player data from breaches and unauthorized access. Encrypt sensitive data and regularly update security protocols.

1. **Data Retention**:

Establish clear data retention policies and timeframes. Delete or anonymize data that is no longer needed for game improvement purposes.

1. **Third-Party Services**:

If using third-party analytics or advertising services, carefully review their data handling practices and ensure they comply with ethical standards.

1. **User Control**:

Give players control over their data. Allow them to opt-out of data collection or delete their data if they choose to do so.

1. **Children's Data**:

If your game is targeted at children, comply with legal regulations such as COPPA (Children's Online Privacy Protection Act) when collecting and handling data.

1. **Sensitive Data**:

Avoid collecting sensitive personal information such as social security numbers, addresses, or financial data unless absolutely necessary.

1. **Data Ownership**:

Clearly state in your terms of service that players own their data and have the right to access or delete it.

1. **Data Usage Transparency**:

Inform players how their data is being used for game improvements, such as level design, bug fixing, or gameplay balancing.

1. **Data Ethics Committee**:

Consider establishing an internal data ethics committee to oversee data practices and ensure ethical compliance.

1. **Ethical Dilemmas**:

Be aware of potential ethical dilemmas, such as using player data to manipulate behavior or unfairly monetize players. Prioritize fair play and player satisfaction.

1. **Community Feedback**:

Listen to and consider community feedback regarding data practices. Address concerns and demonstrate a commitment to ethical data usage.

1. **Legal Compliance**:

   Stay informed about data protection laws and regulations in the regions where your game is available. Comply with legal requirements to protect player rights.

1. **Regular Audits**:

   Conduct regular audits of your data practices to ensure ongoing ethical compliance and data security.

1. **Public Accountability**:

   Maintain transparency in your data practices, and be prepared to publicly address any concerns or questions from players or the gaming community.

1. **Ethical Data Partnerships**:

   Collaborate with data partners and service providers who share your commitment to ethical data usage.

1. **Continuous Education**:

   Keep your development team educated and aware of evolving ethical standards and best practices in data usage.

By adhering to ethical principles in player data usage, you not only build trust with your player community but also contribute to the responsible and ethical development of the gaming industry as a whole. Ethical considerations should be an integral part of your game development process from data collection to data-driven decision-making.

Section 14.5: Real-Time Analytics and Reporting

In the rapidly evolving landscape of game development, real-time analytics and reporting have become indispensable tools for developers and publishers. These tools provide valuable insights into player behavior, game performance, and other critical aspects of game development. In this section, we will explore the importance of real-time analytics and reporting and how they can benefit your game development process.

1. **Immediate Feedback**:

Real-time analytics offer the advantage of immediate feedback. Developers can monitor player actions, in-game events, and performance metrics as they happen. This immediacy allows for timely responses to emerging issues or opportunities.

1. **Player Engagement**:

Understanding player engagement is crucial for game success. Real-time analytics provide insights into which game features are most engaging, helping developers tailor their updates and content to match player preferences.

1. **Performance Monitoring**:

Real-time reporting enables developers to monitor the performance of their games across different platforms and devices. This includes tracking frame rates, loading times, and other performance metrics that can impact player experience.

1. **In-Game Events**:

Tracking in-game events and player interactions in real-time can help identify bottlenecks, balance issues, or unexpected behavior. Developers can use this data to refine gameplay and enhance player satisfaction.

1. **Player Retention**:

Real-time analytics help in tracking player retention rates. By identifying when and why players drop off, developers can implement strategies to improve player retention and reduce churn.

1. **Monetization Insights**:

For games with in-app purchases or ads, real-time analytics provide insights into revenue generation. Developers can assess the effectiveness of monetization strategies and adjust them as needed.

1. **A/B Testing**:

Real-time reporting facilitates A/B testing, allowing developers to experiment with different game features or marketing approaches and quickly assess which performs better.

1. **Bug and Crash Detection**:

Identifying bugs and crashes in real-time is essential for delivering a stable gaming experience. Analytics can alert developers to issues and help prioritize bug fixes.

1. **Player Feedback Integration**:

Real-time analytics can be integrated with player feedback systems, allowing developers to correlate player comments and reviews with in-game events and data.

1. **Live Ops**:

For live service games, real-time analytics are essential for managing live events, updates, and ongoing content delivery. Developers can assess event participation and adjust content on the fly.

1. **Community Engagement**:

By monitoring player activity and discussions in real-time, developers can engage with the gaming community more effectively, responding to concerns or celebrating achievements.

1. **Data-Driven Decision-Making**:

Real-time analytics empower data-driven decision-making. Developers can make informed choices about game design, updates, and marketing strategies based on real-time insights.

1. **Competitive Analysis**:

Analyzing real-time data on player behavior and trends can help developers stay competitive by adapting to changing player preferences and market dynamics.

1. **Security and Fraud Detection**:

Real-time analytics can aid in detecting security breaches, cheating, and fraud, protecting both the game and the player community.

1. **Player Support**:

Support teams can benefit from real-time analytics to identify and address player issues more efficiently.

1. **Resource Allocation**:

Developers can allocate resources, such as server capacity, based on real-time player activity to ensure optimal performance during peak times.

1. **Predictive Analytics**:

Advanced analytics can include predictive models that forecast future trends and player behavior, helping developers prepare for upcoming challenges and opportunities.

1. **Privacy Considerations**:

When implementing real-time analytics, ensure that player privacy is respected and sensitive data is handled securely. Compliance with data protection regulations is essential.

1. **Custom Dashboards**:

   Create custom dashboards for real-time reporting tailored to your game's specific metrics and KPIs. This allows you to focus on the data that matters most.

1. **Continuous Improvement**:

   Real-time analytics should be an integral part of the game development lifecycle, allowing for continuous improvement and adaptation to player needs and market dynamics.

In conclusion, real-time analytics and reporting are invaluable tools for modern game development. By leveraging these tools effectively, developers can enhance player engagement, optimize game performance, and make data-informed decisions that contribute to the success and longevity of their games.

Chapter 15: Advanced Level and World Design

Section 15.1: Techniques for Dynamic Level Generation

Dynamic level generation is a powerful technique that can significantly enhance a player's gaming experience. It involves creating game levels or environments procedurally, rather than designing them manually. This approach offers several advantages, including replayability, reduced development time, and the ability to generate vast and diverse game worlds. In this section, we will explore various techniques and considerations for implementing dynamic level generation in your games.

1. **Procedural Content Generation (PCG)**:

Procedural content generation is the heart of dynamic level generation. It involves using algorithms to generate various aspects of game levels, such as terrain, structures, items, and enemy placement. PCG algorithms can be deterministic or stochastic, producing consistent or random results, respectively.

1. **Randomization**:

Randomization plays a crucial role in dynamic level generation. It introduces unpredictability and variety into each playthrough. By using random seeds or noise functions, you can create unique game worlds for players.

1. **Biomes and Themes**:

To add diversity to your game world, consider implementing different biomes or themes. Each biome can have its unique terrain, vegetation, weather, and challenges, creating a rich and immersive experience.

1. **Tile-Based Level Generation**:

Tile-based level generation involves dividing the game world into smaller tiles or chunks. These tiles can be assembled to create larger levels dynamically. This approach is common in 2D games and can be extended to 3D as well.

1. **Cellular Automata**:

Cellular automata algorithms, such as Conway's Game of Life, can be used to generate terrain and vegetation patterns. They are suitable for creating natural-looking environments with a sense of organic growth.

1. **L-Systems**:

L-systems (Lindenmayer systems) are used for generating complex and branching structures, like trees or caves. They are particularly useful for creating detailed and realistic environments.

1. **Perlin Noise and Voronoi Diagrams**:

Perlin noise and Voronoi diagrams are essential tools for generating natural-looking terrain and distributing elements like resources or enemies. These techniques can simulate realistic landscapes and spatial distributions.

1. **Procedural Generation of Assets**:

In addition to terrain and structures, you can procedurally generate various in-game assets, such as textures, models, and animations. This helps maintain the cohesive look and feel of your dynamically generated levels.

1. **Player Progression and Scaling**:

Consider the player's progression when generating levels dynamically. Levels should become progressively challenging or change in complexity as the player advances, keeping the gameplay engaging.

1. **Scripted Events and Storytelling**:

While dynamic level generation is excellent for creating gameplay spaces, scripted events and storytelling elements can be integrated to add narrative depth and cinematic moments to your game.

1. **User-Defined Parameters**:

Allow players to customize certain aspects of the level generation, such as difficulty, biome selection, or world size. This adds replayability and personalization to the experience.

1. **Balancing and Playtesting**:

Dynamic level generation requires extensive playtesting and balancing. Ensure that generated levels are fair, enjoyable, and free from game-breaking issues.

1. **Data Serialization and Persistence**:

Implement mechanisms for serializing and persisting generated levels. This allows players to revisit or share their favorite procedurally generated worlds.

1. **Performance Optimization:**

Generating levels dynamically can be computationally intensive. Optimize your algorithms and data structures to ensure smooth gameplay performance.

1. **Procedural Audio and Music:**

Extend dynamic level generation to audio by creating procedural soundscapes or adaptive music systems that respond to the player's actions and the generated environment.

1. **Emergent Gameplay:**

Embrace the emergent gameplay possibilities of dynamic levels. Encourage player creativity and exploration by designing systems that react dynamically to their decisions.

1. **Documentation and Tools:**

Document your level generation algorithms and provide tools for other developers to understand, modify, or extend the generation process. Sharing knowledge within your team is essential.

1. **Player Feedback:**

Solicit feedback from players to improve your dynamic level generation. Their input can help you refine algorithms, balance generated content, and address any player frustrations.

1. **Hybrid Approaches**:

Don't limit yourself to purely procedural or manual level design. Hybrid approaches that combine procedural generation with handcrafted elements can provide the best of both worlds.

1. **Iterative Development**:

Dynamic level generation is an iterative process. Continuously refine and expand your generation techniques as you gather more data and insights from player experiences.

Dynamic level generation can be a transformative aspect of game design, opening up new possibilities for creativity and player engagement. When implemented thoughtfully, it can result in memorable and immersive gaming experiences that keep players coming back for more.

Section 15.2: Creating Interactive and Responsive Environments

Creating interactive and responsive environments is crucial for enhancing player immersion and engagement in modern games. Dynamic interactions with the game world, non-player characters (NPCs), and objects contribute to a more lifelike and enjoyable gaming experience. In this section, we will explore various techniques and considerations for designing interactive and responsive environments in your games.

1. **Physics and Collisions**:

Implement physics simulation and collision detection to make the game world feel tangible and believable. Ensure that characters and objects respond realistically to forces and interactions.

1. **Environmental Effects**:

Enrich your game environments with interactive elements such as weather, day-night cycles, and environmental hazards. These effects can influence gameplay and create a more immersive atmosphere.

1. **Dynamic Lighting**:

Utilize dynamic lighting systems to create realistic shadows and light interactions. Adjust lighting conditions based on the time of day or specific in-game events.

1. **Interactable Objects**:

Populate your game world with interactable objects that players can manipulate. These objects can serve various purposes, from puzzle-solving to enhancing storytelling.

1. **NPC Behavior**:

NPCs should exhibit lifelike behavior and react to the player's actions. Implement AI routines that make NPCs responsive to environmental changes and the player's choices.

1. **Ecosystem Simulation**:

For open-world games, consider simulating ecosystems with flora and fauna. These systems can create dynamic interactions between different species and add depth to the game world.

1. **Dynamic Terrain**:

Implement terrain deformation and modification based on in-game events or player actions. This can include digging, building, or destructible environments.

1. **Realistic Weather Systems**:

Create dynamic weather systems that affect gameplay and visuals. Rain can make surfaces slippery, and storms can change visibility and soundscapes.

1. **Procedural Destruction**:

Utilize procedural techniques to simulate object destruction realistically. Debris, crumbling structures, and dynamic damage can enhance combat and environmental storytelling.

1. **Fluid Dynamics**:

For games with water bodies, implement fluid dynamics to simulate realistic water behavior, including waves, currents, and buoyancy.

1. **Dynamic Audio**:

Match audio cues to in-game events and interactions. Sounds should respond dynamically to changes in the environment and player actions.

1. **Emergent Gameplay**:

Encourage emergent gameplay by allowing players to interact with the environment in unexpected ways. Reward creativity and experimentation with unique outcomes.

1. **Environmental Storytelling**:

Use the environment itself to tell stories and convey information. Scattered notes, graffiti, or visual cues can provide context and engage players in the narrative.

1. **Interactive UI**:

Ensure that the user interface (UI) elements are responsive and interactive. Visual feedback, tooltips, and interactive menus can enhance the player's connection with the game world.

1. **Multiplayer Environments:**

In multiplayer games, synchronize dynamic interactions across all players. Ensure that environmental changes are consistent for everyone in the session.

1. **Gameplay Consequences:**

Make sure that interactions with the environment have meaningful consequences in the game. Choices made by the player should impact the storyline, gameplay, or character relationships.

1. **Testing and Iteration:**

Rigorously playtest and iterate on interactive systems to ensure they are balanced and enjoyable. Collect player feedback to refine environmental interactions.

1. **Performance Optimization:**

Efficiently manage the computational resources required for interactive and responsive environments. Optimize code and assets to maintain smooth gameplay.

1. **Accessibility Considerations:**

Ensure that interactive elements are designed with accessibility in mind. Provide alternative ways for players with disabilities to engage with the game environment.

1. **Documentation and Modding Support:**

If applicable, document environmental systems and provide modding tools for the community to create custom interactions and environments.

Interactive and responsive environments have the potential to elevate your game to new heights by immersing players in a dynamic and engaging world. By carefully designing and implementing these systems, you can create memorable and immersive gaming experiences that keep players coming back for more.

Section 15.3: Narrative-Driven World Building

Narrative-driven world building is a vital aspect of game development, particularly in titles where storytelling and immersion play key roles. Crafting a rich and engaging game world that captivates players and complements the narrative is a multifaceted task. In this section, we will explore various techniques and considerations for creating narrative-driven game worlds that enhance storytelling and player engagement.

1. **Thematic Consistency**:

Establish a consistent thematic foundation for your game world. Consider the game's genre, setting, and narrative to ensure that all elements align cohesively.

1. **Lore and History**:

Develop a deep lore and history for your game world. This background information can be used to enrich storytelling, provide context, and create a sense of depth.

1. **Character Backstories**:

Create backstories for significant characters and factions within the game world. Understanding their histories, motivations, and conflicts can inform narrative choices and character development.

1. **Geography and Geography**:

Design the geography and topography of the game world to support the narrative. Terrain, climate, and landmarks can influence the storyline and gameplay.

1. **Cultural Diversity**:

Populate your game world with diverse cultures and societies. Each culture should have unique customs, beliefs, and traditions that contribute to world-building.

1. **Environmental Storytelling**:

Use environmental details, such as architecture, graffiti, or decay, to tell stories without words. Players can deduce past events and character backgrounds by observing the environment.

1. **Interactive NPCs**:

NPCs should not only serve as quest givers but also provide insights into the world's lore and history. Conversations with NPCs can reveal valuable information.

1. **Quests and Side Stories**:

Craft quests and side stories that are intricately woven into the game world's narrative. These should feel like organic parts of the world rather than isolated tasks.

1. **In-Game Books and Documents**:

Scatter books, scrolls, and documents throughout the world. These can contain stories, legends, or historical accounts that players can discover and read.

1. **Dynamic Events**:

Implement dynamic events that change the game world based on player actions or in-game triggers. These events should have narrative significance and consequences.

1. **Storytelling Through Art**:

Incorporate visual storytelling through concept art, loading screens, and in-game art. These images can convey additional narrative details.

1. **Non-Linear Storytelling**:

Allow for non-linear storytelling where player choices impact the narrative's direction and outcome. Multiple story branches can lead to various endings.

1. **Easter Eggs and Secrets**:

Include hidden easter eggs and secrets in the game world. These can reward observant players with insights, lore, or humor.

1. **Sound and Music**:

Use soundscapes and music to enhance the narrative experience. Audio cues can evoke emotions and reinforce storytelling elements.

1. **Progressive World Changes**:

As the narrative progresses, introduce changes to the game world. These can be physical alterations or shifts in the behavior of NPCs and factions.

1. **Player Agency**:

Empower players to influence the game world's narrative. Choices made by the player should have a meaningful impact on the storyline.

1. **Quest Chains**:

Create quest chains that gradually unveil important aspects of the game world's history and lore. Completing these chains should feel rewarding and informative.

1. **Collaboration with Writers**:

Collaborate with experienced writers or narrative designers to ensure that the game world's storytelling is compelling and well-executed.

1. **Consistent Tone**:

Maintain a consistent tone throughout the game world and narrative. Sudden shifts in mood or style can disrupt immersion.

1. **Iterative Development**:

Continuously iterate on the game world's narrative elements based on playtesting and player feedback. This process helps refine the storytelling experience.

Narrative-driven world building is a delicate balance of creativity, storytelling, and design. When executed effectively, it can transport players to captivating and immersive game worlds, leaving a lasting impression and a desire to explore every corner of the narrative-rich environment.

Section 15.4: Integrating Levels with Game Mechanics

Integrating game levels seamlessly with core gameplay mechanics is crucial for creating an engaging and immersive gaming experience. This section explores the principles and best practices involved in designing game levels that complement and enhance the underlying game mechanics. Whether you're developing a platformer, RPG, or first-person shooter, these guidelines will help you achieve a harmonious relationship between levels and gameplay.

1. **Alignment of Themes**:

   Ensure that the theme and aesthetics of each level align with the overall game narrative and mechanics. Consistency in visual and thematic design enhances player immersion.

1. **Learning Curve**:

   Introduce gameplay mechanics gradually as players progress through levels. Start with simpler challenges to help players understand core mechanics before presenting more complex ones.

1. **Progressive Difficulty**:

   Increase the level of difficulty as players advance. Gradually introduce new obstacles, enemies, or puzzles that require mastery of existing mechanics.

1. **Environmental Puzzles**:

Use level design to create environmental puzzles that require players to apply game mechanics creatively. These puzzles should feel integrated into the game world.

1. **Player Agency**:

Allow players to use their acquired skills and mechanics to overcome challenges in meaningful ways. Encourage creative problem-solving and reward experimentation.

1. **Contextual Storytelling**:

Use level design to convey narrative elements and lore. Environmental details can provide context for the game's story without relying solely on cutscenes or dialogue.

1. **Game Mechanics Variability**:

Introduce variations or twists to existing mechanics within levels. This keeps gameplay fresh and prevents monotony.

1. **Revisiting Mechanics**:

Revisit and build upon previously introduced mechanics throughout the game. Challenge players to apply what they've learned in new and inventive ways.

1. **Level Flow**:

Ensure smooth transitions between levels to maintain the pacing of the game. Avoid abrupt changes in difficulty or gameplay style.

1. **Player Feedback**:

Provide immediate and clear feedback to players when they interact with game mechanics. Visual and audio cues can enhance the player's understanding of their actions.

1. **Checkpoint System**:

Implement a fair checkpoint system to prevent frustration. This ensures that players don't need to replay long sections of a level due to failures.

1. **Dynamic Elements**:

Include dynamic elements in levels that respond to player actions or game mechanics. These elements can surprise and challenge players in unexpected ways.

1. **Optional Challenges**:

Offer optional challenges or side objectives that encourage players to explore and experiment with game mechanics. These can provide additional rewards or story insights.

1. **Balancing Act**:

Strive for a balance between gameplay mechanics and level design. Avoid overloading levels with too many mechanics, as it can overwhelm players.

1. **User Testing**:

Conduct playtesting to gather feedback on the integration of game mechanics and level design. Observing how players interact with your levels can lead to valuable insights.

1. **Accessibility**:

Ensure that the game's mechanics and levels are accessible to a wide range of players. Consider different skill levels and playstyles when designing challenges.

1. **Consistency in Controls**:

Maintain consistent controls across levels to provide a cohesive gameplay experience. Sudden changes in control schemes can disrupt player immersion.

1. **Iterative Design**:

Iterate on level design and mechanics integration based on player feedback and testing. Continuously refine the relationship between levels and gameplay.

1. **Embrace Constraints**:

Embrace design constraints and limitations, as they can lead to creative solutions that enhance the connection between levels and mechanics.

1. **Player Empowerment**:

Empower players to feel in control of their actions and the game world. When mechanics are integrated seamlessly with levels, players are more likely to become deeply engaged with your game.

The integration of game levels with core mechanics is an art that requires careful consideration, creativity, and a deep understanding of your game's unique identity. When executed thoughtfully, it results in a gaming experience where levels not only serve as stages but also as dynamic playgrounds for players to explore and conquer using the mechanics at their disposal.

Section 15.5: Balancing Aesthetic Appeal and Functionality

Balancing aesthetic appeal with functionality is a crucial aspect of level and world design in game development. Games are a visual medium, and creating visually stunning environments is essential to draw players into the game world. However, aesthetics should not come at the expense of gameplay or functionality. This section explores the delicate equilibrium between making levels visually captivating and ensuring they serve their intended gameplay purpose effectively.

1. **Theme Consistency**:

   Ensure that the aesthetic choices made in level design align with the overarching theme of the game. Consistency in theme maintains immersion.

1. **Visual Storytelling**:

   Use the environment's visual elements to convey narrative and world-building aspects. Details such as environmental storytelling can engage players in the game's lore.

1. **Player Orientation**:

   Design levels with visual cues that guide players naturally through the game world. Visual markers can help players understand objectives and navigate without the need for excessive HUD elements.

1. **Clarity of Obstacles**:

Make sure that obstacles and interactive elements are visually distinct from the background. Players should easily identify objects or areas they can interact with.

1. **Accessibility Considerations**:

Keep in mind that players may have varying visual abilities. Ensure that your level's aesthetics do not hinder accessibility or gameplay for those with visual impairments.

1. **Lighting and Mood**:

Utilize lighting to set the mood and atmosphere of your levels. Lighting can dramatically impact the visual appeal and emotional tone of a scene.

1. **Balance of Detail**:

Strike a balance between adding intricate details for immersion and maintaining a level's clarity. Overly cluttered environments can confuse players.

1. **Color Palette**:

Choose a color palette that complements the game's tone and helps convey information. Consistent use of colors can assist in conveying emotions or highlighting gameplay elements.

1. **Dynamic Environments**:

Create environments that feel alive with dynamic elements such as moving objects, weather effects, or day-night cycles. Dynamic changes can make levels more engaging.

1. **Interactive Props**:

Use interactive props or objects in the environment that enhance gameplay and provide opportunities for player interaction. These props should blend seamlessly with the level's aesthetics.

1. **Distracting Elements**:

Be mindful of visually distracting elements that can draw players' attention away from the main objectives or gameplay. Ensure that critical elements are prioritized visually.

1. **Performance Optimization**:

High-quality visuals can be resource-intensive. Optimize the level's visuals to maintain good performance on a variety of hardware configurations.

1. **Aesthetic Variety**:

Introduce variety in aesthetics across levels or areas of the game to keep players engaged and prevent visual monotony.

1. **Player Feedback**:

Use visual cues to provide feedback to players when they perform actions or interact with the environment. This enhances the player's sense of agency and connection with the game world.

1. **Iterative Design**:

Continuously iterate on level aesthetics based on player feedback and testing. Strive for a balance that enhances the overall gaming experience.

1. **Playtesting**:

Conduct playtesting sessions to gather feedback on how players perceive the aesthetic elements of your levels. Pay attention to their emotional responses and preferences.

1. **Accessibility Options**:

Include accessibility options that allow players to customize certain visual aspects, such as contrast or text size, to cater to individual preferences and needs.

1. **Storytelling Through Environment**:

Explore opportunities to tell parts of the game's story or provide context through the environment's visuals. This can deepen the player's engagement with the narrative.

Balancing aesthetic appeal and functionality is an art that requires consideration of both the player's experience and the game's narrative. When executed effectively, it results in levels that not only look stunning but also enhance the overall gameplay and immersion, creating memorable gaming experiences for players.

Chapter 16: Monetization and Business Models

Section 16.1: Innovative Monetization Strategies

Monetization is a critical aspect of game development, ensuring that your hard work and creativity are rewarded. While traditional monetization methods like one-time purchases still have their place, innovative monetization strategies have become increasingly prevalent in the gaming industry. These strategies not only maximize revenue but also enhance the player experience. In this section, we'll explore some innovative monetization strategies that can help you achieve success in the competitive world of game development.

1. **In-Game Advertising**: One of the most prevalent innovative monetization strategies is in-game advertising. By incorporating non-intrusive advertisements within your game, you can generate revenue without directly charging players. Options include banner ads, interstitial ads, and rewarded video ads. Careful placement and relevance are key to maintaining a positive player experience.
2. **Gacha Systems**: Gacha systems, inspired by capsule-toy vending machines, have gained popularity. Players spend virtual currency to receive randomized in-game items or characters. This can create excitement and anticipation, encouraging players to make more purchases to get their desired items. However, ensure that the system is balanced and not perceived as pay-to-win.
3. **Season Passes and Battle Passes**: Many successful games now offer season passes or battle passes. These time-limited subscriptions provide players with exclusive rewards, cosmetics, or in-game currency as they progress through

the pass tiers. This strategy encourages player engagement and spending while offering tangible benefits.

4. **Limited-Time Events and Sales**: Creating limited-time in-game events and sales can drive urgency and FOMO (Fear of Missing Out) among players. These events can offer exclusive items, discounts, or bonus content, enticing players to spend during a specific window.
5. **Cosmetic Microtransactions**: Selling cosmetic items such as skins, costumes, and emotes allows players to personalize their in-game characters or avatars without affecting gameplay. Cosmetic microtransactions are popular because they don't provide a competitive advantage, making them more acceptable to players.
6. **Subscription Models**: Some games adopt subscription models that offer ongoing benefits, such as premium currency, early access to content, or ad removal. Subscriptions can provide a stable source of income and build a loyal player base.
7. **Crowdfunding and Early Access**: Platforms like Kickstarter and Patreon enable developers to engage with their community and secure funding for game development. Offering exclusive rewards or early access builds a dedicated player base and provides financial support.
8. **Playable Ads**: This innovative approach allows players to experience a portion of a game as an advertisement. If they enjoy the brief gameplay, they might choose to download and continue playing the full game.
9. **Non-Fungible Tokens (NFTs)**: While controversial, NFTs have gained attention in the gaming industry. Game developers can tokenize unique in-game assets or characters, allowing players to buy, sell, or trade them.

Implementing NFTs requires careful consideration and transparency to avoid backlash.

10. **Dynamic Pricing**: Implementing dynamic pricing based on player behavior, demand, or other factors can optimize revenue. For example, offering discounts to lapsed players or pricing items differently for different regions can maximize profitability.

Remember that the success of these innovative monetization strategies depends on balancing revenue generation with player satisfaction. Be transparent with your players about how monetization works in your game, and actively seek their feedback to refine your approach. By finding the right balance, you can create a win-win situation where players enjoy your game while supporting its continued development and success.

Section 16.2: Balancing Profit and Player Experience

In the world of game development, finding the right balance between profit and player experience is essential for the long-term success and sustainability of your game. While monetization is crucial, it should never come at the expense of player enjoyment or fairness. In this section, we'll explore strategies to strike that delicate equilibrium.

1. **Value-Based Pricing**: When offering in-game items or content for purchase, consider their perceived value to players. Pricing should align with the perceived value, ensuring players feel they are getting their money's worth. Conduct player surveys or gather feedback to determine what players consider valuable.
2. **Free-to-Play (F2P) Foundations**: If you choose a free-to-play model, focus on providing a complete and enjoyable experience for free players. Ensure that the core gameplay is engaging without requiring purchases. Offer in-game purchases as optional enhancements rather than necessities.
3. **Transparency and Fairness**: Transparency is key when it comes to monetization. Clearly communicate how in-game purchases work, including drop rates for random items and the impact of purchases on gameplay. Avoid pay-to-win mechanics that create an unfair advantage for paying players.
4. **Player Choice**: Empower players with choices regarding how they monetize within your game. Provide multiple options for obtaining in-game items or currency, including both free and paid methods. This gives players a sense of

control and reduces frustration.

5. **Regular Updates**: Keep players engaged by delivering regular updates and new content. These updates can include free content accessible to all players and premium content for those who choose to purchase it. This approach ensures ongoing monetization opportunities while maintaining a vibrant player community.
6. **Community Engagement**: Foster a strong community around your game. Engaging with players through forums, social media, and live events builds trust and loyalty. Players are more likely to support a game they feel emotionally connected to.
7. **Anti-Addiction Measures**: Consider implementing features that discourage excessive play or spending. Limiting daily playtime, providing spending alerts, and encouraging breaks can help players maintain a healthy balance.
8. **Limited-Time Offers**: Create urgency with limited-time offers or events. These can encourage players to make purchases or engage more actively in the game. However, ensure that these events do not create pressure to spend excessively.
9. **Regularly Review Metrics**: Continuously analyze player data and metrics related to monetization. Understand player behavior, spending patterns, and player satisfaction. Use these insights to make informed adjustments to your monetization strategy.
10. **Testing and Iteration**: Experiment with different monetization strategies through A/B testing. This allows you to assess the impact of changes on player behavior and revenue. Be willing to iterate and refine your approach based on the results.

11. **Ethical Monetization**: Avoid manipulative or exploitative monetization practices that can harm vulnerable players. Uphold ethical standards in your monetization strategies, and be mindful of the potential impact on players' mental and financial well-being.
12. **Player Feedback**: Actively seek and listen to player feedback regarding monetization. Understand their concerns and address them where possible. This collaborative approach can lead to a more positive player perception of your monetization efforts.

Remember that a sustainable and ethical approach to monetization will contribute to the long-term success of your game. Balancing profit with player experience is an ongoing process that requires careful planning, continuous evaluation, and a commitment to delivering value to your players. When done right, monetization can enhance player engagement and support the growth of your game's community.

Section 16.3: Exploring Subscription and Freemium Models

In the ever-evolving landscape of game monetization, subscription and freemium models have gained significant popularity. These models offer unique opportunities for game developers to generate revenue while providing value to players. In this section, we'll delve into the concepts of subscription-based and freemium monetization, exploring their benefits and considerations.

Subscription-Based Monetization

Subscription-based models involve charging players a recurring fee in exchange for access to premium content, features, or services within the game. These subscriptions can come in various forms, such as monthly, quarterly, or annually. Here are some key aspects to consider:

1. **Premium Content Access**: Subscribers typically gain access to exclusive in-game content, such as additional levels, characters, cosmetics, or virtual currency. This content is often gated behind the subscription paywall.
2. **Steady Revenue Stream**: Subscriptions provide a predictable and regular income stream for game developers. This stability can help support ongoing development and updates.
3. **Player Retention**: Subscribers are incentivized to continue playing the game to make the most of their subscription. This can lead to increased player retention and engagement.
4. **Tiered Subscriptions**: Offer multiple subscription tiers with varying benefits. Higher tiers may provide more

exclusive content or faster progression. This allows players to choose the level of commitment that suits them.

5. **Trial Periods**: Consider offering a free trial period to allow players to experience the subscription benefits before committing. This can help attract new subscribers.
6. **Communication**: Clearly communicate the value of the subscription to potential subscribers. Regularly update them on the exclusive content and benefits they receive as part of their subscription.
7. **Community Building**: Subscribers often form a dedicated community within the game. Encourage interaction and engagement among subscribers to strengthen this community.

Freemium Monetization

Freemium models involve offering a game for free with the option for players to make in-game purchases. While the core gameplay is accessible without spending money, players can enhance their experience through microtransactions. Here are some considerations for freemium monetization:

1. **In-App Purchases (IAPs)**: Implement a range of in-game items, cosmetics, or virtual currency that players can purchase. Ensure that these purchases are not necessary for basic gameplay.
2. **Ad Revenue**: Consider integrating ads into your free game. Players can choose to watch ads voluntarily in exchange for rewards, such as in-game currency or power-ups.
3. **Balance and Fairness**: Maintain a fair playing field by avoiding pay-to-win mechanics. In-app purchases should provide convenience or cosmetic enhancements rather than gameplay advantages.

4. **Virtual Currency**: Implement a virtual currency system that players can buy and spend in various ways. This can make purchases more accessible and appealing.
5. **Limited-Time Offers**: Create time-limited promotions and discounts on in-game items. This encourages players to make purchases during specific events or periods.
6. **Energy Systems**: Some freemium games use energy or stamina systems that limit gameplay unless players wait or make a purchase to refill their energy. Use this mechanic judiciously to avoid frustrating players.
7. **Progression Balance**: Ensure that players who choose not to make in-game purchases can still progress and enjoy the game. Balance the difficulty curve accordingly.
8. **Data Analytics**: Monitor player behavior and spending patterns through analytics. This data can inform your monetization strategy and help you tailor offers to player preferences.
9. **Ethical Monetization**: Adhere to ethical monetization practices, making sure that players are not pressured or coerced into making purchases.
10. **Player Feedback**: Be open to player feedback and adjust your monetization strategy based on their preferences and concerns.

Both subscription-based and freemium models have their merits, and the choice between them depends on your game's genre, target audience, and content. Some games even combine elements of both models to offer players a variety of choices for monetization. The key is to strike a balance between generating revenue and delivering an enjoyable and fair gaming experience.

Section 16.4: Managing In-Game Economies

In-game economies play a pivotal role in the success of freemium and many online multiplayer games. They are the systems that govern the distribution, acquisition, and use of virtual goods and currency within the game world. Managing an in-game economy effectively requires careful planning and balance to ensure player engagement, progression, and monetization. This section explores the strategies and considerations involved in managing in-game economies.

Core Components of In-Game Economies

1. **Virtual Currency**: Most in-game economies revolve around a virtual currency. This currency can be earned through gameplay, purchased with real money, or a combination of both. It serves as the primary medium of exchange within the game.
2. **Virtual Goods**: These are the items, assets, or enhancements that players can acquire or purchase using virtual currency. Virtual goods can include weapons, skins, outfits, power-ups, and more.
3. **Monetization Mechanics**: In-game economies include various monetization mechanics, such as in-app purchases (IAPs), loot boxes, battle passes, or premium subscriptions. These mechanics offer players the opportunity to spend real money to acquire virtual goods or currency.
4. **Earning Opportunities**: Game developers must provide players with opportunities to earn virtual currency through gameplay. This can include rewards for completing missions, achievements, winning matches, or participating in events.
5. **Trading and Marketplaces**: Some games allow players to

trade virtual goods with each other or utilize virtual marketplaces where they can buy and sell items. This adds depth to the in-game economy and encourages player interaction.

6. **Economy Balancing**: Balancing the economy is crucial to prevent inflation or deflation of virtual currency. Developers must carefully adjust the rate at which players earn currency and the prices of virtual goods.

Strategies for Effective In-Game Economy Management

1. **Economy Design**: Start by designing a well-defined economy that aligns with the game's goals and player experience. Consider the types of virtual goods available, their rarity, and their impact on gameplay.
2. **Player Progression**: Ensure that the in-game economy contributes to player progression. Allow players to earn virtual currency and valuable items through skill and effort, creating a sense of achievement.
3. **Monetization Balance**: Maintain a delicate balance between monetization and player engagement. Avoid creating a pay-to-win environment where players can purchase a significant advantage.
4. **Limited-Time Offers**: Implement limited-time offers and events that create a sense of urgency and encourage spending. These can include sales, bundles, or exclusive items available for a short duration.
5. **Data Analysis**: Continuously analyze player behavior and spending patterns. Use data to identify trends and optimize the in-game economy, pricing, and offers accordingly.
6. **Economic Feedback Loop**: Encourage player feedback on the in-game economy. Engage with the community to

understand their concerns and preferences, and be open to making adjustments based on their feedback.

7. **Regular Updates**: Keep the in-game economy fresh by regularly introducing new virtual goods, cosmetics, or content. This keeps players engaged and provides opportunities for monetization.
8. **Fairness and Transparency**: Be transparent about the odds of acquiring rare items from loot boxes or gacha systems. Ensure that players understand the value of their purchases.
9. **Anti-Fraud Measures**: Implement anti-fraud measures to prevent cheating or exploiting the in-game economy. This includes monitoring and taking action against illegitimate transactions.
10. **Ethical Monetization**: Prioritize ethical monetization practices. Avoid exploiting player psychology and adhere to industry standards for fair pricing and engagement mechanics.

A well-managed in-game economy can enhance player engagement, extend the lifespan of your game, and drive revenue. However, it's crucial to strike a balance between monetization and player satisfaction to maintain a positive player experience and foster a loyal player base.

Section 16.5: Ethical Considerations in Game Monetization

Ethical considerations in game monetization are of paramount importance in today's gaming industry. Developers and publishers must prioritize player well-being and fair play while generating revenue. This section delves into various ethical aspects to keep in mind when designing your game's monetization strategies.

Player-Centric Ethical Practices

1. **Transparency**: Be transparent about your game's monetization methods. Clearly communicate how in-game purchases work, including the odds of acquiring specific items from loot boxes or gacha systems.
2. **Informed Consent**: Ensure that players provide informed consent before making purchases. Avoid misleading or coercive tactics that pressure players into spending money.
3. **Fair Pricing**: Set fair and reasonable prices for in-game items and currency. Avoid exploiting players with exorbitant prices for virtual goods.
4. **No Pay-to-Win**: Avoid creating a pay-to-win environment where players can gain a significant advantage by spending money. Monetization should not disrupt the game's balance or fairness.
5. **No Predatory Practices**: Do not engage in predatory practices, such as targeting vulnerable players, including children, or using manipulative tactics to encourage spending.
6. **Refund Policies**: Have clear refund policies in place. Allow players to request refunds for accidental purchases or dissatisfaction with their purchases.

7. **Limiting Spending**: Implement spending limits to prevent excessive spending by players. Encourage responsible spending habits.
8. **Age Ratings**: Adhere to age ratings and regional regulations for your game's monetization practices. Ensure that your game is suitable for its intended audience.

Community and Social Responsibility

1. **Community Feedback**: Listen to player feedback regarding monetization practices. Engage with the gaming community to address concerns and make improvements.
2. **Anti-Cheating Measures**: Implement anti-cheating measures to maintain a fair and competitive gaming environment. Cheating can undermine fair play and discourage honest players.
3. **Data Privacy**: Safeguard player data and privacy. Comply with data protection regulations and clearly communicate your data usage policies to players.
4. **Support for Vulnerable Players**: Provide support and resources for players who may be vulnerable to excessive spending or addiction. Offer options for self-imposed spending limits or temporary suspensions.

Ethical Advertising and Marketing

1. **Honest Advertising**: Ensure that advertisements for your game accurately represent its content and gameplay. Avoid using deceptive or clickbait marketing tactics.
2. **Age-Appropriate Ads**: Display age-appropriate ads within your game. Ensure that ads targeting minors are suitable for their age group.
3. **No Exploitative Ads**: Do not display ads that promote

scams, harmful products, or illegal activities. Verify the legitimacy and ethics of advertising partners.

4. **Ad Frequency**: Limit the frequency of in-game ads to maintain an enjoyable player experience. Excessive ad interruptions can deter players.

Social Responsibility

1. **Charitable Initiatives**: Consider charitable initiatives or collaborations to give back to the community or support relevant causes.
2. **Environmental Impact**: Be mindful of the environmental impact of your game development and distribution processes. Implement eco-friendly practices where feasible.
3. **Diversity and Inclusion**: Promote diversity and inclusion in your game content, development teams, and player communities. Create a welcoming and inclusive environment.

Ethical game monetization practices not only contribute to a positive player experience but also foster trust and long-term loyalty among your player base. By prioritizing ethical considerations, you can build a reputation for fairness, responsibility, and social consciousness in the gaming industry.

Chapter 17: Advanced Debugging and Error Handling

Section 17.1: Complex Bug Tracking and Resolution

In the world of game development, complex bugs are inevitable. These issues can range from obscure crashes and performance bottlenecks to unexpected gameplay behaviors. Effectively tracking and resolving such bugs is a critical skill for developers. This section explores advanced techniques for identifying, tracking, and resolving complex bugs in your game code.

1. Logging and Instrumentation

Implement comprehensive logging and instrumentation in your game code. This involves strategically placing log statements and tracking metrics to gather data on the game's behavior during runtime. Use logging levels (e.g., debug, info, warning, error) to categorize log messages and prioritize them based on severity.

Example (C++):

```
// Logging a debug message

LogDebug("Player health decreased by 10 points.");

// Logging an error message

LogError("Failed to load game assets.");
```

Logging and instrumentation provide valuable insights into the game's execution flow, making it easier to pinpoint issues.

2. Crash Dump Analysis

When your game crashes, generate crash dumps that capture the state of the application at the time of the crash. Analyze these dumps using debugging tools like WinDbg or GDB. Crash dumps can reveal the exact location and cause of crashes, helping you fix them more efficiently.

3. Profiling Tools

Utilize profiling tools to identify performance bottlenecks and memory leaks. Profilers like Intel VTune, NVIDIA Nsight, or built-in profiling tools in game engines provide detailed performance analysis. Addressing performance issues can lead to smoother gameplay experiences.

4. Reproducible Test Cases

Encourage the creation of reproducible test cases for bugs. Repro steps make it easier to isolate the problem and verify fixes. Collaborate with QA teams and testers to gather detailed steps to reproduce complex bugs.

5. Static Analysis

Employ static analysis tools to scan your codebase for potential issues. These tools can detect code patterns that may lead to bugs, such as uninitialized variables or null pointer dereferences. Static analysis can help catch issues early in the development process.

6. Code Reviews and Pair Programming

Collaborate with team members through code reviews and pair programming. A fresh set of eyes can catch issues that you might overlook. Discussing code with peers can lead to insights and solutions for complex problems.

7. Version Control and Issue Tracking

Use version control systems (e.g., Git) and issue tracking systems (e.g., Jira, Bugzilla) to manage code changes and track bug reports. Linking issues to specific code changes helps in monitoring bug progress and ensures that fixes are properly documented.

8. Automated Testing

Implement automated tests, including unit tests and integration tests, to catch regressions and verify fixes. Continuous integration (CI) pipelines can automatically run tests whenever code changes are submitted.

9. Root Cause Analysis

When investigating complex bugs, aim for root cause analysis rather than superficial fixes. Understand the underlying cause of the bug to prevent similar issues in the future.

10. Documentation

Document complex bug resolutions comprehensively. This documentation aids future developers who may encounter similar issues. Include details on the problem, the analysis performed, and the solution applied.

11. Post-Mortems

Conduct post-mortem reviews after resolving complex bugs **or** critical issues. Post-mortems help teams learn **from** their experiences **and** improve development processes.

Mastering the art of tracking and resolving complex bugs is a continuous journey in game development. By leveraging advanced techniques and collaborating effectively with your team, you can enhance your debugging and error handling skills, resulting in more stable and polished games.

Section 17.2: Automated Testing and Continuous Integration

Automated testing and continuous integration (CI) are fundamental practices in modern game development that play a pivotal role in identifying and preventing bugs, ensuring code quality, and streamlining the development process. This section delves into the importance of automated testing and CI pipelines in advanced debugging and error handling.

1. Types of Automated Tests

Automated tests come in various forms, each serving a specific purpose:

- **Unit Tests:** These tests focus on small, isolated components of your code, such as functions or classes. They ensure that individual pieces of code work as intended. Unit tests are particularly useful for identifying logical errors.

- **Integration Tests:** Integration tests verify the interactions between different parts of your game or system. They help ensure that components work together harmoniously. For example, you might test the integration between the physics engine and character controller.

- **Functional Tests:** Functional tests examine the game's functionality from an end-user perspective. They validate that features and gameplay mechanics behave as expected. These tests can catch gameplay bugs early.

- **Regression Tests:** Regression tests check whether recent code changes introduce new bugs or regressions. They help maintain the stability of existing features while new ones are added.

2. Test Automation Frameworks

Choose appropriate test automation frameworks and tools based on your game's programming language and engine. Popular choices include:

- **Unity Test Framework:** For Unity game development, the Unity Test Framework allows you to create and run unit tests within the Unity Editor.

- **Unreal Engine Testing Framework:** Unreal Engine provides its testing framework for creating functional and unit tests for your game logic.

- **Third-Party Frameworks:** Depending on your programming language (e.g., NUnit, PyTest, JUnit), you can use third-party testing frameworks to write and execute tests.

3. Continuous Integration (CI) Pipelines

Implement CI pipelines that automatically build, test, and validate your game code whenever changes are committed to the version control system. CI pipelines typically consist of several stages, including:

- **Build Stage:** Compiles the game code and assets to create executable files or game builds.

- **Unit Test Stage:** Runs unit tests to verify the correctness of individual code components.

- **Integration Test Stage:** Executes integration tests to validate interactions between game systems.

- **Functional Test Stage:** Conducts functional tests to ensure gameplay features work as expected.

- **Deployment Stage:** Deploys the game to target platforms or environments for further testing.

4. CI Platforms

Several CI platforms cater to different game engines and programming languages. Examples include:

- **Travis CI:** A cloud-based CI service that supports various languages and platforms.

- **Jenkins:** An open-source automation server that can be customized to suit your game development needs.

- **GitHub Actions:** Integrated directly into GitHub repositories, it enables CI/CD workflows for your game projects.

- **GitLab CI/CD:** A built-in CI/CD solution within GitLab for seamless integration with your Git repositories.

5. Benefits of CI

CI offers several advantages in the context of advanced debugging and error handling:

- **Early Bug Detection:** Automated tests catch bugs early in the development cycle, reducing the likelihood of critical issues reaching production.

- **Consistency:** CI ensures consistent and reproducible builds and tests across different development environments.

- **Faster Feedback:** Developers receive rapid feedback on code changes, making it easier to identify and resolve issues promptly.

- **Confidence:** CI instills confidence in code changes, knowing that automated tests validate their correctness.

6. CI Best Practices

To maximize the benefits of CI in advanced debugging:

- Maintain a suite of meaningful tests that cover critical game functionality.

- Configure CI pipelines to run tests on multiple platforms and configurations.

- Monitor CI pipelines for failures and investigate issues promptly.

- Integrate CI with your issue tracking system to link code changes to bug reports.

Automated testing and continuous integration are indispensable tools for improving the reliability and stability of your game code. By incorporating these practices into your development workflow, you can streamline the debugging process and ensure a higher quality gaming experience for players.

Section 17.3: Handling Runtime Errors and Crashes

Handling runtime errors and crashes is a crucial aspect of game development, ensuring that your game remains stable and provides a seamless experience to players. This section explores strategies and best practices for detecting, diagnosing, and mitigating runtime errors and crashes in your game.

1. Runtime Errors vs. Crashes

Runtime errors and crashes are distinct issues:

- **Runtime Errors:** These are errors that occur while your game is running but do not terminate the application. Examples include null reference exceptions, out-of-bounds array access, or division by zero. Runtime errors can lead to unexpected behavior and negatively impact gameplay.

- **Crashes:** Crashes result in the abrupt termination of your game application. They can be caused by various factors, such as unhandled exceptions, memory leaks, or hardware-related issues. Crashes can frustrate players and tarnish your game's reputation.

2. Error Reporting and Logging

Implement a robust error reporting and logging system to capture information about runtime errors and crashes. Key elements of this system include:

- **Logging Severity Levels:** Use different severity levels for log messages to categorize issues. Common levels include INFO, WARNING, ERROR, and CRITICAL.

- **Stack Traces:** Include stack traces in error logs to pinpoint the location of the issue within your code. This information is invaluable for debugging.

- **User Feedback:** Encourage players to report errors and crashes, providing an easy mechanism within the game to submit feedback. Collecting user data can help identify common issues.

3. Exception Handling

Proper exception handling is essential for gracefully managing runtime errors. Implement try-catch blocks to catch exceptions and handle them appropriately:

```
try

{

// Code that may throw an exception

}

catch (Exception ex)

{

// Handle the exception (e.g., log it, display an error message)

}
```

Handle exceptions based on their type, and consider whether it's safe to continue the game's execution or if it should gracefully exit.

4. Memory Management

Memory-related issues, such as memory leaks or accessing deallocated memory, can lead to crashes. Utilize memory profiling tools and best practices to manage memory effectively:

- Use smart pointers or garbage collection (depending on your programming language) to automate memory management.

- Regularly profile memory usage and look for memory leaks using tools like Valgrind, Instruments (for macOS), or your game engine's built-in profiler.

5. Crash Dumps and Minidumps

When your game crashes, it's beneficial to generate crash dumps or minidumps. These files contain valuable information about the state of the game at the time of the crash, including memory contents and call stacks. Developers can analyze these dumps to diagnose the root cause of crashes.

6. Automatic Crash Reporting

Implement automatic crash reporting tools and services that allow players to send crash reports directly to your development team. Services like Sentry, Bugsnag, or custom solutions can help collect crash data efficiently.

7. Continuous Testing

Incorporate continuous testing into your development pipeline. This includes both automated and manual testing to identify and address runtime errors and crashes during development and before releasing updates.

8. User-Friendly Error Handling

When a runtime error occurs, provide user-friendly error messages or feedback instead of cryptic technical details. This helps players understand the issue and prevents frustration.

9. Debugging Tools

Equip your development team with powerful debugging tools and profilers to identify and resolve runtime issues efficiently. Common debugging tools include Visual Studio Debugger, GDB, and Unity Profiler.

10. Monitoring in Production

After your game is live, monitor for runtime errors and crashes in the production environment. Implement remote logging and error reporting to gather data from players' devices.

Handling runtime errors and crashes requires a proactive approach throughout the development lifecycle. By implementing robust error reporting, effective exception handling, and continuous testing, you can enhance your game's stability and provide a smoother gaming experience for players.

Section 17.4: Debugging Multiplayer and Network Issues

Debugging multiplayer and network issues is a critical aspect of game development, particularly for online multiplayer games. Ensuring that the networked components of your game function correctly is essential for providing players with a smooth and enjoyable gaming experience. This section discusses common challenges, tools, and strategies for debugging multiplayer and network-related problems in your game.

1. Understanding Networked Systems

Before you can effectively debug network issues, it's crucial to have a deep understanding of the networked systems in your game. This includes:

- **Client-Server Architecture:** Familiarize yourself with how your game's client and server components interact. Understand the flow of data between clients and the server.

- **Protocols and Data Serialization:** Know the communication protocols and data serialization formats used for network messages. Ensure consistency between clients and the server.

- **Latency and Bandwidth Considerations:** Be aware of the impact of latency and limited bandwidth on networked gameplay. Implement techniques to mitigate these issues, such as interpolation and bandwidth optimization.

2. Network Emulation and Simulation

Network emulation tools like tc (Traffic Control) on Linux or network simulators can be invaluable for testing your game under various network conditions. Simulate high latency, packet loss, or low bandwidth to identify how your game behaves in adverse network environments.

3. Logging and Diagnostics

Implement extensive logging and diagnostics for your network code. Log important events, messages sent and received, and any errors or exceptions that occur during network communication. Use different log levels to categorize messages for easier analysis.

```
# Example of logging network messages in Python

import logging

logging.basicConfig(level=logging.DEBUG)

logger = logging.getLogger("network")

def send_message(message):

# Send the message

logger.debug("Sent: %s", message)

def receive_message():

# Receive a message

message = "Received message from server"

logger.debug("Received: %s", message)

return message
```

4. Packet Inspection and Wireshark

Wireshark is a powerful tool for capturing and analyzing network traffic. You can use it to inspect packets exchanged between your game clients and server. Look for anomalies, unexpected data, or communication errors that may be causing network issues.

5. Reproducible Test Cases

To debug network problems effectively, strive to create reproducible test cases that trigger the issue consistently. Having a reliable way to recreate the problem simplifies the debugging process.

6. Peer-to-Peer Debugging

In peer-to-peer networking scenarios, enable peer-to-peer debugging tools that allow you to view the state of each peer and their interactions. This can help identify synchronization issues or discrepancies between peers.

7. Latency Compensation

Implement latency compensation techniques in your game to minimize the perceived impact of network latency on gameplay. Techniques like client-side prediction and server reconciliation can improve the responsiveness of your game.

8. Synchronization and Authoritative Server

Ensure that your server is authoritative and responsible for critical game logic to prevent cheating or synchronization issues. Clients should send input and receive updates from the server to maintain consistency.

9. Load Testing

Perform load testing to evaluate how your server handles a high volume of concurrent players. Identify performance bottlenecks and optimize your server code to handle the load gracefully.

10. Cross-Platform Compatibility

Test your game on different platforms and operating systems to verify that network communication works consistently across various environments.

11. Security Audits

Conduct security audits to identify and address potential vulnerabilities in your network code, such as denial-of-service (DoS) attacks or unauthorized access.

Debugging multiplayer and network issues can be challenging due to the complexity of networked systems. However, with a combination of thorough testing, diagnostic tools, and a deep understanding of network protocols, you can ensure that your multiplayer game provides a stable and enjoyable experience for players.

Section 17.5: Establishing Effective QA Processes

Establishing effective Quality Assurance (QA) processes is crucial in game development to ensure the final product meets high standards of quality, functionality, and stability. QA encompasses a wide range of activities, from bug testing to usability testing, and plays a significant role in delivering a polished and enjoyable game. In this section, we'll explore key considerations for establishing robust QA processes.

1. Test Planning and Strategy

Begin by creating a comprehensive test plan that outlines your QA strategy. Define test objectives, scope, test cases, and acceptance criteria. Consider various testing types, such as functional, regression, performance, and compatibility testing, depending on your game's requirements.

2. Test Case Design

Develop well-documented test cases that cover different aspects of your game. Include step-by-step instructions, expected results, and any preconditions necessary for each test case. This documentation ensures that tests are executed consistently.

Example Test Case (Functional Testing):

Test Case ID: TC001

Test Case Name: Player Movement

Test Description: Verify that the player character can move in all directions.

Preconditions: Player character is spawned in the game.

Test Steps:

1. Move the character forward.

2. Move the character backward.

3. Move the character left.

4. Move the character right.

Expected Result: The character moves correctly in all directions without issues.

3. Automated Testing

Implement automated testing where possible, especially for repetitive and time-consuming tests. Automated tests can be used for regression testing, ensuring that new code changes don't introduce old bugs.

```
# Example of an automated test in Python using the unittest framework

import unittest

class TestPlayerMovement(unittest.TestCase):

def test_move_forward(self):

# Simulate moving the character forward
result = move_character_forward()

self.assertEqual(result, "Character moved forward successfully")

def test_move_backward(self):

# Simulate moving the character backward
```

```
result = move_character_backward()

self.assertEqual(result, "Character moved backward successfully")

# Similar tests for left and right movements
```

4. Regression Testing

Continuously perform regression testing to verify that recent code changes haven't introduced new defects or broken existing features. Maintain a regression test suite that covers critical game functionality.

5. Bug Tracking and Reporting

Implement a bug tracking system to record and manage issues identified during testing. Include details such as the bug's severity, steps to reproduce, and a clear description. This helps developers prioritize and address bugs effectively.

6. Usability Testing

Conduct usability testing with real players to gather feedback on the game's user interface, controls, and overall experience. Use this feedback to make improvements that enhance player satisfaction.

7. Performance Testing

Test your game's performance under various conditions, including different hardware configurations and network conditions. Identify performance bottlenecks and optimize your game code accordingly.

8. Localization and Accessibility Testing

If your game is targeting international markets, perform localization testing to ensure it's culturally and linguistically appropriate.

Additionally, test for accessibility to ensure that players with disabilities can enjoy the game.

9. Continuous Integration and Delivery (CI/CD)

Implement CI/CD pipelines that automate the testing and deployment process. This ensures that builds are automatically tested, and stable versions of the game are regularly delivered.

10. User Acceptance Testing (UAT)

Involve external users or focus groups in UAT to gather feedback from a broader audience. Their insights can uncover issues that internal testing might have missed.

11. Documentation

Maintain comprehensive documentation for your QA processes, including test plans, test cases, bug reports, and testing schedules. Well-documented processes help streamline QA efforts.

12. Feedback Loops

Establish feedback loops between QA, development, and design teams. Encourage open communication to address issues promptly and improve collaboration.

Effective QA processes are iterative and require continuous improvement. Regularly review and refine your QA strategies to adapt to the evolving needs of your game development project. By investing in quality assurance, you can enhance the overall player experience and increase the chances of your game's success in the market.

Chapter 18: Legal and Ethical Considerations

Section 18.1: Intellectual Property Rights in Game Development

Intellectual property (IP) rights play a pivotal role in the game development industry. Understanding these rights is essential to protect your creative work and navigate the legal landscape. In this section, we'll delve into intellectual property rights in game development, including copyrights, trademarks, patents, and trade secrets.

Copyrights

Copyright is one of the most fundamental aspects of intellectual property rights in game development. It provides legal protection for original creative works, including video games, their source code, graphics, music, and storylines. Here are key considerations regarding copyrights:

1. **Ownership**: The creator or team behind a game typically holds the copyright to the game's content. However, if you're working with a team, it's essential to establish clear ownership agreements to avoid disputes.
2. **Registration**: While copyright is automatically granted upon creation, registering your game with the relevant copyright office provides additional legal benefits, such as the ability to sue for statutory damages in case of infringement.
3. **Fair Use**: Understand the concept of "fair use," which allows limited use of copyrighted material for purposes like commentary, criticism, or parody. However, relying solely

on fair use can be legally risky, so it's best to obtain permission or use content that is explicitly licensed for such purposes.

4. **Derivative Works**: Be cautious when creating derivative works based on existing copyrighted content. Seek proper licensing or legal advice to ensure compliance.
5. **Open Source Software**: If your game uses open source software, adhere to the licensing terms of those components. Failure to do so can lead to legal complications.

Trademarks

Trademarks protect branding elements such as logos, game titles, and characters. Here's what you need to know about trademarks in game development:

1. **Distinctiveness**: To qualify for trademark protection, your game's branding elements must be distinctive and not generic. Conduct a trademark search to ensure your chosen name or logo is unique.
2. **Registration**: Like copyrights, registering your trademarks provides stronger legal protection. It prevents others from using similar marks for similar goods or services.
3. **Use in Commerce**: To maintain trademark rights, you must use the trademark in commerce. Neglecting this can result in the loss of your trademark.

Patents

Patents protect inventions, processes, or unique gameplay mechanics. However, obtaining a patent for a game can be complex, and their relevance varies in the gaming industry.

1. **Utility Patents**: These protect new and useful processes, machines, or compositions of matter. In gaming, utility patents might apply to novel hardware devices or unique algorithms.
2. **Design Patents**: These protect the ornamental design of a functional item. In gaming, design patents could cover the visual appearance of game hardware or unique controller designs.
3. **Game Mechanics**: Patents for game mechanics are challenging to obtain, and their applicability is a subject of debate. Courts have ruled differently on whether specific game mechanics are patentable.

Trade Secrets

Trade secrets encompass confidential and valuable information that gives your game a competitive edge. Protecting trade secrets involves taking measures to keep them confidential:

1. **Non-Disclosure Agreements (NDAs)**: Use NDAs when sharing sensitive information with employees, contractors, or partners.
2. **Access Control**: Restrict access to critical game assets and source code on a need-to-know basis.
3. **Encryption**: Encrypt sensitive data to prevent unauthorized access.

4. **Security Policies**: Implement security policies and employee training to safeguard trade secrets.
5. **Non-Compete Clauses**: Include non-compete clauses in contracts to prevent individuals from using your trade secrets to create competing games.

Enforcement

Infringement of intellectual property rights is a common concern in the game industry. To enforce your rights, consider these actions:

1. **Cease and Desist Letters**: Send a cease and desist letter to alleged infringers, demanding they stop the infringing activities.
2. **Legal Action**: If necessary, take legal action to protect your rights, which may include filing lawsuits for copyright, trademark, or patent infringement.
3. **Alternative Dispute Resolution**: Explore alternative dispute resolution methods, such as arbitration or mediation, to resolve IP disputes without going to court.
4. **Licensing**: Consider licensing your IP to others, which can be a revenue source while allowing you to maintain control over your creations.
5. **Regular IP Audits**: Periodically review your intellectual property portfolio and assess its value and legal protection.
6. **Stay Informed**: Keep abreast of changes in IP law and industry trends to adapt your strategies accordingly.

Remember that the legal aspects of intellectual property can be complex, and it's advisable to consult with legal professionals who specialize in intellectual property law to ensure your game's protection and compliance with the law. Properly managing intellectual property rights is vital for the long-term success and sustainability of your game development endeavors.

Section 18.2: Navigating Licensing and Compliance

Navigating licensing and compliance is a crucial aspect of game development, as it involves adhering to legal and contractual requirements related to third-party assets, software libraries, and platforms. In this section, we'll explore the key considerations and best practices for licensing and compliance in the game development industry.

Licensing of Third-Party Assets

Game development often relies on various assets, including music, sound effects, graphics, and 3D models, which may be created by third-party artists, musicians, or studios. When using such assets, it's essential to understand the licensing terms and obtain the appropriate permissions or licenses.

1. **License Types**: Common license types for third-party assets include royalty-free, creative commons, and exclusive licenses. Ensure you choose a license that aligns with your project's needs and budget.
2. **Attribution**: Some licenses require attribution to the original creator. Ensure you provide proper credit as specified in the license agreement.
3. **Exclusive Licenses**: If you require exclusive rights to an asset, negotiate and document the terms carefully to prevent others from using the same asset in similar projects.
4. **Rights Transfer**: Understand whether the license allows you to transfer or sublicense the asset. This can be essential

if your game is sold, acquired, or developed by multiple parties.

5. **License Duration**: Determine the duration of the license. Some licenses may be perpetual, while others are limited in time.
6. **License Fees**: Be aware of any license fees or royalties associated with third-party assets. Factor these costs into your budget.
7. **License Renewal**: If your project has a long development cycle, check if the license needs renewal during development and plan accordingly.

Open Source Software (OSS) Compliance

Many game developers use open source software components and libraries to streamline development. However, using OSS requires compliance with its respective licenses. Here's what you need to consider:

1. **License Compatibility**: Ensure that the OSS licenses used in your project are compatible with each other and your game's intended distribution method.
2. **License Review**: Conduct a comprehensive review of OSS licenses within your project to identify any potential conflicts or compliance issues.
3. **Attribution**: If required by the OSS license, provide proper attribution in your game's documentation or credits.
4. **License Documentation**: Maintain documentation that clearly outlines the OSS components used, their licenses, and any modifications made.
5. **License Disclosure**: Some licenses may require you to

disclose the use of OSS in your game's distribution. Ensure you comply with these requirements.

6. **Contribution Policies**: If your project allows external contributions, establish clear policies and guidelines for contributors to ensure their work aligns with your project's licensing.

Platform and Storefront Compliance

Publishing games on platforms and digital storefronts like Steam, Apple App Store, Google Play, and others comes with specific compliance requirements:

1. **Content Guidelines**: Review and adhere to the content guidelines provided by the platform or storefront. Failure to comply can lead to the removal of your game.
2. **Age Ratings**: Obtain the appropriate age ratings and content descriptors for your game to ensure it's suitable for the target audience.
3. **In-App Purchases and Monetization**: Follow the platform's rules regarding in-app purchases, advertisements, and monetization practices.
4. **User Data**: Safeguard user data and privacy in compliance with relevant data protection regulations, such as GDPR.
5. **Updates and Patching**: Be prepared to release updates or patches to address any compliance issues or bugs identified by the platform.
6. **Digital Rights Management (DRM)**: Consider DRM options if necessary, but balance their use with user experience and potential impact on legitimate customers.

Legal Counsel and Compliance Review

Engaging legal counsel experienced in the game industry is highly recommended to ensure compliance with licensing agreements, intellectual property rights, and industry regulations. Legal professionals can review contracts, offer guidance on compliance matters, and assist in dispute resolution if needed.

In summary, navigating licensing and compliance in game development involves careful consideration of licensing agreements for third-party assets, compliance with open source software licenses, adherence to platform and storefront requirements, and legal counsel to ensure your game's compliance with industry regulations and intellectual property rights. Proactive compliance measures can help mitigate legal risks and ensure the successful release and distribution of your game.

Section 18.3: Addressing Privacy and Data Protection

Addressing privacy and data protection is a fundamental aspect of modern game development, as games often collect and process user data. In this section, we'll delve into key considerations and best practices for safeguarding user privacy and complying with data protection regulations.

User Data Collection and Consent

1. **Transparency**: Clearly communicate to players what data you collect, why you collect it, and how it will be used. This information should be easily accessible, such as through a privacy policy.
2. **Explicit Consent**: In regions like the European Union (EU), ensure you obtain explicit consent from players before collecting personal data. Implement a consent mechanism that allows players to opt in or out of data collection.
3. **Age Verification**: If your game is targeted at children or has content suitable for children, implement age verification mechanisms to prevent data collection from minors without parental consent.
4. **Data Minimization**: Collect only the data necessary for the game's functionality. Avoid excessive or unnecessary data collection.

GDPR Compliance

If your game is accessible to players in the EU, it must comply with the General Data Protection Regulation (GDPR). Key considerations include:

1. **Data Protection Officer (DPO)**: Appoint a Data Protection Officer if required by GDPR. This individual oversees data protection activities within your organization.
2. **Data Subject Rights**: Understand and facilitate data subject rights, including the right to access, rectify, or delete personal data.
3. **Data Processing Records**: Maintain records of data processing activities, including purposes, categories of data, and third-party recipients.
4. **Data Breach Notification**: Develop a data breach response plan and notify relevant authorities and affected individuals promptly in the event of a data breach.

Data Security

1. **Encryption**: Implement encryption for sensitive data both in transit and at rest. Use secure protocols for data transfer.
2. **Access Control**: Restrict access to user data based on roles and responsibilities. Only authorized personnel should have access to sensitive data.
3. **Data Storage**: Store user data securely, ensuring that databases and cloud storage solutions are configured with strong security measures.
4. **Regular Auditing**: Conduct regular security audits and vulnerability assessments to identify and address potential

weaknesses.

Data Retention and Deletion

1. **Data Retention Policy**: Develop a data retention policy that specifies how long user data will be retained. Delete data that is no longer necessary for the purposes for which it was collected.
2. **User Data Deletion**: Allow users to request the deletion of their data. Implement procedures to fulfill such requests promptly.

Third-Party Services and SDKs

Be cautious when integrating third-party services, analytics tools, or software development kits (SDKs) into your game. Ensure that these services also comply with privacy regulations and follow best practices.

Consent and Opt-Out Mechanisms

1. **Granular Consent**: Provide players with granular options to consent or opt out of specific data collection activities, such as location tracking or personalized ads.
2. **Opt-Out at Any Time**: Allow players to change their data preferences or withdraw consent at any time through in-game settings.

Privacy by Design

Incorporate privacy considerations into the game's design and development from the outset. Conduct privacy impact assessments to identify and mitigate potential risks.

Privacy Policy

Draft a clear and comprehensive privacy policy that explains your data practices to players. Ensure that it is easily accessible within the game, on your website, or through app stores.

Compliance Verification

Consider seeking legal counsel or consulting privacy experts to verify your game's compliance with relevant privacy laws and regulations.

In conclusion, addressing privacy and data protection is paramount in modern game development. Game creators must be transparent about data practices, comply with regulations like GDPR when applicable, secure user data, and provide mechanisms for data control and deletion. Prioritizing user privacy not only helps maintain legal compliance but also builds trust with players, fostering a positive gaming experience.

Section 18.4: Ethical Dilemmas in Game Content

Ethical considerations in game content have gained prominence in recent years as the gaming industry faces scrutiny over various aspects of game design and storytelling. This section explores some of the ethical dilemmas game developers may encounter and offers guidance on addressing them.

Representation and Diversity

1. **Inclusive Representation**: Strive for diverse and inclusive representation of gender, race, ethnicity, sexual orientation, and other identities in both characters and storylines. Avoid stereotypes and tropes that perpetuate harmful biases.
2. **Sensitivity and Cultural Respect**: Be culturally sensitive and respectful when portraying different cultures, traditions, and beliefs. Collaborate with cultural consultants or experts to ensure accuracy.
3. **Player Customization**: Allow players to customize their characters' appearances, genders, and identities to create a more inclusive experience.

Violence and Graphic Content

1. **Content Warnings**: Provide appropriate content warnings for violent or graphic content. Allow players to opt in or out of such content, especially in games that explore mature themes.
2. **Realistic Violence**: Be cautious when depicting realistic

violence, especially if it serves as entertainment rather than a narrative tool. Avoid gratuitous violence.

3. **Impact on Mental Health**: Consider the potential impact of violent or disturbing content on players' mental health and well-being. Provide resources or support for players who may be affected.

Monetization Practices

1. **Loot Boxes and Gambling**: Be transparent about the presence of loot boxes or randomized microtransactions. Ensure they are not designed to exploit players or encourage gambling-like behavior, especially among minors.
2. **Pay-to-Win**: Avoid pay-to-win mechanics that give paying players a significant advantage over non-paying players. Strive for a balanced and fair gameplay experience.
3. **Predatory Practices**: Steer clear of predatory monetization practices that manipulate players into spending excessively. Implement spending limits and encourage responsible spending.

Inclusivity and Accessibility

1. **Accessibility Features**: Implement accessibility features, such as customizable controls, subtitles, and colorblind modes, to ensure that players with disabilities can enjoy the game.
2. **Inclusive Gameplay**: Consider the needs of players with different skill levels and gaming experiences. Provide options for both casual and hardcore gamers.

Social and Online Interactions

1. **Toxic Behavior**: Implement measures to combat toxic behavior, hate speech, and harassment within online communities. Encourage positive and respectful interactions among players.
2. **Reporting and Moderation**: Provide reporting tools and effective moderation systems to address problematic behavior. Take appropriate actions against offenders.

Narrative Choices

1. **Moral Choices**: Present players with meaningful moral choices in the game's narrative. Avoid scenarios that promote harmful behaviors or attitudes.
2. **Consequences**: Ensure that player choices have consequences within the game world. Show the impact of their decisions on characters and the story.

Cultural Sensitivity

1. **Research and Consultation**: When creating narratives or settings inspired by real-world cultures, conduct thorough research and consult with members of those cultures to avoid misrepresentation and cultural appropriation.
2. **Acknowledgment**: Give credit to the cultures and sources of inspiration that contributed to your game's content.

Ethical Game Testing

1. **Informed Consent**: Obtain informed consent from playtesters and ensure they understand the content they

will experience during testing, particularly if it includes sensitive or disturbing themes.

2. **Support and Debriefing**: Offer support and debriefing sessions to playtesters after exposure to emotionally challenging content.

In conclusion, navigating ethical dilemmas in game content requires careful consideration and a commitment to creating a positive and inclusive gaming experience. By prioritizing representation, avoiding exploitative practices, promoting inclusivity, and respecting player choices, game developers can contribute to a healthier and more responsible gaming industry. Ethical game design not only benefits players but also strengthens the reputation of developers and the industry as a whole.

Section 18.5: Promoting Fair Play and Community Standards

Promoting fair play and community standards is essential for creating a positive gaming environment and ensuring the long-term success of online games. In this section, we will explore various aspects of maintaining a healthy gaming community and fostering an atmosphere of sportsmanship and inclusivity.

Code of Conduct

Establishing a clear and enforceable code of conduct is a fundamental step in promoting fair play and maintaining community standards. Your code of conduct should outline expected behavior, consequences for violations, and the values that the gaming community upholds. Some key points to consider include:

1. **Respect**: Emphasize the importance of respecting fellow players, regardless of their background, skill level, or opinions.
2. **Sportsmanship**: Encourage sportsmanship, which includes fair competition, acknowledging opponents' skills, and accepting defeat graciously.
3. **Anti-Harassment**: Explicitly prohibit harassment, hate speech, and toxic behavior. Make it clear that such actions will not be tolerated.
4. **Inclusivity**: Promote inclusivity by welcoming players from diverse backgrounds and ensuring they feel valued and represented.
5. **Reporting Mechanisms**: Provide clear instructions on

how to report inappropriate behavior and a system for addressing reports promptly.

Moderation and Enforcement

Creating a safe gaming environment requires active moderation and enforcement of community standards. Some best practices in this regard include:

1. **Moderator Training**: Ensure your moderation team is trained to handle various situations, from minor disputes to severe code of conduct violations.
2. **Consistency**: Apply rules and consequences consistently to all players. Avoid favoritism or bias in moderation decisions.
3. **Transparency**: Be transparent about the moderation process and decisions, while respecting privacy and confidentiality when necessary.
4. **Temporary and Permanent Bans**: Implement a system of temporary and permanent bans for players who repeatedly violate community standards or engage in egregious behavior.
5. **Community Involvement**: Involve the gaming community in discussions about rules and consequences, seeking input and feedback when appropriate.

Player Education

Educating players about the code of conduct and the importance of fair play is crucial. Consider these strategies:

1. **In-Game Notices**: Display the code of conduct

prominently within the game, and periodically remind players of its existence.

2. **Tutorials and Tips**: Include tutorials or tips on sportsmanship and positive behavior during loading screens or game sessions.
3. **Rewards for Good Behavior**: Reward players who consistently exhibit fair play and sportsmanship to incentivize positive conduct.
4. **Community Events**: Organize community events that promote fair play, cooperation, and a sense of belonging.

Reporting and Feedback

Encourage players to report inappropriate behavior and provide feedback on their gaming experiences. Establish channels for communication, such as:

1. **In-Game Reporting**: Implement an in-game reporting system that allows players to report harassment or rule violations directly.
2. **Player Surveys**: Conduct periodic player surveys to gather feedback on the community environment and identify areas for improvement.
3. **Community Forums**: Maintain official forums or social media groups where players can discuss community standards and provide feedback.

Continuous Improvement

Regularly evaluate and update your code of conduct and community standards to adapt to changing player expectations and evolving online environments. Consider forming a community council or advisory group to assist in these efforts.

Positive Reinforcement

Lastly, use positive reinforcement to reward players who actively promote fair play and contribute to a positive gaming community. Recognize and celebrate good behavior through in-game achievements, leaderboards, or other forms of acknowledgment.

In conclusion, promoting fair play and community standards in the gaming industry is an ongoing commitment. By setting clear expectations, enforcing rules consistently, educating players, and fostering open communication, game developers can create a welcoming and inclusive environment that enhances the overall gaming experience and contributes to the success of their games.

Chapter 19: Post-Launch Management and Evolution

Section 19.1: Strategies for Post-Launch Game Support

After a game's initial launch, the journey is far from over. Post-launch management and evolution are critical to maintaining a successful game and keeping players engaged over time. In this section, we'll explore various strategies and best practices for effectively managing your game after it's been released.

Continuous Updates and Content

One of the most effective ways to keep players engaged is by regularly releasing updates and new content. This can include bug fixes, balance adjustments, new features, levels, characters, or any other form of in-game content. Consider the following:

- **Roadmap**: Create a post-launch roadmap outlining your plans for upcoming updates. Share this roadmap with the community to build anticipation.

- **Community Feedback**: Listen to player feedback and prioritize updates based on their input. Engage with your community through forums, social media, or surveys.

- **Bug Fixes**: Address critical bugs and issues promptly to ensure a smooth gaming experience. Maintain a public list of known issues and their status.

- **Seasonal Events**: Host seasonal or themed in-game events to keep players engaged and excited. These events can introduce exclusive content or rewards.

Monetization Strategies

Post-launch is an opportunity to refine your game's monetization strategies. It's crucial to strike a balance between generating revenue and providing value to players. Consider the following approaches:

- **Microtransactions**: If your game includes microtransactions, ensure they are fair, transparent, and not pay-to-win. Offer cosmetic items or optional content that doesn't disrupt gameplay balance.

- **Subscription Models**: Explore subscription-based models that provide players with ongoing benefits, such as early access to new content or premium in-game currency.

- **In-Game Advertising**: If you use ads, optimize their placement and frequency to minimize disruptions to gameplay. Offer ad-free options for premium players.

Community Engagement

Maintaining an active and engaged player community is essential for the long-term success of your game. Consider these community engagement strategies:

- **Community Managers**: Appoint community managers or moderators to foster a positive and welcoming atmosphere. They can facilitate discussions, organize events, and address concerns.

- **Player-Created Content**: Encourage players to create and share their content, such as mods, skins, or user-generated levels. Support user-generated content platforms if applicable.

- **Developer Updates**: Regularly communicate with your community through developer blogs, patch notes, or livestreams. Share insights into the game's development process.

- **Player Support**: Provide efficient player support to address issues, inquiries, or account problems promptly. A responsive support team helps build trust.

Data-Driven Decision Making

Use player data and analytics to inform your post-launch strategies. Analyze player behavior, engagement metrics, and financial data to make informed decisions:

- **Player Retention**: Identify factors that contribute to player retention and engagement. Adjust your content and features accordingly.

- **A/B Testing**: Experiment with different features, pricing models, or content releases using A/B testing to determine what resonates best with your audience.

- **Economy Balancing**: Continuously monitor your in-game economy to ensure it remains fair and balanced. Adjust rewards, pricing, and progression systems as needed.

Cross-Platform and Cross-Progression

Consider enabling cross-platform play and cross-progression to broaden your game's appeal and retain players. This allows players to access their progress and content on different devices:

- **Cross-Platform Play**: Enable players on different platforms to play together seamlessly, expanding your game's player base.

- **Cross-Progression**: Allow players to transfer their progress and purchases between platforms, providing flexibility and convenience.

Marketing and Promotion

Sustained marketing efforts are vital for keeping your game visible and attracting new players post-launch:

- **Content Marketing**: Produce regular content, such as blogs, videos, or social media posts, to keep your game relevant and inform players about updates.

- **Influencer Partnerships**: Collaborate with influencers or content creators to showcase new content and reach a broader audience.

- **Seasonal Campaigns**: Run seasonal marketing campaigns tied to in-game events or updates to generate excitement.

Player Feedback and Iteration

Lastly, maintain a feedback loop with your players. Act on their feedback, iterate on your game's features, and demonstrate your commitment to improving the player experience.

In conclusion, post-launch management and evolution require a combination of player-focused strategies, data-driven decision-making, and ongoing community engagement. By consistently delivering quality updates, maintaining transparent monetization practices, and fostering a thriving player community, you can ensure the long-term success of your game in a competitive market.

Section 19.2: Managing Community Feedback and Expectations

Managing community feedback and expectations is a crucial aspect of post-launch game support. Your player community can be a valuable resource for improving your game, but it can also present challenges. In this section, we'll explore effective strategies for handling player feedback and setting realistic expectations.

Active Communication

Open and active communication with your player community is key. Here are some practices to consider:

- **Official Forums and Social Media**: Maintain official forums and social media channels where players can provide feedback and discuss the game. Assign community managers or moderators to monitor and engage in these spaces.

- **Feedback Channels**: Create dedicated channels for players to submit feedback, bug reports, and suggestions. Implement a clear and user-friendly system for players to communicate with the development team.

- **Regular Updates**: Keep players informed about ongoing development and upcoming changes. Share developer blogs, patch notes, and progress reports to demonstrate your commitment to the game.

- **Transparency**: Be transparent about the status of reported issues and the timeline for addressing them. Transparency builds trust with your community.

Prioritizing Feedback

Not all feedback is equal, and it's essential to prioritize and categorize player feedback effectively:

- **Bug Reports**: Quickly address critical bugs that impact gameplay or cause crashes. Maintain a public list of known issues and their status.

- **Gameplay Balancing**: Consider player feedback on gameplay balance, but use data and analytics to make informed decisions. Avoid knee-jerk reactions to individual complaints.

- **Feature Requests**: Track feature requests and gauge their popularity among players. Some requests may align with your game's vision, while others may not.

- **Community Voting**: Implement a community voting system for feature requests and changes. This allows players to have a direct influence on the development roadmap.

Feedback Analysis

Analyze player feedback and data to gain insights into player sentiment and preferences:

- **Sentiment Analysis**: Use sentiment analysis tools to assess whether player feedback is positive, negative, or neutral. Identify trends in sentiment over time.

- **Player Surveys**: Conduct surveys to gather structured feedback on specific aspects of the game, such as new features or changes.

- **Data-Driven Decisions**: Combine player feedback with in-game analytics to make data-driven decisions. For example, if players complain about a particular level's difficulty, analyze completion rates to confirm the issue.

- **User Testing**: Consider conducting user testing sessions with a diverse group of players to gather in-depth feedback and observe their interactions with the game.

Handling Negative Feedback

Negative feedback is inevitable, but how you handle it can make a significant difference:

- **Constructive Responses**: Respond to negative feedback professionally and constructively. Acknowledge the issue, thank the player for their input, and explain the steps you're taking to address it.

- **Avoid Arguments**: Avoid engaging in arguments or becoming defensive. Maintain a respectful tone and focus on solutions.

- **Community Guidelines**: Enforce community guidelines and rules to prevent toxic behavior or harassment within the player community.

- **Feedback Resolution**: Keep players updated on the resolution of reported issues. Share patch notes and confirm when bugs have been fixed.

Setting Realistic Expectations

Setting realistic expectations with your player community is essential to avoid disappointment and frustration:

- **Roadmap Sharing**: Share a clear roadmap outlining your plans for upcoming updates and content releases. Be transparent about what players can expect in the short and long term.

- **Release Timing**: Communicate estimated release timings for updates and new content, but emphasize that they are subject to change based on development needs.

- **Scope Management**: Avoid overpromising or setting unrealistic expectations regarding the scope of future updates. Ensure that you can deliver on your commitments.

- **Managing Hype**: While hype can be beneficial, be cautious not to overhype updates or features. Manage player expectations to minimize disappointment.

- **Surprise Content**: Occasionally, surprise players with unexpected content or features to create excitement and positive surprises.

In summary, managing community feedback and expectations requires a combination of active communication, effective prioritization, feedback analysis, and professionalism in handling negative feedback. By fostering a collaborative relationship with your player community and maintaining transparency, you can create a more positive and engaged player base while navigating the challenges of post-launch support.

Section 19.3: Iterative Development and Updates

Iterative development and regular updates are essential components of post-launch game management. In this section, we'll delve into the importance of iterative development, how to plan and execute updates effectively, and strategies for keeping your game fresh and engaging.

The Power of Iteration

Iterative development is a continuous improvement process that allows you to refine and expand your game based on player feedback and evolving market trends. Here's why it's crucial:

- **Player-Centric Focus**: Iteration puts players at the center of development. By listening to their feedback and adapting, you can create a game that resonates with your audience.

- **Adapting to Change**: The gaming industry is dynamic, with new technologies and trends emerging regularly. Iteration ensures your game can adapt to these changes.

- **Longevity**: Games with ongoing development tend to have longer lifespans. Players are more likely to stay engaged when they know there's more to come.

Planning Updates

Effective updates begin with thoughtful planning:

- **Roadmap**: Maintain a development roadmap that outlines your post-launch plans. Include details on the frequency of updates, the type of content or features you intend to add, and any overarching goals.

- **Player Feedback**: Continuously collect and analyze player feedback. Identify pain points, desired features, and areas for improvement. Use this data to inform your update plans.

- **Prioritization**: Prioritize updates based on player feedback, the impact on gameplay, and your game's strategic goals. Consider both quality-of-life improvements and content updates.

- **Testing**: Thoroughly test updates to ensure they are stable and bug-free. Consider using public test realms or beta versions to gather additional feedback from dedicated players.

Content Updates

Content updates are a core part of post-launch game management:

- **New Features**: Introduce new gameplay mechanics, features, or systems that enhance the player experience. This could include new characters, maps, game modes, or customization options.

- **Events and Seasons**: Implement special in-game events, seasons, or challenges to keep players engaged. These can offer exclusive rewards and create a sense of excitement.

- **Balancing**: Continuously balance gameplay elements to ensure fair competition. Adjust character abilities, weapon stats, or other variables based on player feedback and data analysis.

- **Storytelling**: Expand the game's narrative with episodic content or story arcs. Engaging storytelling can captivate players and keep them invested in the game world.

Community Involvement

Involving your player community in the update process can be highly rewarding:

- **Player Councils**: Consider establishing player councils or advisory groups composed of dedicated players. These individuals can provide valuable insights and act as liaisons between the community and development team.

- **Feedback Channels**: Maintain open feedback channels for players to suggest ideas and provide input on upcoming updates. Acknowledge and credit players for their contributions when appropriate.

- **Community Challenges**: Organize community challenges or contests that encourage players to create content or participate in events. Highlighting player contributions can foster a sense of ownership and pride.

Post-Launch Monetization

While offering free updates is important, you can also monetize post-launch content:

- **DLC and Expansion Packs**: Create downloadable content (DLC) or expansion packs that offer substantial additions to the game. Ensure that paid content is optional and doesn't fragment the player base.

- **Cosmetic Items**: Offer cosmetic items, such as skins, outfits, or customization options, that allow players to personalize their experience. Cosmetic microtransactions can be a sustainable revenue stream.

- **Battle Passes**: Implement battle passes or season passes that provide a structured way for players to unlock premium content through gameplay or purchase.

- **Subscription Models**: Explore subscription models that provide players with ongoing benefits, such as early access to updates, exclusive content, or in-game currency.

Community Celebrations

Celebrate milestones and anniversaries to maintain a sense of community:

- **Anniversary Events**: Host special in-game events and rewards to celebrate the game's launch anniversary. Reflect on the journey and achievements with your player community.

- **Player Appreciation**: Show gratitude to your players with exclusive gifts or in-game rewards during milestone celebrations. Acknowledge their role in the game's success.

- **Developer Insights**: Share developer insights, retrospectives, and behind-the-scenes content during anniversaries. This can provide players with a deeper connection to the development team.

Conclusion

Iterative development and regular updates are fundamental to post-launch game management. By planning updates strategically, involving the player community, monetizing content thoughtfully, and celebrating milestones, you can ensure that your game remains engaging and relevant in a competitive gaming landscape.

Section 19.4: Keeping Your Game Relevant in a Changing Market

In a constantly evolving gaming industry, keeping your game relevant is an ongoing challenge. This section explores strategies to ensure your game remains competitive and appealing to players in a changing market.

Market Research and Trends

To stay relevant, you must keep a close eye on market trends and player preferences:

- **Competitor Analysis**: Regularly analyze your competitors' games. Identify what makes them successful and assess areas where your game can excel or differentiate itself.

- **Player Surveys**: Conduct surveys or gather player feedback to understand their changing preferences. Ask about their expectations, favorite features, and areas where they'd like to see improvements.

- **Market Reports**: Study industry reports and trends to identify emerging technologies, gaming genres, and player demographics. Adapt your strategy to align with the shifting landscape.

Continuous Innovation

Innovation is key to maintaining player interest:

- **Feature Updates**: Regularly introduce new features, mechanics, or gameplay modes to keep the experience fresh. Experiment with innovative ideas that align with your game's identity.

- **Technology Integration**: Embrace new technologies, such as VR/AR, haptic feedback, or AI, when appropriate. These innovations can provide unique experiences that captivate players.

- **Storytelling Evolution**: If your game has a narrative component, evolve the story over time. Unexpected twists and character development can rekindle player engagement.

- **Cross-Platform Play**: Consider enabling cross-platform play to expand your player base and create a more inclusive gaming environment.

Community Engagement

A vibrant and engaged player community is a valuable asset:

- **Regular Communication**: Maintain open lines of communication with your community. Use social media, forums, and official channels to update players on upcoming changes and events.

- **Player-Driven Content**: Involve players in content creation through contests, user-generated content (UGC) features, or community challenges. Highlight player creations to foster a sense of ownership.

- **Live Streams and Q&A**: Host live streams, developer Q&A sessions, or AMAs (Ask Me Anything) to connect with your player base. Share insights and updates directly with the community.

Data-Driven Decision Making

Leverage player data and analytics to inform your decisions:

- **Player Behavior Analysis**: Continuously analyze player behavior and engagement metrics. Identify patterns, drop-off points, and areas where players struggle or excel.

- **A/B Testing**: Conduct A/B testing for new features or changes. Compare player responses and adoption rates to make informed decisions about what resonates with your audience.

- **Player Segmentation**: Segment your player base based on demographics, playstyles, or preferences. Tailor updates and content to specific segments to maximize relevance.

- **Feedback Integration**: Use player feedback as a valuable source of data. Consider implementing in-game feedback mechanisms to gather insights and bug reports.

Consistent Quality Assurance

Maintain a high standard of quality with each update:

- **Bug Fixes and Optimization**: Allocate resources to bug fixes, performance optimization, and quality assurance.

A polished and stable game contributes to player satisfaction.

- **Testing and Feedback Loops**: Establish thorough testing processes and feedback loops before releasing updates. Public test realms or beta versions can help identify issues early.

- **Community Bug Bounties**: Encourage players to report bugs and provide incentives for valuable bug reports. Acknowledge and reward players for their contributions to the game's quality.

Monetization Considerations

While monetization is important, it should be balanced with player experience:

- **Value-Based Monetization**: Focus on value-based monetization, where players perceive a fair exchange between spending money and receiving in-game content or benefits.

- **Transparency**: Be transparent about monetization methods. Avoid predatory practices that negatively impact player trust and enjoyment.

- **Regular Free Content**: Continue to offer free updates and content to all players. Monetized content should complement the overall experience rather than gating essential gameplay elements.

Evolving Marketing Strategies

Your marketing efforts should evolve with the changing market:

- **User Acquisition**: Stay informed about evolving user acquisition channels and strategies. Adapt your marketing campaigns to target new player demographics effectively.

- **Community-Driven Promotion**: Encourage your community to promote the game through word of mouth, user-generated content, and social sharing. Player advocacy can be a powerful marketing tool.

- **Influencer Collaborations**: Collaborate with influencers and content creators to reach broader audiences. Ensure that influencer content aligns with your game's values and target audience.

Conclusion

Keeping your game relevant in a dynamic gaming market is an ongoing process that requires adaptability, innovation, and player-centricity. By staying attuned to market trends, engaging with your community, making data-driven decisions, maintaining quality, and evolving marketing strategies, you can ensure that your game continues to thrive and capture the hearts of players, even in the face of evolving competition.

Section 19.5: Planning for Longevity and Legacy

Planning for the longevity and legacy of your game is essential for its sustained success and impact. In this section, we'll explore strategies and considerations for ensuring your game leaves a lasting mark in the gaming industry.

Sustainability in Game Development

Sustainability encompasses various aspects of game development, including environmental, economic, and cultural considerations:

- **Environmental Sustainability**: As game developers, it's important to minimize the environmental impact of your operations. Consider energy-efficient hardware, sustainable office practices, and eco-friendly packaging for physical releases.

- **Economic Sustainability**: Ensure that your game's financial success is sustainable. Maintain a healthy revenue stream through a combination of sales, in-game purchases, and other monetization methods.

- **Cultural Sustainability**: Your game can contribute to cultural sustainability by preserving and celebrating cultural heritage or by fostering diverse and inclusive gaming communities.

Post-Launch Support and Updates

Continuously supporting and updating your game is key to its longevity:

- **Regular Updates**: Continue releasing updates, bug fixes, and new content to keep players engaged. Plan a content roadmap that extends beyond the initial release.

- **Community Engagement**: Maintain an active presence within your game's community. Listen to player feedback, address concerns, and involve the community in shaping the game's future.

- **Expansions and DLCs**: Consider creating expansion packs or downloadable content (DLCs) to extend the game's storyline and features. These can generate additional revenue and provide fresh experiences.

- **Live Events**: Organize live events, in-game festivals, or special challenges to bring players together and create memorable moments within your game.

Legacy Support

Preserving your game's legacy is crucial for future generations of players and developers:

- **Archiving and Preservation**: Consider contributing to game preservation efforts by archiving your game's source code, assets, and historical documents. This ensures that future generations can study and appreciate your work.

- **Compatibility and Ports**: Make efforts to keep your game compatible with modern hardware and operating systems. Consider porting your game to new platforms to reach wider audiences.

- **Documentation**: Maintain comprehensive documentation for your game's development, design, and code. This documentation can be invaluable for future developers or enthusiasts who want to understand and build upon your work.

Building a Community and Brand

Creating a strong community and brand around your game can extend its impact:

- **Community Building**: Foster a passionate and engaged player community. Encourage fan creations, fan art, and fan fiction to strengthen the emotional connection players have with your game.

- **Merchandise and Licensing**: Consider licensing your game's intellectual property for merchandise, novels, comics, or other media. This can expand your game's reach and generate additional revenue.

- **Legacy Projects**: Collaborate with other developers, modders, or enthusiasts to create legacy projects, such as mods, fan games, or remakes. These projects can breathe new life into your game and keep it relevant.

Ethical Considerations

As you plan for longevity and legacy, remember the ethical responsibilities associated with game development:

- **Data Privacy**: Ensure that you handle player data ethically and responsibly. Comply with data protection regulations and prioritize player privacy.

- **Content Moderation**: Implement effective content moderation mechanisms to maintain a safe and inclusive gaming environment. Address issues related to harassment, hate speech, and toxicity.

- **Accessibility**: Continue to improve accessibility features to make your game enjoyable for players with disabilities. Prioritize accessibility in both new content and updates.

- **Community Standards**: Enforce community standards that promote fair play, inclusivity, and respect among players. Take actions against toxic behavior and hate speech.

Leaving a Lasting Impact

By adopting a holistic approach that encompasses sustainability, post-launch support, legacy preservation, community building, ethical considerations, and more, you can ensure that your game leaves a lasting impact on players, the gaming industry, and future generations of developers. Plan for your game's longevity and legacy with care, and it will continue to shine in the gaming world long after its initial release.

Chapter 20: Future Directions in Game Development

Section 20.1: Emerging Trends and Technologies

In the ever-evolving landscape of game development, staying informed about emerging trends and technologies is vital for keeping your games relevant and engaging. This section explores some of the exciting directions that the gaming industry is heading toward.

1. Metaverse and Virtual Worlds

The concept of the metaverse, a collective virtual shared space, has gained momentum. It presents opportunities for immersive social experiences, commerce, and entertainment. Virtual worlds like Decentraland and Roblox are pioneering this concept, enabling users to create, interact, and monetize within these digital realms.

2. Cloud Gaming

Cloud gaming services have the potential to revolutionize how games are played and accessed. Platforms like Google Stadia, Microsoft's Project xCloud, and NVIDIA GeForce NOW allow players to stream games without the need for powerful hardware. This trend can lead to more accessible and flexible gaming experiences.

3. Augmented Reality (AR) Gaming

AR gaming, popularized by games like Pokémon GO, continues to evolve. Advances in AR technology, such as improved device capabilities and better integration with the physical world, promise more immersive and engaging gaming experiences.

4. Blockchain and NFTs in Gaming

Blockchain technology and non-fungible tokens (NFTs) are making their way into the gaming industry. These technologies enable verifiable ownership of in-game assets, creating new opportunities for player-driven economies and unique in-game items.

5. AI and Procedural Content Generation

AI-driven game design and procedural content generation are becoming more sophisticated. Games can use AI to adapt to a player's style, create dynamic narratives, and generate diverse and expansive game worlds.

6. Cross-Platform Play and Compatibility

The demand for cross-platform play is on the rise. Players want the ability to enjoy games seamlessly across various devices and platforms. Game developers are working to provide this unified experience to their audiences.

7. Sustainability and Environmental Initiatives

Game developers are increasingly aware of their environmental impact. Initiatives for sustainability include eco-friendly game development practices, reduced carbon footprints, and green game hosting solutions.

8. Neurogaming and Brain-Computer Interfaces (BCIs)

Advancements in neurogaming and BCIs are opening new possibilities for gaming. These technologies can detect brain signals and translate them into in-game actions, potentially leading to novel gaming experiences.

9. Accessibility and Inclusivity

Game developers are prioritizing accessibility features to ensure that games can be enjoyed by a wider audience, including players with disabilities. This includes options for customizable controls, visual aids, and more.

10. AI-Generated Content and Stories

AI is being used to generate content, quests, and even entire narratives in games. This allows for dynamically changing storylines and personalized experiences for players.

11. Ethical Game Development

Ethical considerations in game development are gaining prominence. Developers are focusing on inclusivity, diversity, and responsible data handling to create more ethical and socially responsible games.

12. Remote and Distributed Development

The COVID-19 pandemic accelerated the adoption of remote and distributed development practices. Many studios are embracing this approach, which can offer flexibility and access to a broader talent pool.

13. Retro and Nostalgia Gaming

Nostalgia-driven gaming experiences, such as remakes, reboots, and retro-inspired games, continue to thrive. Players are drawn to familiar titles reimagined with modern technology.

14. Sandbox and User-Created Content

Games with extensive sandbox modes and user-generated content platforms empower players to become creators. Titles like Minecraft and Dreams allow players to shape their own gaming experiences.

15. Game Streaming and Content Creation

The rise of platforms like Twitch and YouTube Gaming has led to the growth of gaming content creation. Game developers are increasingly collaborating with content creators and streamers to reach wider audiences.

These emerging trends and technologies represent just a glimpse of the future of game development. As a game developer, staying adaptable and embracing innovation will be crucial for success in this dynamic and ever-changing industry.

Section 20.2: SDL's Role in Future Game Development

In the ever-evolving landscape of game development, the role of SDL (Simple DirectMedia Layer) remains significant. SDL has been a reliable and versatile library for game developers, providing a cross-platform framework for creating games and multimedia applications. As we look to the future, SDL continues to offer valuable features and benefits that align with emerging trends in game development.

1. Cross-Platform Development

SDL has always excelled in cross-platform development, allowing developers to write code that runs on multiple operating systems with minimal modifications. This capability becomes increasingly crucial as the gaming industry embraces a wider range of platforms, from traditional PCs and consoles to mobile devices, cloud gaming services, and emerging technologies like AR and VR.

2. Performance and Optimization

Performance optimization remains a top priority in game development. SDL offers tools and libraries that enable developers to achieve high performance while maintaining portability. As games become more complex and resource-demanding, SDL's focus on efficient rendering, input handling, and multimedia capabilities is invaluable.

3. Multi-Threaded and Asynchronous Programming

With the growth of multi-core processors, multi-threaded and asynchronous programming becomes essential for maximizing performance. SDL provides support for multi-threading and asynchronous operations, helping developers harness the full potential of modern hardware.

4. Integration with Emerging Technologies

As new technologies like cloud gaming, blockchain, and AR/VR continue to evolve, SDL's adaptability ensures it can be integrated into projects that leverage these innovations. SDL's flexibility and open-source nature make it an ideal choice for experimenting with and incorporating cutting-edge technologies into games.

5. Community and Ecosystem

SDL boasts a robust community of developers, contributors, and users. This active community ensures that SDL remains up-to-date, well-maintained, and responsive to industry changes. Leveraging this community can be a valuable resource for staying informed about new developments and best practices.

6. Open Source and Accessibility

SDL's open-source nature promotes accessibility and encourages developers to collaborate and share their knowledge. This ethos aligns with the industry's increasing focus on inclusivity, ethical game development, and responsible data handling.

7. Simplicity and Versatility

SDL is known for its simplicity and ease of use. While it provides powerful capabilities, its straightforward API makes it accessible to developers of all levels of experience. This versatility is essential in an industry that values rapid prototyping and iteration.

8. Legacy Support

SDL has a legacy of reliability and stability. For developers maintaining or updating older games, SDL's backward compatibility ensures that previous projects can continue to run on modern systems without major overhauls.

9. Middleware Integration

SDL's compatibility with various middleware solutions, including physics engines, audio libraries, and networking frameworks, streamlines game development. This integration capability remains valuable as developers seek to create feature-rich games efficiently.

10. Licensing and Business Models

SDL's open-source licensing options provide flexibility for various business models, from indie developers to large studios. The freedom to choose the appropriate licensing model aligns with the industry's diverse monetization strategies.

In conclusion, SDL's role in future game development is as vital as ever. Its cross-platform support, performance optimization, adaptability to emerging technologies, and strong community make it a resilient choice for game developers navigating the ever-changing landscape of the gaming industry. Whether you're a veteran developer or just starting your journey, SDL continues to be a reliable and valuable tool for creating the next generation of interactive experiences.

Section 20.3: Preparing for Next-Generation Platforms

The landscape of game development is constantly evolving, and as technology advances, new platforms and opportunities emerge. Preparing for next-generation platforms is crucial for staying relevant and successful in the industry. In this section, we'll explore the key considerations for game developers as they prepare to embrace the future of gaming.

1. Hardware Advancements

One of the defining characteristics of next-generation platforms is the significant hardware advancements they bring. These platforms typically feature more powerful processors, enhanced graphics capabilities, and increased memory. To prepare for these platforms, developers must optimize their games to take full advantage of the improved hardware. This includes implementing advanced rendering techniques, leveraging multi-core processors, and optimizing resource management.

2. Resolution and Display Technologies

Next-generation platforms often introduce higher screen resolutions and new display technologies. Developers should consider how their games will adapt to these changes. This may involve creating assets at higher resolutions, implementing scalable UI elements, and ensuring that graphics are compatible with the latest display technologies such as OLED or high-refresh-rate displays.

3. Ray Tracing and Realistic Graphics

Ray tracing is becoming more prevalent in gaming, delivering realistic lighting, reflections, and shadows. Game developers should explore the integration of ray tracing techniques into their games to achieve a higher level of visual fidelity. SDL (Simple DirectMedia Layer) provides support for ray tracing, making it a valuable tool for next-generation graphics.

```
// Example code for enabling ray tracing in SDL

SDL_SetHint(SDL_HINT_RENDER_RAY_TRACE, "1");
```

4. Input and Interaction

Next-generation platforms often introduce new input methods and interaction paradigms. Game developers should be prepared to support these innovations, whether it's through gesture controls, voice commands, or haptic feedback. SDL's versatility allows developers to adapt their input handling to these emerging technologies.

5. Cross-Platform Compatibility

As new platforms emerge, developers should continue to prioritize cross-platform compatibility. SDL's cross-platform capabilities make it easier to maintain a single codebase that can run on various devices and operating systems. This approach ensures a broader reach for your games and maximizes your potential audience.

6. Networking and Multiplayer

Next-generation platforms often emphasize online multiplayer and social gaming experiences. Developers should invest in robust networking solutions and implement features that enhance the social aspects of their games. SDL provides networking libraries that can simplify the development of multiplayer functionality.

```
// Example code for setting up a multiplayer game using SDL_net

SDLNet_Init();
```

7. Performance and Optimization

With the increased capabilities of next-generation hardware, players expect smooth and immersive experiences. Performance optimization remains a top priority. SDL's performance optimization tools can help developers identify and address bottlenecks, ensuring that games run seamlessly on advanced platforms.

```
// Example code for profiling and optimizing with SDL

SDL_SetHint(SDL_HINT_RENDER_VSYNC, "0");
```

8. Scalability

Next-generation platforms can reach a wide range of hardware specifications, from high-end gaming PCs to more modest devices. Game developers should design their games with scalability in mind, allowing them to run smoothly on a variety of systems without compromising on quality. SDL's adaptable features support scalability.

9. Accessibility and Inclusivity

As the gaming industry grows, so does the importance of accessibility and inclusivity. Game developers should consider the needs of diverse audiences, including players with disabilities. SDL's commitment to open source and community collaboration aligns with the industry's focus on creating more accessible and inclusive gaming experiences.

10. Ethical Considerations

Lastly, game developers should be mindful of ethical considerations, including data privacy, content moderation, and fair play. SDL's open-source nature allows developers to implement ethical practices and transparency in their games.

In conclusion, preparing for next-generation platforms involves a combination of technical readiness, adaptability, and ethical considerations. SDL, with its cross-platform support, performance optimization tools, and versatile features, can be a valuable ally for game developers as they embrace the future of gaming on advanced platforms. By staying proactive and forward-thinking, developers can position themselves to thrive in an ever-evolving industry.

Section 20.4: The Evolving Landscape of Game Design

The landscape of game design is in a constant state of evolution, driven by advancements in technology, changes in player preferences, and shifts in the gaming industry. In this section, we'll explore the evolving trends and considerations that game developers should be aware of to create engaging and successful games.

1. Immersive Experiences

As technology continues to advance, players have come to expect more immersive experiences. Virtual reality (VR) and augmented reality (AR) are gaining traction as platforms that can deliver unparalleled immersion. Game developers should explore how these technologies can be integrated into their games to provide players with more immersive and interactive worlds.

2. Narrative Complexity

Storytelling in games has grown in complexity and sophistication. Players are drawn to games with intricate narratives, well-developed characters, and branching storylines that allow them to make meaningful choices. Game developers should invest in strong narrative design and explore techniques such as non-linear storytelling to engage players on a deeper level.

3. Live Services and Continuous Content

Live services and the concept of games as a service have become prevalent in the gaming industry. Developers are expected to provide ongoing content, updates, and events to keep players engaged over the long term. This approach requires a shift in development strategies, emphasizing post-launch support and community engagement.

4. User-Generated Content

The rise of user-generated content (UGC) platforms and tools empowers players to create their own content within games. Game developers should consider implementing UGC features that allow players to contribute to the game's ecosystem, fostering creativity and increasing player retention.

```
// Example code for implementing user-generated content in a game

public void CreateCustomLevels(User user, LevelData levelData) {

// Code to save and integrate user-created levels

}
```

5. Esports and Competitive Gaming

Esports has become a massive industry, and many games are designed with competitive play in mind. Developers should explore esports features, including spectator modes, tournament support, and balanced gameplay, to tap into the growing esports market.

6. Accessibility and Inclusivity

Game developers should prioritize accessibility and inclusivity in their designs. This includes accommodating players with disabilities, offering a range of difficulty options, and considering diverse representation in characters and narratives. SDL's commitment to inclusivity aligns with these industry trends.

7. Ethical Game Design

Ethical considerations, including the impact of microtransactions, loot boxes, and the addictive nature of games, have come to the forefront of game design discussions. Developers should strive for ethical game design practices that prioritize player well-being and transparency.

8. Sustainability and Environmental Responsibility

Environmental sustainability is an emerging concern in game development. Developers should consider the carbon footprint of their games and explore ways to reduce energy consumption and waste. This aligns with the broader trend of environmental responsibility in the tech industry.

9. Cultural Sensitivity and Global Markets

The global nature of gaming means that developers should be culturally sensitive and aware of the diverse preferences of players worldwide. Localization, cultural consultation, and respectful representation are essential aspects of game design in a global market.

10. Emerging Platforms and Technologies

Finally, game developers should keep an eye on emerging platforms and technologies, such as cloud gaming, blockchain, and artificial intelligence. These innovations have the potential to reshape the gaming landscape, and developers should be prepared to adapt and innovate.

In conclusion, the evolving landscape of game design offers both challenges and opportunities for developers. By staying informed about industry trends, embracing new technologies, and prioritizing player engagement and well-being, developers can create games that resonate with audiences and stand the test of time. The future of game design is dynamic and promising, and developers who are proactive and adaptable will thrive in this ever-changing landscape.

Section 20.5: Visionary Thinking for Future Game Creators

As we look ahead to the future of game development, it's essential for game creators to adopt a visionary mindset. The industry is constantly evolving, and those who dare to think outside the box and envision new possibilities will be at the forefront of innovation. In this section, we'll explore some visionary ideas and concepts that future game creators can consider.

1. Metaverse and Virtual Worlds

The concept of a metaverse, a shared, persistent virtual universe, has gained significant attention. Future game creators can explore the development of interconnected virtual worlds where players can socialize, work, and play. This vision extends beyond traditional gaming, offering a new form of online existence.

```
# Pseudocode for creating a basic metaverse interaction

def interact_with_metaverse(player, virtual_world):

virtual_world.connect(player)

player.chat_with_other_players()

player.build_virtual_objects()
```

2. AI-Generated Worlds and Stories

Artificial intelligence (AI) has the potential to revolutionize game design by generating unique worlds and narratives in real-time. Future game creators can leverage AI algorithms to craft dynamic game environments and stories that adapt to each player's choices, ensuring a truly personalized gaming experience.

3. Haptic Feedback and Immersion

Advancements in haptic feedback technology offer the promise of more immersive gaming experiences. Game creators can explore the integration of advanced haptic feedback devices that provide tactile sensations, enhancing realism and player immersion. Imagine feeling the texture of virtual objects or the impact of in-game actions.

4. Neurogaming and Brain-Computer Interfaces

The field of neurogaming is emerging, where brain-computer interfaces (BCIs) enable direct communication between the brain and games. Future game creators can envision games that respond to players' thoughts and emotions, offering unprecedented levels of interactivity and personalization.

```
// Hypothetical code for a neurogaming interface

const playerThoughts = readBrainSignals(playerBCI);

game.respondToPlayerThoughts(playerThoughts);
```

5. Blockchain and Ownership

Blockchain technology introduces the concept of true ownership of in-game assets. Game creators can explore blockchain-based ecosystems where players have verifiable ownership of digital items and can trade them across multiple games. This concept empowers players and enhances the value of in-game assets.

6. Sustainable Game Development

With a growing focus on environmental sustainability, future game creators can prioritize eco-friendly game development practices. This includes reducing energy consumption, minimizing waste, and supporting renewable energy sources in the gaming industry.

7. Mixed Reality Experiences

The boundary between the physical and digital worlds continues to blur with mixed reality experiences. Game creators can envision games that seamlessly blend virtual and real-world elements, creating entirely new forms of gameplay and interaction.

8. Ethical AI and Inclusivity

Future game creators should consider the ethical implications of AI in games, ensuring that AI-driven experiences are fair, inclusive, and transparent. Ethical AI can help address biases, create diverse representations, and promote responsible game design.

9. Education and Skill Development

Games have the potential to become powerful tools for education and skill development. Future game creators can design games that not only entertain but also impart valuable knowledge, fostering learning and personal growth.

10. Global Collaboration

The future of game development may involve global collaboration among creators from different cultures and backgrounds. Cross-cultural game design teams can bring diverse perspectives to game development, leading to innovative and culturally rich gaming experiences.

In conclusion, the world of game development is filled with exciting possibilities for future game creators who dare to dream big and embrace visionary thinking. Whether it's the creation of metaverses, AI-generated experiences, or ethical and sustainable game design, the future holds immense potential for those who are willing to push the boundaries of what is possible in the world of gaming. By staying curious, open-minded, and innovative, game creators can shape the future of the industry and deliver unforgettable experiences to players around the world.

www.ingramcontent.com/pod-product-compliance
Lightning Source LLC
LaVergne TN
LVHW090257210926
848480LV00001B/51
9798224062935